# An Uncensored Chronicle that Vividly Portrays the Life-and-Death Career of the . . .
## LADY COP
★

In the tradition of Mark Baker's *Cops: In Their Own Words*, *Lady Cop* emerges from hundreds of hours of interviews with women police officers to present a searing portrait of the deeply felt emotions and vivid, often moving, experiences of real women on the police force. You'll discover what makes them take a "man's job." You'll learn how their Academy training prepares them—or fails to prepare them—to keep the peace on the meanest streets in America. You'll understand how they handle the pressures, the danger, and the violence of undercover work; what it is like to be a detective; and what sacrifices they must make to wear a badge.

★

And in this exciting, fascinating book, you'll become actively involved in the private and professional struggles of these courageous, committed women—brave enough to confront a mugger alone on the midnight streets, yet woman enough to comfort a dying child . . . as each day they fight to earn the name *Lady Cop*.

★

"Portrays with admirable understanding the complex relationships between the women and men who inhabit th............ subculture inside the law."

*..........le*

"A searching book............

*..........kly*

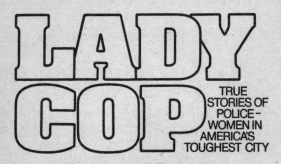

# LADY COP

TRUE STORIES OF POLICE-WOMEN IN AMERICA'S TOUGHEST CITY

## BRYNA TAUBMAN

WARNER BOOKS

A Warner Communications Company

WARNER BOOKS EDITION

Cover design by Anthony Russo
Cover photograph by Bill Charles

Warner Books, Inc.
666 Fifth Avenue
New York, N.Y. 10103

A Warner Communications Company

Printed in the United States of America

This book was originally published in hardcover by Warner Books.
First Printed in Paperback: February, 1988

10  9  8  7  6  5  4  3  2  1

To the women and men of the
New York City Police Department
and their colleagues everywhere.

# FOREWORD

This is a work of journalism, of reporting and organizing facts. It is based on long, taped interviews with dozens of women in the New York Police Department and on many hours of observing them at work, on patrol and in the precinct. All of the stories involving police action are true, although the locations of these stories have been changed. The attitudes expressed about the job, about male colleagues and about bosses are taken directly from the interviews.

For the most part, and always in matters of substance, the conversations as presented here are verbatim accounts of what police officers said to me or to each other during those interviews. The stories are based on interviews and, as nearly as possible, use the words of the storyteller.

The opinions expressed by male officers about the women they work with are excerpted both from taped interviews and from conversations with men who have worked with women partners. The attitudes of men who dislike working with women come mostly from stories related to me by women and, in a few cases, from interviews with the men themselves.

The only instances in which I am not directly quoting from

interviews are when the needs of setting a scene or structuring the book into a coherent format prevented me from doing so. These are mostly scenes of transition, based on what I know from my research to be true about police work.

Because so much of the book is excerpted from interviews, it is laced with the special phrases and jargon of police work. As much as possible, I have marked these terms with an asterisk the first time they are used. These words are defined in the Glossary at the back of the book.

A second point about language: Police officers, both men and women, use a lot of four-letter words when they are working. But few of the women I interviewed used those words to me unless such language was part of a specific story. To maintain the integrity of the quotes, I did not feel free to interject those words when they had not been said to me. As a result, however, the book reflects a misleading politeness of language. The reader should therefore feel free to add as many obscene words or terms as she knows, and then double that, to get the full flavor of police language.

I think I should also explain a bit more about the special powers and training of New York City police officers, who deal with the special demands of a city of eight million residents and a daily influx of eight million visitors. Although, in general, a crime is a crime is a crime, the enormous population of New York and its physical complexity add extra dimensions. In New York, a crime is a violation, misdemeanor or felony.

No police officer ignores a felony, a serious crime punishable by a term in jail. Violations and misdemeanors—involving lesser offenses—are another matter, however. Because of overcrowding in New York's courts and jails, these are usually punished by fines, suspended sentences, probation and the like. Police officers who patrol the streets have discretionary powers when they come across violations and misdemeanors. They can write tickets to the offender, bring the individual to the precinct for a Desk Appearance Ticket (which requires a later court appearance) or take other action, depending on the seriousness of the situation.

During their training at the Police Academy, the new recruits are told over and over again to use their common sense to know what is possible and reasonable. Thus, in some instances reported in the book, a New York City police officer chooses not to take official action when a peace officer in a smaller community might feel justified in making an arrest in a similar situation. None of these instances involve felonies or even crimes against another person.

This book describes, in the officer's own words, the work and feelings of some of the women who serve as police officers on the streets of New York City. The women I interviewed represent a broad spectrum of races, ages and ethnic backgrounds. They hold jobs ranging from detective to patrol duty. Many have had non-patrol assignments at times in their careers. Several of them serve on special details. I have endeavored to give their voices a forum for being heard while maintaining their anonymity.

As a journalist in New York City for the past twenty years, I have worked closely with the Police Department. I began as a general assignment reporter for the *New York Post* and observed firsthand the police handling criminal investigations and riots, protests and parades. Later, as a writer and producer of local radio and television news for CBS in New York, I had more opportunities to know the NYPD.

This book is intended to describe the job of being a police officer, particularly as it affects women who work on patrol. During my research I got to know many of these women well. We talked about personal problems as well as professional ones, about the similarities and differences between reporting and policing. I had thought myself informed about police procedure and the criminal justice system from my reporting experience, but I learned a great deal more than I had expected.

As a reporter, I was able to see patterns and attitudes about the job that were not usually visible to the women who were in the middle of it. Several women expressed opinions or related stories that each thought personal and individual, but which, over the course of my research, had grown familiar to me. At the same time, not being a Member of the Service (MOS) presented me with some obstacles in understanding and describing the special bonds that tie all police officers together. There is no way to deny that I am a civilian.

I think it will come as a revelation to most readers to see how much the job differs from the image presented on television and in books and movies. Police work is more exciting, challenging and routine than civilians can imagine. I wrote this book because I believe it is important for civilians to better understand the world of police officers and learn that the fiction presented on films and TV is just that—fiction meant to be entertaining, but not necessarily accurate.

Most of the police officers I know have told me over and over how much they dislike dramatic police shows on television and in the movies. The most frequently cited favorite TV series was the comedy *Barney Miller*. Few police officers I spoke with watch the action police shows or read detective fiction because their reality is so very different. But they are often frustrated and even harassed by civilians whose image of police work has been shaped by those books, television series and films.

As a result of this research and the friendships I have developed, I have a new view of police officers, both men and women. I admire them for taking the risks that keep the rest of us safer than we would be otherwise. I respect the devotion to the job that allows them to put in long hours—often outdoors —in all kinds of weather, and to work on holidays and weekends and through the night while the rest of us are enjoying our leisure. I better understand their frustration and anger when reporters focus on the cops who have gone bad, and everyone on the job has to live with the contempt of a public that views all police as corrupt or brutal—until the next act of bravery or special intelligence.

This book would not have been possible without the cooperation of the New York Police Department, the Policewomen's Endowment Association and especially the individual women who gave up their free time to talk to me. I am grateful for their openness and interest in this project. I hope they will feel that I kept my promises to them to present an accurate picture of their lives and work, its special rewards and problems.

After a year of interviews, conversations and observation, I am in awe of their bravery, compassion and devotion to duty. I admire their patience and stubbornness in the face of official and unofficial harassment. I am grateful that they, and the men they work with, have chosen to put their safety and lives at risk for the protection of the rest of us. I wish each of them good luck and hope that every reader will remember that all but a very few police officers want to be the good guys.

# CHAPTER 1

It was just after midnight when Police Officer Mary Frances Devlin Riley went off-duty and left the precinct, turning east toward Columbus Avenue. The night was colder than it had been a half hour earlier when she came in from patrol, but then she had been in a car most of the night. She pulled her scarf tighter around her neck and her wool ski cap down further on her head, tucking her hair under it. Her feet were already cold in her sneakers, despite the leg warmers and knee-high socks she was wearing. She was sorry she was not wearing boots as she turned the corner on Columbus Avenue and walked south.

She threaded her way through the pedestrians strolling down the crowded street, window-shopping in the trendy boutiques or stopping to look at menus in the bewildering variety of restaurants. She passed a sidewalk vendor, another one of the immigrants selling pocketbooks, leather belts and beaded necklaces, displayed on a blanket spread on the sidewalk. Most of them could speak only enough English to give the price of their goods. This one had a vendor's license pinned to his coat.

The sidewalks were busier than they would be in the middle of the afternoon. Mary Frances noted a gypsy fortune-teller set up on a corner and made a mental note to check on her the next evening during her tour* to see if she was doing no more than telling fortunes. Some of the gypsies sold cheap gold necklaces as 14-karat chains.

Mary Frances entered Ray's, a crowded pizza restaurant, and got in line while she looked at the booths, searching for the two friends who were meeting her there. She spotted Sophia, who had called to suggest they meet after work. Sitting next to her in an orange booth in the back was Geri, who spotted Mary Frances and smiled.

Out of habit, Mary Frances glanced around as she waited for her order, watching people in the strip of mirror that lined the walls just above the top of the booths. It was the usual Columbus Avenue mix on a late weeknight, residents in jeans and sweatshirts, tourists in pants suits or sport jackets and theatergoers in dressier clothes. Down coats and furs hung on wall hooks.

Mary Frances balanced her pizza and soda carefully as she made her way to the booth where Sophia and Geri waited. She was glad to see them, but wondered why Sophia had called. Soph was her oldest friend on the job and Geri was her oldest friend, period. She and Geri were really cousins, but she was four years younger than Geri and had always followed her lead, even on to the police force. Mary Frances sat down with her pizza, and they exchanged the usual greetings and small talk of old friends.

Mary Frances noticed that Geri's light brown hair was hanging in ringlets from a recent perm. Geri was wearing a wool jacket over her turtleneck, which made her broad shoulders look even wider. As usual, she looked relaxed, but ready for anything. Her expression was good-humored but concerned, and Mary Frances wondered if she knew why Sophia had suggested their meeting.

Sophia looked annoyed, even angry. Her short black hair was more disordered than usual. She was small and thin, which Mary Frances knew was an advantage to her on the job. Now that she was working in plainclothes, no one would make* her for a cop. When they had met, Mary Frances couldn't believe such a delicate-looking person even wanted the job. Now she knew Sophia better.

"Have you been waiting long?" she asked, noting the empty

plates and half-finished beers in front of them. Both shook their heads.

"I stayed late to catch up on some paperwork," Sophia said. "I didn't get here until almost eleven-thirty and Geri wasn't here yet."

Sophia took the last cigarette from the pack in front of her, then crumpled and tossed it on a plate. The tin star-shaped ashtray was already full of cigarette butts—mostly Sophia's brand, Mary Frances noticed.

"What's going on?" Mary Frances asked, getting right to the point. "Something happen today?"

"You know me too well," Sophia said with a tired smile.

"It's not a question of knowing you," Mary Frances replied. "I do like seeing both of you, but when I get a message at midnight to meet you two for a pizza, I know something must be wrong."

"She won't tell me," Geri said. "She said I have to wait until you get here, because she didn't think she could go through the whole thing again."

"It's just I'm so damn angry I can't even think straight," Sophia said. "This job, or maybe the system, is really getting to me."

"Okay, what happened?" Mary Frances asked again.

Sophia smiled sheepishly. "I know I shouldn't get so upset about these things, but I just can't seem to help it. I want things to be right, not subject to some stupid whim of a district attorney."

"For God's sake, what happened?" Geri said. She had known Sophia since Mary Frances had met her at the Academy.* Over the past few years they had become good friends, and she knew both Sophia and Mary Frances relied on her experience on the job. This wasn't the first time the three of them had met to talk about problems, but she couldn't give advice if she didn't know what was wrong.

With a sigh, Sophia told them the story. She had been working in plainclothes the day before, as usual, when a man, obviously disturbed, started threatening people on the street with a broken bottle. He was a big guy—more than six feet and nearly two hundred pounds—standing on one of the meridian strips running down the center of Broadway, waving the jagged bottle top and cursing at people trying to cross the street. Sophia and her partners had moved to stop him.

"I tried to talk to him, but he wasn't having any of it," she related. "He just kept waving that damn bottle and scratched Norm in the face and Van on the hand. A sector car* arrived and the two uniforms* came up while I was hanging on to his arm, trying to get the bottle away from him. He cut one of the uniforms, too. We finally got the bottle away from him and put the cuffs on, but it took all five of us to do it."

"How badly were the guys hurt?" Mary Frances asked, concerned.

"Not too bad, just scratches really, but they went to the hospital and I took the collar,"* Sophia replied. "I took him downtown and booked him for resisting arrest and assaulting a police officer and all the rest. Then this bitch of an assistant district attorney tells me she's knocking it down to harassment."

"You're kidding?" Mary Frances was horrified. "Three cops hurt and she calls it harassment."

"Yeah, but that's not all." Sophia grimaced. "You know me. I got pissed off and refused to sign the complaint as harassment. I mean, she's willing to let him off with a misdemeanor when we had a good case on a felony. We had a yelling match and the duty captain came over to see what's wrong. I explained the whole thing and he looked at me like I'm just off the farm. I told him I wouldn't sign a harassment complaint, so he did. And I'm ready to resign, I'm so mad."

"Sophia, you know you don't mean that," Mary Frances said. "What would I do without you on this job? You can't quit on me now." She looked at Geri for help. It wasn't the first time the two of them had calmed Sophia down. Sophia Amadetto had a fiery temper and a sharp wit, and was frequently angry at what she considered injustice or in trouble for making a smart comment.

"Come on, Soph, it's not like it's something new," Geri added. "We go through this all the time, having the DA knock a good collar down so they don't have to go to court. I can understand how angry you must be on this one, with three cops hurt, but that's the way the system works."

"I know and that's why I'm thinking about quitting," Sophia said. "It seems like I'm always angry lately. I get mad at the bosses and the rules and the prisoners and the poor kids who are just operating the computers. I can't seem to calm down because as soon as I get over one thing, something else comes up."

Geri was concerned to hear how serious Sophia sounded. She had often listened to the younger woman voice her frustrations, but she couldn't remember Sophia wanting to leave the force before. "You've been on the job six years now. Surely you know better than to let this kind of thing get to you so much. There isn't anything you can do and it's just part of the job."

"But it's a part I don't like and it's only one of the things I don't like," Sophia answered. "Every day I find something else. The DA's office is only a small part of the whole thing. I feel like one of those things that runs on a wheel in a cage, a hamster or gerbil or whatever they are. Just going around in circles and never getting anywhere. I swear some of the people I arrest are out on the street before I finish doing the paperwork. I'll probably arrest this creep again in two weeks, only this time he'll have a knife or a gun and really hurt someone."

"Come on, Soph, you know you don't mean it." Mary Frances looked carefully at her friend. She could see the tension on Sophia's face, but hoped talking about the frustration would help her. "Nothing's changed since we came on and your leaving won't change anything either. Give it some more time."

"Oh, I'm not going to quit tomorrow," Sophia admitted. "It's just that when I get this upset and angry I can't think of anything else to do. I guess that's why I called you guys to meet me. Talking to you two always seems to help. It did this time. I'm not as upset as I was, but I'd still like to get that bitch in the DA's office fired."

"Yeah, well, there are a couple of ADA's I'd like to bring up on charges, too. And I'd like to make all lawyers responsible for the crimes committed by clients they get off," Geri said. "If you wait long enough, the ADA's will be gone. Most of them are just working there until they can find a fancy law firm to take them on."

"Enough of my problems." Sophia shrugged her shoulders as though to push off her anger. "I promise not to resign without telling you two and I'm not about to do it right away. I'm just feeling extra put-upon today." She turned to Geri. "What's happening in Sex Crimes?"

"Nothing new, just the usual rapes and sodomies." Geri grimaced and lit another cigarette from the pack of Mores lying on the table. "A couple of hookers filed 61's* in your area in the last week. They both claimed to have been raped, and it sounded like they were describing the same guy—a male Hispanic, short, well-built, with a couple of homemade tattoos and straight black hair. I think he's getting a blow job, then knocking them out when he's through to avoid paying, and they're coming in crying that they've been attacked.

"I understand that prostitutes can be raped, but I just can't seem to feel the same sympathy for them. This is their profession and I can't believe it's all that frightening for them. Personally, if they want to file charges, I think it should be theft of services," she concluded.

"I don't know how you stay in Sex Crimes," Mary Frances said, taking another piece of pizza. "I'd go nuts listening to details of rapes all day long." Geri had been in Sex Crimes for a couple of years, and from the beginning Mary Frances had wondered why she stayed. Geri rarely talked about her cases, but then she always seemed so calm and in control. Mary Frances continued: "At least boring as it can be on patrol, there's always a different job. Even if it's only another noise complaint, it's not something as depressing and personal as rape."

"I know what you mean," Geri said. "Sometimes I hear myself asking questions and I sound so bored and uninterested. It's not fair, I know, but when you hear the same thing every day, it becomes run-of-the-mill. It's the only kind of crime we deal with, and after a while they all sound the same.

"It's not that I don't feel for these girls, not the hookers maybe, but the real rape victims, the ones who have really been terrified by the experience. But I've heard so many of them and there's just so much empathy one person, even one cop, can give. I'd like to get off this detail,* but I don't know where I'd like to go."

"It sounds like you're as frustrated as Sophia," Mary Frances said. "I guess we all are. I've been going crazy lately, too. I'm sick and tired of working all hours of the day and night. I'd like to work a steady shift, but I'd have to take midnights or get on a special detail." She twisted her wedding ring. Her long auburn hair veiled her face, so she could not see her two friends looking at each other. Mary Frances glanced up in time to watch her cousin blow a smoke ring and squint her eyes.

"I thought you liked being on patrol," Geri observed.

"I do like patrol, I don't like the hours," Mary Frances replied. "Look at us. It's twelve-thirty in the morning. I just got off work and I'm still wide awake. I'm lucky it was a dull night. If I'd gotten a collar, I'd be spending the rest of the night with a bunch of degenerates at Central Booking.*

"That's one of the nicer things about this job. If you do it right, you spend your time with creeps most people would step over in the gutter. I have a two-year-old son and a husband at home and I'm sitting in a pizza joint. I'm just tired of missing so much time with my family." Mary Frances sounded bitter and Geri and Sophia looked at each other again.

"But why are you upset about it now?" Geri asked. "You've been a policewoman for six years and you've been working around-the-clock* all that time, except when you were pregnant. Why is it getting to you now?"

Sophia ran her fingers through her short black hair and glanced again at Mary Frances. Her friend had a stubborn look on her face, one Sophia had seen often.

"I don't know," Mary Frances admitted. She twisted her ring again, then drummed her carefully manicured nails on the table. "I guess it's just the time away from home, the crazy hours, never knowing when I'll have to work overtime, the whole thing.

"Neal is working a steady eight to four weekdays since he was assigned to Community Affairs in his precinct. I'm on four to midnights for the next two weeks and he'll be asleep when I get home and I'm asleep when he leaves. He has weekends off, but my days off are in the middle of the week. We never even have time to go see a movie. He's on the job, too, so he knows the problems, but it's some way to run a marriage.

"I'm eligible for steady midnights,* and I'm thinking about it seriously. I could spend most of the evening with Neal and Stevie before going to work. But I'm really more of a morning person and making the adjustment to working midnight to eight all the time would be really hard."

"I used to love working midnights when I was on patrol," Sophia remembered. "I liked the early-morning quietness. The streets were empty just as I was getting tired and I loved seeing the sunrise every day. But I didn't care about getting home to Greg. Our marriage was already on the rocks and I was just as happy not seeing him." She grinned sheepishly at her companions.

Geri watched her cousin through the smoke. She knew she was responsible for Mary Frances going into police work in the first place. Geri's father and uncles were cops and she had grown up hearing about the job. Mary Frances heard the stories secondhand, from her. As they were growing up, Geri had told her younger cousin stories heard at the dinner table and enjoyed the admiration. Geri had joined right out of school, knowing she was going into a job that required a lot of flexibility. Mary Frances had followed when she decided she didn't like nursing.

"Why don't you try midnights?" Geri suggested. "If you don't like it, you can always change back. I'm like Soph. I always liked them, too. You work with the same people most of the time and you really have a chance to get to know everyone, even the bosses."

"I am thinking about it," Mary Frances answered. "I haven't talked to Neal about it yet. He wants me to do something to have more time at home. He knows I like the job and I was a cop before we got married, so he can't say he didn't know what he was getting. Still, sometimes I think he would like it if I stayed home and didn't work at all, like his mother."

"He doesn't mean that, Mary Frances. You know he just

says that to tease you," Sophia said. Her brown eyes looked worried and she was watching Mary Frances very carefully.

"I know. It's just that sometimes I think he really does mean it. When I told him I was going out with you guys tonight he sounded almost jealous and upset because he'll be asleep when I come home." Mary Frances shook her head, then looked at her two friends.

"But if I went to steady midnights, I wouldn't be able to have Paul as a partner," she reminded them. "I'm not sure I could stand midnights, but working like this I can't seem to make out a schedule. I feel so disorganized all the time, like I'm living day-to-day without any planning."

"You still have your big book, don't you?" Geri asked, with a grin at Sophia. It was an old joke among them that Mary Frances always had a notebook in which she liked to make lists, detailing chores or shopping, appointments and social plans, whereas Geri and Sophia were more spontaneous. Both had been known to go away for a weekend at the last minute, never planned vacations and dressed according to her mood that day.

"Yes, but it doesn't help much when I can't keep appointments even if I remember them. For Stevie's last two appointments with the pediatrician I was stuck at Central Booking and my mother had to take him at the last minute." Mary Frances smiled sadly. "I swear the pediatrician's receptionist thinks my mother is Stevie's mother.

"I don't want to find out twenty years from now that I've missed out on his growing up." She looked up. "When he started to talk his first words were Da-Da and cookie. After all, Neal was home with him every evening, but I only saw him every couple of weeks because of these damn shifts. It was several weeks until he tried Mama. Now, I usually see him in the afternoon, when he's at his liveliest, and at this age all I seem to do is tell him 'no.' I feel like a wicked stepmother sometimes."

"You won't be working around-the-clock forever, Mary Frances," Sophia pointed out. "Even if you don't want to work midnights, you can get on a special detail or get a desk job like Neal has. Something will turn up. You've got five years on the job and you can move off patrol if you want."

"I can always get pregnant again." Mary Frances laughed. "Then I'll be back inside and working days for a while. But that's even more boring. I've already lost a year because of Stevie. If I go on maternity leave again, I'll just lose more seniority and be no further from working around-the-clock."

Someone put money in the jukebox and a rock song blared out. The noise level in the restaurant increased, making it hard to hear.

Geri covered her ears with her hands, grimacing. "I can't stand this music. Are you ready to leave?"

"No," Mary Frances answered. "We have to stay here. I invited someone else to meet us."

"Who?" Geri asked.

"Sally Weston," Mary Frances said. "She asked if we could talk and when I told her I was meeting you two, she asked if she could come along, but then the sergeant wanted to talk to her about something."

"Who is she?" Geri asked.

"She's one of the new kids in the precinct," Mary Frances answered. "Very quiet, almost shy. I was surprised when she came up to me tonight because I don't remember hearing her say anything before. I'm not sure why she wants to talk to me." They chatted for a few minutes about mutual friends until Sally appeared.

The frail-looking blonde smiled as she spotted Mary Frances and walked to the table. Her blue eyes were very pale and her skin looked like alabaster. She was wearing a white down coat and a light yellow scarf and hat that accented her fairness. She was of average height, but thin, and looked a little nervous. She twisted the ends of the yellow scarf as she glanced at Geri and seemed to hesitate before she sat down.

"Hi, Sally. Do you want a slice of pizza or something to drink?" Mary Frances greeted her. "This is my cousin, Detective Geri Casey. If you want to talk about the job, she can probably help more than I can. She's got twelve years."

"No thanks, I don't want anything," Sally said. She smiled slightly at Geri and nodded hello to Sophia as she slipped off her coat. "Thank you for letting me join you. I just didn't feel like going straight home tonight."

"Did Sergeant Bailey want you for something special?" Mary Frances asked.

"No, nothing," Sally said. "He just asked if everything was all right. He said I never say anything and he wanted to be sure nothing was wrong. He sounded like my mother."

"Well, it's true you never say anything," Mary Frances commented sympathetically.

"Oh, it's just I never know what to say," Sally said. "Everyone seems so sure of themselves and knows what they're doing and I feel so dumb. I don't say anything because I don't want to look stupid. I don't know how to fill out forms or take fingerprints or do anything, it seems."

"Don't feel bad," Geri reassured her. "We all felt that way when we started. I bet your first day you worried about someone coming at you with a gun in the middle of a crowd of people."

"I did." Sally smiled again. "I was sure everyone knew I was a rookie and would take advantage of me. Another rookie and I were directing traffic because of an accident and we weren't watching each other. We both motioned cars forward from opposite directions and almost caused another accident. I was sure the sergeant would take my badge and gun right there. Luckily, the two drivers stopped in time, but I felt so stupid."

"We all made mistakes when we started," Geri assured Sally as she watched the girl, who was looking around the restaurant. "It's natural. You've seen so many cop shows on television and think you know what the job is. Then you go out there in a uniform and find it's not the same."

"Oh, I knew those things weren't real," Sally said. "I don't think I would have taken the test if I'd thought the job was going to be like on television, with all that shooting.

"It's just that I don't think I can remember everything. I don't know the radio codes* and I can never remember the difference between larceny* and robbery.* I forget to salute sometimes and I never really learned how to do an about-face.

We learned first aid at the Academy, but I'm sure when I'm faced with something serious I'll forget it all.

"Then there are the guys." Sally grimaced. "I'm sure they all laugh every time I try to salute. I always feel so silly, like I'm playing soldier and they know it."

"Ignore them," Geri said. "When I came on in 1973 we were the first girls in the precincts and the guys were really nasty. I left my coat on a table once before inspection and when I picked it up, someone had peed on it. They don't do things like that anymore, thank God. You'll get used to them."

Sally looked horrified and Geri wondered if she had been too graphic. But if Sally wanted to be a cop, she had better learn to expect even blunter language.

"I know what you mean, Sally," Mary Frances said. "I came on because I thought I could help people. I went into nursing when I got out of high school. I read all the Sue Barton books as a kid and thought it sounded really wonderful, comforting sick people and helping them get well.

"But I hated it," Mary Frances continued, frowning at the memory. "The work was routine and had little to do with patients. I spent a lot of time counting sheets and listening to complaints from relatives of patients instead of talking to the patients themselves. There was so little freedom of action and I didn't like taking orders from dumb doctors all day long, so I listened to my big cousin Geri and joined the Police Department. Now I take orders from dumb sergeants for eight hours a day."

"I don't mind the sergeant," Sally said. "I like Sergeant Bailey. He's been really nice. And I know I can ask him questions. It's the other guys. I feel so dumb asking them how to fill out forms and they look at me like I'm an idiot for not knowing. I've been working inside almost every day since I was assigned to the precinct and I'm sure some of those guys resent that I'm not on patrol. That I have a cushy desk job and it's because I'm a woman."

Geri laughed. "You both should remember that the guys who bitch the loudest are the ones who never do anything no matter what they're assigned."

"That's true," Sophia agreed. "Don't forget, most of the

guys who yell the loudest about not wanting to work with a woman are the guys you wouldn't want to work with anyway. Remember Irv Rosen, Mary Frances?"

"Yeah. You should have seen this guy, Sally. He was a real hairbag* in Soph's first precinct, in Brooklyn." She grinned at the memory. "He hated the idea of women on the job and made sure everyone knew his feelings.

"Then his partner got transferred and they put him with Soph one midnight. She called me right after the tour to tell me what happened." Mary Frances glanced at Sophia, who had also started to laugh. "Irv had tried everything with the sergeant to avoid riding with her, but everyone else without a partner on that tour was either out sick or on vacation or due in court the next day. The sergeant finally told him to just work with her for one night. Then Soph went up to the sergeant and said she didn't want to work with Irv." She smiled at Sophia and leaned back to let her finish the story.

"He had this hurt look on his face and finally said, 'Why don't you want to work with me?' " Sophia giggled. "I told him I didn't know how good a cop he was, but I was willing to try for one tour if he was. So we went out and we were partners for more than a year.

"We were very good friends. He got me through my divorce," she recalled. "Just after I transferred here he retired. He said he retired because he could never find another partner like me. Of course, it helped that he had twenty years on the job and was eligible for a half-pay pension." Geri and Mary Frances laughed with her. Sally joined in the general laughter at the story, too, and Mary Frances was glad to see her relax a little.

"I think it takes a woman on this job a lot longer to develop the confidence you need," Geri remarked.

"What do you mean?" Sophia asked. "We can do the job as well as anyone."

"You know I don't mean that," Geri said. "If I didn't think I could do the job, I wouldn't have stayed on for as long as I have. I just think it takes women longer to develop the instinct for physical or mental combat that you need."

"I don't agree," Mary Frances said. "You sound like some of the guys Sally was talking about."

"Come on." Geri sounded angry now. "You two, of all people, should know I think women belong on this job. I'm not talking about that. It's just that men are taught as little boys to be physical, to be aggressive. Women who come on this job have to teach themselves to do that. We have to take on qualities we weren't taught as children."

"I see that," Sally said. "But I've had so little patrol time so I'm not getting that experience to learn those instincts and I'm not sure I can do it. I went through the Academy and NSU* and that seemed to go okay, but being in the precinct and seeing the way some of the people live in this area really shocked me.

"I come from a very traditional middle-class background. I didn't know anyone who was divorced when I was growing up. I thought everyone grew up with both parents and their own house. Then I came on and saw that some people can't even imagine the life I took for granted." Sally frowned and looked around sheepishly.

"I went into apartments and saw three or four kids running around with no father there, and sometimes they all have different fathers and the mother is the same age I am." Sally's expression showed how deeply this all still surprised her. "They don't have clothes or heat or even food sometimes. Everyone in the family is yelling at and hitting each other all of the time, even the children. It never occurred to me that people live like that."

"I know." Mary Frances smiled sympathetically at Sally. "I wasn't really prepared for it either, even after working as a nurse. There are times when I wish I could take the kids and isolate them from the family. I feel bad for the children because it's not like they know any better. They only know what they're brought up in. The kids really bother me. I think they bother everyone on the job."

"I didn't mean to imply that you were used to those conditions," Sally said, blushing.

"You will get used to it," Geri told her, taking another cigarette.

"That's my tough cousin, Geri the cop, talking," Mary Frances said. "Come on, you're not really as cold as you just sounded."

Geri grinned and looked at Sally, who again seemed shocked by what she had said. "No, I don't mean that you'll get totally callous. It's just that you'll get used to the conditions that upset you now. There will always be someone who gets to you, but after a few more months, or even weeks, it won't be everything and everyone you see. I know that sounds hard, but you just can't let every little thing bother you. If you do, you won't be a very good cop."

"Don't tell me they've stopped giving the standard speech about leaving the job in the locker with your uniform," Sophia interjected. "They tell that to everyone at the Academy and it's true. You can't take everything home with you or you'll go nuts." Sophia remembered how upset she had been earlier and grinned somewhat sheepishly as the two older women laughed and Sally smiled. Sophia looked at her watch and then at the other three. "I hate to break up this happy hour, but I'm due in court tomorrow morning. It's already past one and I've got to drive home to the Bronx."

"Yeah, I've got to be leaving, too," Mary Frances said. "Do you want to stay, Sally, or are you ready to leave?"

"I'm ready. I just wanted to talk to someone. Thanks for listening, all of you. I really appreciate it."

"That's okay. If you need someone to talk to, just ask," Geri replied sympathetically. "Remember, we all went through the same thing." She turned to her cousin. "Mary Frances, can you drop me off?"

"Sure, let's go."

The four women walked to the door, sidestepping customers carrying paper plates loaded down with slices of pizza. They shrugged on their coats and stepped out on to Columbus Avenue, which was still filled with strolling pedestrians despite the late hour.

"I'm parked on Amsterdam," Sophia said. "Mary Frances, I'll talk to you soon. Maybe I can convince you to try midnights." She hugged her briefly and waved good-bye to Geri and Sally. Sophia looked like a teenager in her striped leg warmers and down vest as she walked off down the street with a bouncy stride that belied her thirty-three years.

The other three headed downtown. Sally stopped and again thanked Mary Frances for inviting her to come along. "My car is on this block. Good-bye, Detective Casey, nice meeting you. I appreciate your advice. I'm glad you were here." She walked off down the side street, and Mary Frances and Geri continued down the avenue.

"She seems like a nice kid, but I think she's worried about more than living conditions," Geri said to Mary Frances. "How long has she been on the job?"

"She's only been in the precinct a couple of months after four months in NSU," Mary Frances answered. "She's been inside a lot because she's a really fast typist, so she gets stuck with the paperwork. I think she's just worried about handling herself."

"Here's the car."

Mary Frances unlocked the door of the hatchback and walked around to the driver's door. She slid into the seat, hooked up her seat belt and started the engine, then turned to look at her cousin. Her long nails drummed on the steering wheel.

"What are you waiting for?" Geri asked.

"Put on your seat belt. I don't want to get a ticket," Mary Frances said, mock seriousness in her tone.

Geri laughed and hooked the seat belt. "I hate the damn things. I think I sold my car just because New York State passed the law about wearing them a couple of years ago."

"I don't like them either, but they do save lives," Mary Frances said with a scolding grin. "And we've both sworn to uphold the laws of this state. I'd feel very dumb if I got a ticket because you weren't wearing a seat belt. In fact, I'd feel so dumb, I'd probably make my cousin the detective pay it." They laughed together.

Mary Frances drove through the park. She stopped in front of a brownstone on East Seventy-seventh Street, just off First Avenue.

"I can't believe you've had this apartment for eight years now," she remarked to Geri. "I remember being so mad when that head nurse left the hospital and I was just a poor little nurse who couldn't afford this apartment. At least you got it. I think that's when I decided to take the test for the department. I've moved four times since then and you're still here."

"It's convenient, comfortable and cheap," Geri said as she unhooked the seat belt, then turned to her cousin. "Do you think Sophia is serious?" she asked.

"Oh, you know Soph." Mary Frances shrugged. "She's always getting upset about something. I can't imagine her taking anything calmly. I'm not worried about her quitting as much as I'm worried about her being forced out."

"What do you mean?" Geri asked.

"Sophia doesn't know when to shut up," Mary Frances replied. "I can almost imagine what she said to the duty captain today. If she was as angry as she said, she probably really let him have it. I've told her one of these days she's going to get into real trouble with some boss."

"I knew she used to be like that," Geri said. "I thought she had outgrown it in six years."

"Not really," Mary Frances answered. "She can't seem to help herself. She just gets mad and whatever she's thinking pops out. Remember when we were in NSU and had that lieutenant who was so nasty about appearances and uniforms. Sophia had long hair then and put it up, but there were wisps hanging down from her cap. He started screaming at her and she just looked at him and said, 'Lieutenant, when you shave your legs I'll shave my neck.' I thought he was going to explode. I don't know where she got the nerve to say that. I was sure he'd write her up, but he just screamed at her after inspection and let it go."

"She was lucky," Geri said, shaking her head. "I don't remember hearing that before. She's too good a cop to lose, but she should be more careful. Saying things like that to a boss could really get her in trouble. I'll call her tomorrow to see if she's still in the same mood. How about you?"

"I guess I'm okay," Mary Frances answered. "I just can't make up my mind what to do. I used to like patrol but lately it's been boring, and I'd miss Paul terribly if I transferred to something else. But the routine and the hours are really getting

to me, and I'm really beginning to worry about my marriage."
She shrugged. "I'll have to think about it some more and talk
to Neal before I make up my mind."

Geri leaned over and hugged Mary Frances, then got out
of the car. She already had her keys in her hand as she ran up
the front steps of the building. She went in the first door, turned
the key in the lock of a second one, then waved Mary Frances
away and went inside.

# CHAPTER 2

**G**eri ran up a flight of stairs, taking them two at a time as usual, a habit she had picked up to get extra exercise whenever she could. She unlocked the door to her apartment, slipped her hand inside to turn on the light and walked in. A black Scottie greeted her by running madly in circles and barking sharply. She leaned down to pet him and after he had quieted down, she hung up her coat.

"Glad to see me, Mac?" she asked. "I guess it's been a long wait for you. You must be starving. We'll go for a run tonight. I just want to change my shoes."

She went into the tiny kitchen and opened a can of dog food for the Scottie. While he gobbled it up, Geri walked into her bedroom, took off her jacket and looked at the clock as she tied her shoes. It was nearly 2 A.M., but she wasn't a bit sleepy and really wanted to go for a run, despite the cold outside. Besides, Maguire needed the exercise after being cooped up in the apartment all day. She had found the little Scottie on the street a few years before while she was still working in uniform and had named him after the police commissioner* at the time.

She returned to the living room of the small apartment to find the dog sitting quietly by the door, but with a hopeful look in his eyes. He held his leash in his mouth and she smiled at his eagerness. Geri checked the gun holstered in the waistband of her slacks, then replaced it. She usually resented the departmental regulations requiring her to carry her gun as long as she was in the city, but at this hour she didn't mind. She put on a light jacket, then took her police ID card and shield from her handbag and put them in her pocket. As long as she had her gun with her, she also needed the shield and ID card.

"Okay, Mac, let's go."

Geri put the leash on the dog before they went out the front door of the building. She put her heavy key ring in a jacket pocket. It was cold, but she would get warm once she started running. They walked up a block, crossing York Avenue, and continued toward the East River. The streets were nearly deserted, with only a few cars going by. The side street was totally empty, but brightly lit with the high-intensity street lamps found all over New York.

This block of East Seventy-eighth Street was one of Geri's favorites in the city. Several six-story, old-fashioned stone apartment buildings lined both sides, two with arched walk-throughs to Seventy-seventh Street that suggested an earlier and more gracious time. These walk-throughs also offered a haven for muggers, so Geri walked close to the curb, as far away from the front of the buildings as possible. It was one of the cautions she had learned since becoming a cop. This block had no trees, so Geri made a point of looking down the alleys and doorways she passed in case anyone was there, waiting for an unwary pedestrian. Few of the apartment windows showed lights.

Mac frisked and pulled as they walked along and Geri tugged him quiet, promising they would run when they got to the park. One of the things she liked about being a cop was that she could go for runs early in the morning, without having to worry as much as unarmed civilians about muggers and other criminals. Still, because of the chance of danger on the empty streets of the city at such an hour, she didn't do it often.

Geri rarely mentioned her late-night runs to friends and family because she knew how upset they would be. She knew that most people, even other cops, found the city eerie, even frightening, in the early hours of the morning, especially if they were alone. She wasn't afraid, but she was cautious whenever she went running after midnight. Geri was willing to take her chances occasionally because she liked the exercise.

As a cop, she needed to be active. Whenever something bothered her, she would work out to the point of exhaustion. She really preferred swimming to running, but either worked. Her job gave her a lot of things to exorcise with exercise—the unexpected violence, the unwary victims, the ingratitude of some people, the intransigence of the organization. Over the years, Geri had learned to get the anger and frustration out of her system physically, with running or swimming or even calisthenics. Then, when she was exhausted, she could think more rationally about the situation and put it in perspective.

It was something to be grateful for. She was thirty-four years old but was in excellent shape. She smoked, but running and swimming had helped keep the consequences of that to a minimum. She looked ten years younger than her sister-in-law, who was the same age but had four children. Secretly, Geri was rather proud of keeping her figure compared to the rest of the women in her family and some of her women classmates at the Academy.

Geri only occasionally used a night out to release energies fed by her job. When she had worked with regular partners, they sometimes had gone out drinking and dancing together after a rough day. Usually there were a bunch of cops, all involved in a situation or a bust or something that had pushed them. They would go to a local bar, stand around buying each other beer and telling loud jokes, laughing uproariously at stories that non-cops never understood. For a lot of cops, male and female, drinking was the only release they had. Geri never minded those outings, but she wasn't much of a drinker.

Geri and Mac passed the small playground on Cherokee Place, then walked up a ramp that crossed the FDR Drive and led down to a narrow park along the East River. Geri looked carefully in both directions from the top of the ramp. There was no one in the park. She unleashed Mac, ignoring the city law requiring dogs to be leashed at all times. She could get away with it at this hour and he liked to run by himself.

Geri walked down a flight of steps. At the bottom she did a few stretching exercises while Mac used a tiny plot of grass. She pulled out a plastic bag, picked up his mess and put it in a litter basket: at no time of day did she ignore the law requiring dog owners to clean up after their pets. She started north in a slow trot. Mac trotted along next to her, occasionally stopping to sniff at park benches and light poles.

As she ran, Geri watched the river. A couple of tugboats were moving slowly south. She really liked being out at this time of night. She felt as though she had all of New York City to herself. She remembered Sophia's comment about enjoying the emptiness of the streets when she worked midnight tours. The streetlights made pools of brightness that dimmed and grew as she ran past them. Geri could hear the water lapping the bank and see the city lights reflecting on it. Across the river, the lights of Queens gleamed. It was very quiet; the only sound was the soft plop of her jogging shoes on the pavement.

Geri thought about the conversation with Mary Frances, Sophia and Sally. She remembered her cousin calling her tough and cold, and she wondered if that was true and if it was so bad. She had been on the job more than a dozen years. Sometimes she felt as though she had seen everything—all the evil, cruel things people could do to each other. Then something would happen to remind her there was no apparent limit to man's viciousness.

Geri still had some civilian friends. Not many though, after twelve years of police schedules. But a few friends from high school still called every once in a while. And even after all those years, they sometimes seemed surprised that she was still on the job. One old girlfriend had even commented on it the last time they had gotten together, reminding Geri of her former naïveté. It was true. Geri used to think things would always work out for the best, that people wanted to do good and be honest. Now, she realized, she expected them to be lying.

How could she not be more cynical? she wondered. As she

ran, Geri thought about the kinds of cases she had to deal with, the details of rapes and sodomies, the abuse of children and elderly women, the violence and violation of other people that she listened to daily.

A couple of days ago, she had gone out to dinner with two other women in the Sex Crimes Unit. They had all talked about work and the problem of dealing with rapes all day. Geri had admitted to them that she often found herself thinking about it when she was making love. She would think about turning the gentleness of lovemaking into violence; that something she was doing willingly and with love was forced on women at gunpoint, in fear of their lives. It upset her that it could intrude on her private life that way.

One of the other women, Alice Sanders, agreed. She, too, found that the details of their daily work often invaded her private life in unexpected ways. She said she carried her gun with her when she went to the basement of her apartment building to do her laundry. Alice had not been nervous about that before she came to Sex Crimes, but she was a lot more conscious of being alone now.

The second woman had denied it. She said she couldn't believe that Geri and Alice allowed it to bother them that way. She had been in Sex Crimes for much longer than either of them and she insisted she never thought about work at home. They had argued for several minutes. The older woman finally remarked that she had noticed only one difference in her life since she started working Sex Crimes: she always slept with the light on. At that, Geri just laughed. How could she possibly think it didn't affect her when she had to keep the lights on at night?

Geri remembered when she first came on the job. She was determined to avoid the callousness and cynicism she had seen in her father and uncles who had been cops. As she grew up listening to their stories and jokes, she was often upset by the bigotry and lack of sensitivity she'd heard from them. Geri remembered being especially furious after hearing the story of a favorite trick of one of her uncles. He always told suspects they could go free if they could answer one question correctly: Which is closer, the moon or Europe? According to her uncle, most of the people he arrested would say the moon because they could see it.

Then she went on patrol and within months realized that she, too, was becoming cynical, less trusting, more cautious about the people around her—and not just on the job, but everywhere in her life. When she started, Geri gave everyone the benefit of the doubt, but that hadn't lasted long. She learned quickly that people would lie about anything that might get them in trouble. She began assuming that everyone was lying until they could prove differently. Geri learned to become immune to tears and to the tales of hard times. She soon found that someone who claimed to be a victim on one day would turn out to be the attacker the next.

She remembered working in a tough Brooklyn neighborhood early in her career. It was like being part of an occupation army in a foreign country. Pedestrians would spit at her as she walked by or call her names. Geri sometimes found it hard to see any humanity in the people around her. Old people were attacked in broad daylight. Men would start knife fights for no apparent reason. Women would steal from stores or trade food stamps for booze or drugs, ignoring their hungry children. The children wore secondhand clothes, played truant constantly and acted like savages. They never seemed to be in school and no one cared. Geri would walk her beat, seeing them playing on the sidewalks or in vacant lots. They looked and played the way she had when she was growing up, but all she could think was that it was just a matter of time before she would be arresting them for a mugging or robbery or narcotics.

No particular time or incident had changed her. It seemed to be an accumulation. Geri thought back to the first time she had been sent to guard a dead body. It was an elderly man who lived alone. He had apparently died of natural causes and she was assigned to stay in the apartment until the morgue attendants came to pick up the body. She had had no experience with dead people. No one in her immediate family had died and the only time she had seen a body was when she went to the morgue while she was at the Academy. Geri was terrified and nervous when the sergeant and the other cops left her alone. They had already reported the death and taken an inventory of the valuables, and now it was just a matter of waiting for the meat wagon.*

Geri sat in a chair by the window in the tiny apartment, trying not to look at the corpse, which was covered with a sheet and lay on the floor a few feet away. She desperately wanted a cigarette but couldn't find any matches. She looked around and noticed matches on a table on the other side of the room. The body was between her and the table, and the room was too small to walk around it. Geri sat for a few more minutes, then stood up, stepped across the sheet-covered body, picked up the matches and stepped back. She was shaking so much she could barely stand, but she had the matches, and smoking the cigarette had calmed her.

It had never been like that again. The first time was always difficult, she supposed. She was a lot less upset the next time she had to stand watch at a DOA.*

Did staying with dead bodies without being nervous mean that she was becoming hard? It seemed a long time ago and there had been a lot of dead bodies since then. A lot of other things as well—abused children, accident victims, all kinds of things. Geri remembered Sally Weston talking about how shocked she had been at what she found when she had gone on patrol. And Sally was working on the Upper West Side, now considered a low-crime precinct.

Geri had started on the job in a high-crime precinct, a slum. Boys hitched rides on the backs of buses to prove their bravery—and because they didn't have the fare. Geri remembered one kid, eleven years old, who didn't make the back of the bus. He hit the side and lost his footing. When he went to step down, he stepped on the wheel and it sucked him in, cutting him in half.

She and her partner Alex had responded to the scene, the first cops to get there. An ambulance was there already; it had been parked on the corner while the crew ate lunch and they had seen the whole thing happen. Now the EMS technicians* were just standing around. They couldn't pick the child up because he was too badly hurt. The kid was dying and nothing could be done.

Geri and her partner had pushed the crowd back. More radio cars showed up and Geri had turned to the boy, lying in the street. She knelt down next to him, looking at his face so she wouldn't have to see the blood and the terrible wound. Still conscious, the boy·was worried about being in trouble with his mother. He knew he was dying and he gave her phone numbers to call. He had talked some more about making his mother angry, getting hurt doing something he had been forbidden to do. Then he died.

Helping that boy die had been one of the hardest things she had ever had to do on the job. Living with the memory had not been easy, either. It was not the kind of memory you could leave behind you. An eleven-year-old had his whole life ahead of him, and now it was over because of a stupid accident. It bothered her a lot. She worked out to the point of exhaustion that day and for days afterward. It helped her sleep, but it didn't help her forget. She still carried the memory with her.

Geri started out on the job determined not to be prejudiced, not to expect the worst just because people were poor or different from her. It didn't take long to learn how naïve that was. It wasn't that people who didn't have jobs or were on welfare were worse than anyone else. It was simply a matter of time and opportunity. If someone didn't have a job to go to, had nothing to do all day but sit home and watch television, something was bound to happen.

The unemployed weren't more violent or less civilized than other people. They were just more bored. And they had more time to get into trouble. Women cooped up all day in a small apartment with young children, with no chance to get out and no hope of anyone coming to take on the chore of disciplining or breaking up the arguments or distracting the kids, were more likely to lose their tempers and their control—especially if they weren't much more than kids themselves.

Men without jobs had nothing better to do than hang out on the streets. Being without a job usually meant they were short of money. It only took a suggestion from someone to make a mugging or purse snatching look attractive—or the offer of some quick money running numbers or selling narcotics. Or if someone had the money for a few six-packs of beer or a bottle of wine, they could get drunk enough to forget the boredom of hanging out all day. Then fights would break out just to give them something to do and talk about the next day.

Geri's belief in these things wasn't racism, just the reality of life. Geri didn't think she was any more bigoted than she had been before she came on the job. But the fact was that most crimes were committed by young men in poor neighborhoods. And most poor people, at least in the city, were from one minority group or another. She didn't think every young black or Hispanic male from a ghetto was a criminal, but the chances that they had been involved in something illegal were greater than if they were college students from the suburbs. That was just a fact.

And it wasn't that she was naturally cynical and therefore attracted to police work. It was, Geri thought, more that she was a cop and had learned about the toughness of life and its problems. She saw the kids in the playgrounds and knew they saw the same things she did. The people with the most success in slum areas—the ones who had cars and clothes and TV's— were those who were breaking the law. Slum society seemed removed in time and space from the middle-class world of the suburbs and the big offices in Manhattan. It was closer to life and death, more aware of the consequences of failure, of starvation and eviction, of violence and insecurity.

She wasn't callous, Geri decided, just realistic. Being a cop made you that way. Cops saw people at their worst, in times of stress and emergency, when their control had disappeared and their emotions were raw. She had often thought that cops and doctors had a lot in common: They both saw things that most other people could avoid and ignore. But their job was to deal with those things, and running was one of the ways she had learned to cope with that.

Geri was back at the ramp by now and feeling better about

herself. Mac was panting as Geri slipped his leash back on, but she wasn't really tired. She had run only a couple of miles, not the five to ten miles she usually did when she was upset.

They walked back up to the top of the ramp. At the top, Geri stopped, looking around. The street seemed as quiet and empty as before . . . until she caught a movement on the other side of the playground at the bottom of the ramp. It looked like someone on a bicycle.

Geri considered going back into the park, but that was too restricting. She would have no escape because the only way out of the park was this ramp, or another a few blocks south. The highway blocked any other exit, so she would be trapped. Her only choice was to go down the ramp and keep walking along East Seventy-eighth Street. Then, at least, she would have some options: running up Seventy-eighth Street or turning on to York.

Geri knew the person on the bike would follow her. Maybe it was her cynicism again, but Geri also knew the rider was a man and she could be reasonably sure he wasn't out at this hour of the morning for a pleasure trip. Still, if she got back to the street, she would have a better chance of getting away. Staying in the park made her more vulnerable, offering less chance of someone else coming by.

She wasn't really worried because she had a gun. If the cyclist threatened her she wouldn't hesitate to use it, but she would prefer not to. This was the first time in years that she had actually seen even a hint of danger on a late-night run. Of course, Geri had always known there was a chance of running into something like this, but now that it had happened, she felt a little surprised. Not that this was a problem yet, but her cop instinct told her the man on the bike was not completely harmless.

Geri unsnapped her holster, putting her hand on the gun as she started down the ramp. The cyclist had spotted her, she was sure. There was a streetlight at the top of the ramp and she might have been standing on a stage. He was coming toward her from Cherokee Place, riding slowly. Geri sensed he was going to give her a hard time, but she had no choice and no place to go. She wrapped Mac's leash around her left hand and kept her right elbow bent, her hand near her waist.

Back on the sidewalk and walking up East Seventy-eighth, her head swiveled to follow the biker as he rode to the end of the street. Maybe if he knew she had seen him, he would leave her alone, but he made a U-turn and came toward her. Geri saw him pull something out of his pants and thought, Oh, God. He's got a gun. She took her gun out of her waistband as a precaution and walked with her hand down, the muzzle pointing to the ground, her fingers curled around the stock. She hoped he didn't have a weapon. She wasn't frightened but uneasy, not knowing what to expect from him. She approached a streetlight and the rider came up on the other side of a parked car.

Geri could see him clearly now: he was white or a light-skinned Hispanic, with curly black hair. He was wearing a khaki parka and riding a ten-speed bike. He had a big grin on his face as he looked at her. Suddenly, she realized he was masturbating. That's what he had taken out of his pants!

A jolt of rage exploded through her, rage and fury that he could be so blatant, so disgusting. Geri brought up her gun hand, pointing the weapon at him, and said, "You bum! I'll put a bullet right between your eyes!"

His erection died instantly. His eyes nearly bulged from his head and the grin turned into a grimace of fear as he started to scream at her: "You're crazy, lady! You must be some kind of nut!" He leaned over the handlebars of the bike and rode away fast, turning on to York Avenue, not even taking the time to put his penis back in his pants.

Geri just stood there, her hand shaking. She put the gun back in her holster, amazed at herself for even pointing it at him. Now that she had had a minute to calm down, she realized she was lucky he had gotten scared and run off. She could have been in a lot of trouble if he had reported her. She could still be in a lot of trouble if he went to the local precinct and told them a crazy woman with a gun was running around on the streets. Geri was supposed to have the gun with her, of course, but she wasn't supposed to point it at someone like that, when she wasn't really in danger. And a masturbator was not considered a deadly threat by the Department Advocate's office, Geri was sure.

She walked home quickly, looking around nervously. She

was still shaky, not so much at running into the little creep but at her reaction. How could she have pulled a gun? How could she have threatened him like that? Geri didn't think she would have used it if he had continued to jerk himself off, but now she felt that she couldn't be sure. She had been so disgusted, so blindingly angry, so furious with him for making her so nervous. She never would have believed she would pull a gun in such a situation until she did it. Without really stopping to think, Geri had just reacted to the rage she felt.

Geri got back to her apartment and locked the door behind her. She sat down in a comfortable chair, petted Mac and thought about the incident again. She had overreacted, sure, and that was dumb, but it wasn't really that bad, now that she had time to think about it. Of course, she was familiar enough with the habits of sex offenders to know that flashers were unlikely to be rapists. The guy on the bike was basically harmless, just disgusting and obnoxious.

Now that the whole thing was over, Geri began to laugh. The look on his face when he saw the gun made her giggle in retrospect. He was jerking himself off on a bike at three o'clock in the morning in front of a totally strange woman and he called *her* crazy!

It would probably be a long time before he tried a stunt like that again. So maybe she had saved other women from being frightened by his weird sex habits—at least for a while.

Geri remembered that when she was still in high school, a Catholic school, she had seen a flasher. She had been terrified. She had run all the way home and when she had gotten there, she was too embarrassed to tell her mother what had frightened her. This kind of made up for that. She had a real sense of satisfaction that she had been the one in control, that he had been frightened and run off. It was one of the advantages of being a cop, especially a woman cop.

Geri stood up. It was over and done with, and unless he reported her to the local precinct no one would ever know about it. She didn't think he would, because he would have to say what he had been doing out at that hour and why she had pulled the gun in the first place. More likely, he would just go home.

After taking the gun out of her holster, she locked it in her desk drawer as usual. She walked into the bedroom and got ready to go to sleep. It was nearly 4 A.M. She wasn't due in to work until four in the afternoon, but thought she might go in a little early. Her boss was a very understanding kind of guy. Maybe she would tell him what happened and admit that it had been stupid to pull the gun.

Then again, maybe she wouldn't. Geri remembered the story Sophia had told that evening. No point in getting tangled up in red tape or making herself vulnerable to trouble. She had been in the department long enough to know that some things were better kept to herself.

That reminded her of her plans to call Sophia and Mary Frances. She would have to think more about what they had said. Maybe she could think of something to help Sophia, suggest ways for her to be more easygoing, less upset by the bureaucracy of the job. And something to help Mary Frances, a way to arrange her schedule or a transfer to a detail so that she would have more time to spend with Neal and Stevie.

And she had her own problems tomorrow. She and another detective were supposed to pick up a rape suspect—a big guy, ID'd by one victim and probably guilty in a couple of other cases. She would have to dress carefully, be ready for trouble. And she had a dinner date later to complicate things.

# CHAPTER 3

**A**fter dropping her cousin off, Mary Frances headed home, thinking about the day. The tour had been boring, one of those days when nothing much happened and what did happen wasn't very interesting. She wondered why she had sounded so bitter while talking to Soph and Geri. She hadn't been aware that she was so upset about the crazy schedules and the boredom of patrol until she heard herself saying it tonight.

Mary Frances's long nails played on the steering wheel as she drove to Queens. Neal had hinted about her quitting, but she knew he really didn't mean it. She was already on the job when they met and he certainly knew she planned to stay, even after Stevie was born. But sometimes Mary Frances thought she detected a resentful tone in his voice when she had to work overtime, or a worried note when she didn't have time to call and tell him she would be late.

Working around-the-clock was what really bothered her. She had to find a way to get off that schedule. Maybe steady midnights was the answer. It would mean changing her whole lifestyle. And if she made a collar during the night, she would lose time with her family.

That didn't seem to be the answer and Mary Frances didn't think Neal would like it either. They would have more time with Stevie, but they would have even less time alone with each other. That wasn't much of a way to save her marriage.

Of course, Neal knew the good and the bad things about the job. He was working as a Community Affairs officer in his precinct now and mostly that meant that he worked weekdays. He talked to community-based groups about crime problems, helped with parking and traffic arrangements for block parties or school fairs, met with the political leaders of the neighborhood concerned about drug sales or prostitution, or attended meetings of businessmen to help improve security. He liked the work and the more regular hours and it was a good job for him. He had enjoyed being on patrol and had been unhappy when he was first assigned as Community Affairs officer, but now he was happier with it.

There had been times when he was still riding in an RMP* that she remembered getting angry because he had to work overtime when she was expecting him home. Neal used to sleep in the precinct or downtown when he made late collars and had to wait to explain the case to an assistant district attorney or had a short turnaround* to his next tour. Mary Frances knew a lot of the guys did that. But the thought of sleeping on the mattress in the women's locker room made her skin crawl. She could only hope the men's cots were cleaner, but she doubted it. She never stayed over like that; she went home if only to take a shower.

That got her thinking about how she had met Neal. Her partner, Doug Green, kept talking about his good buddy from the Academy and how he thought the two of them would hit it off. Mary Frances hadn't been interested. She was having a great time being single, having some money to spend and just enjoying the excitement of being a cop after the boredom of nursing.

In those days, she really didn't want to date cops, but it was hard to find civilian men who understood the special problems of her job. As hard as her schedule was on a marriage, it had made dating almost impossible. And she learned quickly not to admit she was a cop when she first met a civilian guy. They all had a ticket they wanted fixed, a complaint about cop brutality or a comment about police corruption. Or they wanted to see her gun. Or they didn't want her to carry the gun.

Then she had to explain emergencies and overtime. Unless the guy was a lawyer or something, they didn't understand about arrests and Central Booking and all the rest of it. Men who had regular jobs just couldn't seem to cope when she had to work on weekends and holidays or had to cancel a date because of an arrest.

But dating cops wasn't much of a solution, Mary Frances learned early. Cops understood the problems of the job better than civilians, but they knew the job too well. Boyfriends who were cops tended to get jealous of male partners. Or they would begin to believe some of the garbage other cops said about their girlfriends.

There were always stories of some kind. One of the precincts in the Bronx was known as Fort Hump for a while because so many cops had gotten married or divorced after women were assigned to work on patrol there. That kind of thing had died down for the most part by the time Sophia and Mary Frances had gone through the Academy. Of course, some romances developed, but no more than in any other job where men and women work together closely. A lot of the men, though, were apparently willing to believe anything they heard about a woman on the job.

Geri and Mary Frances had often laughed about it, wondering how the bosses downtown reacted when they heard about a romance. The department's official attitude had changed a lot in the past few years. As recently as twenty years ago, a male officer found living with a woman he was not married to could be suspended. It was considered conduct unbecoming to the department. Now, unmarried women who were expecting a baby were routinely given maternity leave and allowed to return to work. In some cases, women officers had had affairs with male cops, gotten pregnant and chosen to have the baby, but neither parent wanted to marry. Both continued to work. The official policy was that the department had no comment on an officer's private life, as long as it did not involve illegal activities.

Mary Frances had known about the gossip, thanks to Geri's warnings, and had not dated men from her own precinct. Doug had told her some of the stories going around in the men's locker room and she knew that most of them weren't true. There was always a hot rumor about a male cop who had been assigned to work with a woman officer for a day or who had acquired a female partner. Sophia was occasionally the subject of the rumors and Mary Frances knew which of the stories about her were true and which weren't. None of those that Doug passed on from the men's locker room were true.

Mary Frances would get furious for Sophia's sake, but Soph just laughed it off. She would say she was like Mae West and preferred being looked over to being overlooked. One time, a really disgusting sketch was put up on the bulletin board in the lounge. It showed a woman cop, one Mary Frances was sure was supposed to be Sophia, on her knees in front of a sergeant. Mary Frances was horrified, but Sophia just commented that she was surprised the drawing showed the woman out of uniform: she should be wearing a hat. The sketch disappeared that day and Mary Frances had to admit that Sophia's joking about it had probably been more effective than her own reaction.

A couple of years later, she and Doug had met for a drink after work one night and he admitted that she had been the subject of just as many rumors, but he had never told her about those. She was stunned. She couldn't believe that everyone in the precinct had assumed they were having an affair because they were good partners.

Doug explained that he had ignored most of the comments: "You can't deny it because they've got their minds made up." He thought about confronting one guy who was really nasty, but realized "the more I confront him the more he's going to believe we are, because I'm defending you. The more you go over and deny it, the more he's going to believe it."

Mary Frances was married to Neal and working in another precinct when Doug finally told her about the gossip, so she just ignored it. When she started working with Paul, she asked him if there was any gossip about them as a team. He was hesitant, but finally admitted that some guys in the precinct just assumed they were sleeping together. Mary Frances realized then that Doug had been right. There really wasn't anything that she could do but ignore it. Their friends knew the truth and Neal trusted her, and the ones who spread the rumors talked that way about everyone.

Cops were terrible gossips and not just within the precincts. That's why Mary Frances had been hesitant to date a cop even from another precinct. Sophia used to say that she sometimes expected to see reports on the latest couples on the orders when she got to work on Mondays. It wasn't quite that bad, but unless both people were being very discreet, word usually got around. So Mary Frances had been insistent when she told Doug that she wasn't interested in cops as dates.

But Doug dragged her off to dinner when they got off a four-to-twelve tour one night. They had been working together about six months then. They had had an early meal and he refused to stop for more than coffee, so she was starving and agreed to go with him. They were sitting at a table and another guy walked up, saying hello to Doug and sitting down. Doug introduced Neal Riley and Mary Frances kicked her partner in the shins for setting her up. She wasn't all that impressed with Neal. He seemed nice enough, six feet two, brown hair, brown eyes—nice brown eyes, in fact. But he was just another guy.

She smiled at herself in the rearview mirror of the car as she remembered how she turned him down the first time he asked her out. They did finally go out, obviously, and it turned out they had a lot in common: they were both Irish Catholics raised in Brooklyn and had attended parochial school. A year after that first date they were married, and a year after that she was pregnant. They had just celebrated their fourth anniversary and she didn't regret it, but at times Mary Frances wondered what her life would be like if she hadn't met Neal.

That wasn't getting her anywhere. What she really had to think about was what she wanted to do about the crazy working schedules. She could resign, but if she quit, what else would she do? Go back to nursing? No way. Stay home? She didn't want to do that either. Besides, they couldn't live on just Neal's salary. Between the two of them, they made nearly seventy thousand dollars last year and they were looking for a house. She would have to find some kind of work, and as long as she was going to be working she preferred what she was doing.

It was just that patrol was so frustrating sometimes, and so demanding. She and Paul had an agreement that gave her the early collars and him the late ones so she wouldn't have to work overtime, unless it was a really good one. Especially when they worked a four to midnight, Mary Frances hated going to Central Booking and having to stay there all night; it was so depressing.

But then so much of the job was depressing. It was almost eerie listening to Sally earlier. Mary Frances remembered feeling the same way. Coming from an Irish Catholic family, growing up in a house in Brooklyn with a backyard and a father who came home every night, going to church and parochial school, then nursing school—she had had such a normal, or protected, life. Even working with sick people in the hospital hadn't really prepared her for what she found when she became a police officer.

Mary Frances remembered her first day on the street in uniform. She had been assigned to walk a foot post on Thirty-fourth Street in front of Macy's, the "World's Largest Department Store." She was very nervous about being by herself. There was another cop a block away, but he was a rookie, too, and she didn't think he would be much help if there was trouble. She was right out of the Academy and hadn't expected to be out on the streets by herself so soon. She thought police officers patrolled with partners, but learned that was only in RMP's.

Mary Frances was very self-conscious in her uniform. She was used to uniforms because she had worn them first in parochial school, then as a nurse, but this one was different somehow. She kept catching glimpses of a female police officer in the big display windows of the department store and wondering who that silly-looking woman was, then realizing it was herself.

Her first day had been in July and it had been very hot. She was wearing a bulletproof vest, of course. It was tight around the middle, from under her arms to below her waist. She remembered wondering if the old-fashioned corsets had felt as uncomfortable.

Mary Frances had been terrified, not so much of getting hurt, but because she didn't know what she was doing. She had a radio, but she was afraid to use it. She could barely understand what was coming over, not that it mattered because she didn't remember the radio code signals anyway. They had gone over them a few times at the Academy, but there were a lot and the instructor told them they would learn them best when they got on the street.

She didn't know the area, beyond that she was on Thirty-fourth Street. Having grown up in Brooklyn, she thought of Manhattan as "The City." She knew Brooklyn very well, but the streets of Manhattan were still a mystery to her.

It was so hot Mary Frances could feel the sweat trickling between her breasts and knew there were wet patches under her arms. They rubbed on the sides of the vest and irritated her. She wasn't used to the uniform or the equipment belt. She had her gun, the radio, a flashlight, handcuffs, a can of Mace, memo book and pens, and a nightstick. It was hard to walk with all that weight on her hips and she felt fifty pounds heavier than usual. Her feet hurt because the leather in the men's-style shoes she was required to wear was stiffer than she was used to. And it was so hot. The sweat on her forehead made her hat slip down over and over again.

A call came over the radio, but Mary Frances couldn't understand most of it. All she heard was Thirty-fourth Street. Her heart was in her throat and she kept looking around in all directions, hoping she could spot whatever the cause of the call had been. She didn't know if she was supposed to answer and she didn't know what to say, so she didn't do anything.

She kept walking back and forth on the street, trying not to think about the quizzical looks she was getting from some passing pedestrians. She felt that she was on display. Everyone who saw her had some kind of reaction. Most people nodded or smiled or even waved, and she returned those greetings. A few people frowned and a couple sneered, but she ignored them. It got hotter and hotter and Mary Frances began to wonder what she was doing out there. She never did find out what the call was about.

She walked past the department store as a door opened, letting out a gust of air-conditioning. It felt so good, Mary Frances decided to just walk back and forth in front of the door. She wasn't sure if that was allowed, but she just couldn't keep walking up and down the street in the heat. The civilians were wearing sleeveless shirts and shorts or cotton skirts and sandals. Her uniform made the day seem twenty degrees hotter to her than it was to everyone else.

Mary Frances knew she couldn't leave the post, but she thought it would be okay if she just stayed in one place, in front of the door. She was still on post, she just wasn't walking. She was probably better off being in the middle of the block than stuck at one end if something happened anyway.

A couple of people asked her for directions. They looked like tourists, with cameras hanging around their necks, and they were looking for the Empire State Building. She could see it down the street, so she was able to point them in the right direction. She wasn't sure if she should, but to be safe, she made a notation in her memo book. So far, she had nothing else to write in it. She hoped no one would ask for anything more complicated. She had no idea of where anything was besides Macy's, Gimbels across the street, the Empire State Building in one direction and Madison Square Garden and Penn Station in the other. Mary Frances made a mental note to look at a map of the area if she was assigned the same post tomorrow.

The patrol sergeant came by after a couple of hours. He signed her memo book, showing she was on post. He waited with her until the air-conditioned door opened again. Then he smiled at Mary Frances and said, "You're learning."

By the time her meal hour came, Mary Frances couldn't wait to get to a bathroom. She went into Macy's to use the ladies' room and realized she had no place to hang her gunbelt. She was afraid to put it on the hook on the door, because someone could grab it while she had her pants off. So she sat on the seat with the gunbelt around her neck. Two women came in and Mary Frances could hear them wondering if a man was using the ladies' room when they spotted her pants and shoes under the stall door. They seemed relieved when she came out. She felt self-conscious, but cops had to go to the bathroom just like anyone else.

Mary Frances had another three hours on the post after

that. When her tour was over, she felt drained. Her shirt was plastered to her back and her hair was soaking wet under her hat. She thought she was used to walking, but eight hours of not being able to sit down was exhausting. Her feet, calves and thighs all hurt. She had managed to get through the day without anything more serious happening. And she came back the next day for more. She bought a tourists' guide to New York and kept it in a pocket so she could answer questions.

Mary Frances smiled at her memories as she drove into the driveway of the house she and Neal rented. That first day on patrol seemed like a lifetime ago. She couldn't believe she had ever been as naïve as that girl. Now, of course, she knew it was okay to stand in the middle of the block on a foot post, at least part of the time. The radio codes came naturally to her and the uniform was more comfortable. Glancing at her watch, she got out of the car. It was after two in the morning. She let herself into the house as quietly as possible.

She tiptoed into her son's room, stopping to touch him on the back of his head. As usual, Stevie was sleeping on his stomach and had kicked most of the covers off. Mary Frances covered him again, then went to the dresser and took out overalls and a long-sleeved shirt. She put the clothes on top of a chair at the foot of the bed. She kissed Stevie on the cheek and left his room.

Mary Frances wasn't sleepy and decided to read for a while before going to bed. She took off her gun and unloaded it. She walked into the bedroom to put it away and Neal woke up. He called to her, so she changed her mind about reading. He was half asleep, but woke up a bit when she kissed him.

"How was the pizza?" he asked.

"Okay. Geri and Soph met me, and a new girl from the precinct. She wanted to talk to someone and I invited her along. She's a bit unsure of herself and the dumb comments the guys in the house* are making aren't helping matters." As she talked, Mary Frances took off her clothes and put on a flannel nightgown.

"Did you girls tell her guys gossip worse than women and she should just ignore them?" he said, grinning. It was an old argument between them and she couldn't help laughing herself.

"That's exactly what we told her. It seemed to help." Mary

Frances crawled into the already warm bed. "Soph was also upset. She was talking about resigning because she had a run-in with an ADA and the duty captain."

"What happened?" he asked. Mary Frances told him briefly and he shook his head. "Your friend Sophia is a good cop, but she doesn't know how to pick her fights. She goes around telling everyone what they're doing wrong. She ought to know by now that people resent that. And it's not just because she's a woman. I hope she changes her mind about resigning. It would be a shame to lose her."

"I don't think she's serious," Mary Frances said. "She's just pissed off. She said she wouldn't make any final decision without talking to me some more. I've told her dozens of times to be more careful about what she says and to whom. She tries, but sometimes, she just can't help herself."

Neal kissed her again, then turned over to sleep. He had to get up in four hours to be at the precinct. She lay awake for a while, thinking again about her own dissatisfaction with the job. It wasn't often that they had even a brief conversation like this. They tried to talk on the phone a couple of times a day, but even that was difficult. She spent her working hours riding in a car and Neal wasn't always in the precinct either. Even when he was at a desk, he couldn't make long personal calls.

They managed somehow. Neal did a lot around the house. He did the laundry all the time and the dishes. Mary Frances hated doing dishes. It ruined her nails and besides, she did most of the cooking. Neal didn't want to learn how to cook and she remembered telling him, "Part of the meal is going to be yours. I cook, you do the dishes. When we get a dishwasher, you'll stack it."

He helped a lot with Stevie, too: feeding him, giving him baths. But she wouldn't let Neal dress him. She often thought Stevie could do better by himself, even at two. Neal couldn't pick a suit and tie that matched to save his life. Sometimes, she thought that was why he became a cop, so he could wear a uniform and not worry about shirts and ties and suits. She always laid out Stevie's clothes the night before.

Sometimes, Neal would have to work weekends or evenings

because of political meetings or block parties. Still, it was more often her schedule that disrupted their life together. And she was getting tired of being on patrol. Even the busiest days were becoming routine.

If she could get a plainclothes assignment her job would be more interesting, and she would probably be working mostly afternoons and evenings. Maybe Neal could adjust his hours. If he worked noon to eight and she worked two to ten, that wouldn't be too bad. Surely it would make sense to the CO* to let him start a bit later every day and work later into the day. It would be worth giving up some overtime money to have more time together.

Mary Frances decided to talk to Neal about changing schedules as long as she was on patrol. He was usually willing to compromise. He would vacuum if she didn't have time, even clean the bathrooms. But whenever that happened, he would wait until she got home and yell, "Don't make me a Harvey!" to tease her. Neal wasn't at all like the Harvey on *Cagney and Lacey*, but he knew he could make her feel guilty that way.

This was something that made sense. She would start thinking about requesting a transfer to something that would take her off round-the-clock patrol. One of the things she liked best about the Police Department was the number of alternatives available. There were a lot of inside jobs Mary Frances could ask for, in Support Services working on payroll or personnel, for example, but she wasn't ready for that yet. Or she might apply to teach at the Academy or the firing range. But she wanted to stay outside, working with people, helping them, being on the street. She liked that part of uniformed patrol but she had had enough of the routine work.

There were some cops—Paul, for example—who loved patrol and never considered anything else. Paul had worked plainclothes, but really didn't like it. He claimed to have more freedom riding in a radio car in uniform. She disagreed, feeling as if every move she made was being judged by a sergeant, then a lieutenant and then everyone else who outranked her. Mary Frances had liked patrol at first, and she would miss Paul a lot, but she had no intention of spending the next fifteen years of her life riding around in an RMP answering noise complaints. It was time to think about moving on.

She could request a transfer to one of the specialized units, Aviation or Mounted or Harbor Patrol, for instance. She liked horses, but she wasn't sure she would be happy scuba diving in the waters around New York City. And she didn't know how to fly a plane or a helicopter. She could apply for a transfer to the Organized Crime Control Bureau (OCCB).* Or she might get assigned to Internal Affairs, checking on reports of corruption among her fellow officers. Mary Frances didn't think she'd like doing that. If she got in the Highway Unit, she could ride a motorcycle.

She had still other options, including pursuing a promotion by taking the Civil Service test for sergeant. But Mary Frances wasn't sure she wanted to be a boss, at least not yet. Her real goal, like most cops, was to earn the promotion to detective, which was based on merit and not on the Civil Service test. And to get that gold shield,* she had to stay on the street.

# CHAPTER 4

**S**ally Weston walked to her car after leaving Geri and Mary Frances. She got her keys out of her purse, switched on the tiny flashlight on the key ring and checked the backseat before she unlocked the door. An instructor at the Academy had told her class to do that, and Sally had ever since, especially when she was in big parking lots, where other women had been attacked by men who hid in the backseats of their cars.

She drove home, going across the Brooklyn Bridge, then taking the Belt Parkway to the Verrazano Bridge to Staten Island. It didn't take long to drive at this hour of the night, but when she worked eight to fours, she was in rush-hour traffic in both directions and she hated driving.

Sally found herself thinking about her conversation with Mary Frances and Sophia. Sally had been somewhat intimidated by Geri Casey's presence and didn't mention what was really worrying her. She just didn't think she could do the job. She was shy and unsure of herself, not just around male cops, but around anyone. The few times she had gone out on patrol, she had let her partner do everything.

She hadn't done too much patrol work in the precinct yet because the administrative lieutenant found out she could type.

Sally typed up the reports on crimes and accidents for Borough Command,* the supervising office for the precinct.

The New York Police Department gathered statistics on everything: the number of crimes, what kinds of crimes, where they happened, when they happened, the victims, the perpetrators. Civilian aides did most of the routine work, but the department preferred that an officer do a lot of the office work. It was necessary, Sally knew, to allocate people and equipment, but she was getting bored doing it all the time.

The problem was, she was too good at it. The CO knew she could do more work than most of the other cops in the precinct and he liked her. She hadn't said anything before because it kept her off midnights. But sooner or later, she was going to have to go on patrol regularly. Besides, she wanted to find out whether she should stay on the job.

She looked at herself in the rearview mirror as she drove. It wasn't that she was afraid, exactly. At least Sally didn't think she was. She just wasn't sure she would say the right thing, or that anyone would listen to her if she did. Why should they? She weighed only 130 pounds. She was twenty-three years old and really didn't know very much. Why should anyone listen to her?

Sally shook her head as she drove. She remembered what the instructors at the Academy had told them: "It's not you talking, it's the uniform. You have to take command, establish a presence, set the tone. If someone doesn't listen, you have to take action to uphold the image of the department, for everyone." But she wasn't sure what action she could take.

She had tried to convince herself. She had been out of the Academy for more than six months. She had gotten through the assignment to the Neighborhood Stabilization Unit. She had some problems, but everyone has problems in NSU. It was like an orientation to patrol after the Academy, to ease the rookie cops into their new world. Mostly, NSU had been fun. Everyone was a rookie and they had often gone out together after work, sharing the problems of getting used to the job and the uniform. They had walked foot posts, been assigned to parades and demonstrations, and ridden in patrols with the training officers. They didn't go after criminals unless they saw something happen in front of them. Instead, the NSU Units, which were assigned by Borough Command, answered the low-priority calls if a precinct team was too busy, things like car alarms or littering problems. If they spotted drug dealers, they would notify Narcotics.* If they noticed groups of suspicious people, they would call in a plainclothes Anti-Crime Unit.

But now Sally was in a precinct. She wanted a chance to go on patrol and put her training to use. She just had to remember what she had been taught and do it.

But she still worried about her abilities. She had taken the Police Department test because she didn't know what else she wanted to do. She had been a Phys Ed major in college, but she didn't want to teach girls' gym classes. The Police Department sounded different. The money was good, the vacations and benefits were terrific, and she didn't mind working nights and weekends. Her father was delighted. He had been a career army man, retiring when she was twelve. Her husband, Jim, was supportive. He worked in a bank and liked the idea of introducing her as my wife the cop. He also thought it would help her to be more self-confident.

The rest of her family had been more doubtful. Her mother didn't think Sally would stick with it. She was afraid of the dark and just too soft, in her mother's opinion. It was true Sally cried at sad movies or at the thought of an animal in pain, or at almost anything upsetting. But she really didn't know what else she wanted to do and this was a way of helping people, and she liked doing that.

While she was still in NSU, Sally remembered calming an old lady who had been knocked down by someone on the street. The woman hadn't been hurt, but she was frightened and upset, and Sally had been sympathetic and understanding while the male cops with her had been brusque. The old lady couldn't believe Sally was a cop, but she was grateful that someone had been nice to her and taken the time to help her.

Sally liked that part of the job, talking to old ladies and

children. It was the thought of people yelling or the confusion of a fight or the kids who ran wild and talked back that worried her. How would she handle that? What would she do in a fight? She had learned self-defense at the Academy, but that was when no one was really trying to hurt her. What would happen in a real fight on the street?

That was really what she wanted to talk to Mary Frances about. She always seemed so sure of herself. Mary Frances wasn't much bigger than Sally, although she was stockier. But she obviously liked being thought of as a woman. She often came to work in a skirt or dress and always had on makeup and nail polish. Some of the other girls in the precinct swore like long-shoremen, wore jeans and heavy hiking boots, and never seemed to care what they looked like.

Sally thought of herself as shy and unassertive. At the Academy, the instructors had praised her for keeping her voice down when they role-played emergencies. But she knew she had really done it only because she just wasn't used to shouting.

Only two blocks away from home, Sally decided to see if she could find an open coffee shop or something. She didn't feel like going to a bar, where she might be approached by strangers. But she was hungry. She turned off Richmond Avenue and drove aimlessly through the side streets, trying to decide if she should find a McDonald's or a real coffee shop.

Sally noticed a double-parked car because it seemed out of place on the nearly empty street. It was a dark, late-model Datsun with Jersey plates. The trunk lock was popped and so was one door lock. It might be stolen. The car had tinted side windows, so she couldn't tell how many people were inside. She noted the license plate and decided she would call the local precinct when she found someplace to eat. She kept going and turned right at the next corner.

As she looked into her rearview mirror, Sally noticed the car that had been double-parked was now behind her. She made another right and found herself stopped at a light. The Datsun pulled up next to her. Sally could see two men in the front seat through the windshield, but she still couldn't see into the backseat. The two guys seemed to be staring at her. At this hour of the night anything could happen in New York, but this was the first time Sally had run into a problem coming home so late.

The light changed and Sally drove off with the Datsun right next to her. The streets were deserted and they had no trouble staying with her. Sally was nervous with the car trailing her like that. She wasn't sure what they wanted. She turned right at the next corner and the Datsun followed. Sally was beginning to get worried and pulled her gun into her lap. The weight was comforting and she was glad she had it.

She was several blocks from a main street and tried honking the horn, hoping someone would get angry and call 911. But she was still driving and the sound probably wasn't loud enough or long enough to wake anyone. Sally thought about stopping and leaning on the horn, but she was sure if she did that the Datsun would stop, too.

At the next light, the Datsun pulled slightly in front of her, at an angle. Sally could not go forward without hitting the other car. The person on the passenger side rolled down the window. Sally kept hers closed, determined not to give him a way to force himself into her car. She yelled through the closed window, "Buddy, move your car!" but she wondered if they could hear her.

"We're not moving. What are you going to do about it?" She heard that through the closed window very clearly.

"Get out of here or I'm calling the police!" Sally knew it was an empty threat. She didn't have a radio and they could tell she didn't have a phone, either. Sure enough, the guy asked how she was going to call the police.

The light changed, and changed again. Sally leaned on the horn, hoping someone would be awake and call the emergency operator or the precinct to complain. It seemed to be hours, and all she could do was try to reason with them. She still didn't roll down the window. She shouted loud enough for them to hear her.

"Come on, guys, just get out of here. I just want to take off and go home."

"We're not moving. What are you going to do about it?"

Sally could see the two in front laughing, but she still didn't know how many others were in the car. She didn't know if they had guns, but she was fairly sure the Datsun was stolen because of the two popped locks. The two people she could see looked like kids, not more than sixteen or seventeen.

There really wasn't too much they could do to her, as long as she stayed in her car with the windows closed. They might ram her car with theirs, but she didn't think they would. They couldn't get to her physically, so she wasn't concerned about rape. Anyway, she had her gun. As she considered the possibilities, the youth on the passenger side spit at her, the saliva sliding down the window in front of her face.

A wave of anger surged through Sally. She felt as if her whole body was on fire, from the inside. She saw a red mist for a few seconds, then felt the white heat of a fury stronger than any she had known before. She was trembling from the force of her rage. No one had ever spit at her before. Even if it hadn't hit her, she felt humiliated. And infuriated. And helpless.

What could she do? If she got out of her car and identified herself as a cop, they might have guns. Approaching an unknown number of people in a probably stolen car by herself violated every procedure and tactic she had been taught. She had no idea how many other people might be in the backseat. She couldn't arrest even the two she could see by herself, and she had no way to call for help as long as she was locked in her car. She pounded furiously at the horn, unable to think of anything else to do.

Suddenly, the Datsun sped away. Sally repeated the license plate to herself, unable to believe her luck. She wondered what had chased them off, then saw the headlights of another car coming up behind her. Sally drove off, following the Datsun. Still raging and humiliated, she looked for a telephone to call 911 and report a stolen car. She wanted to see those jokers arrested if the car was stolen. Even if it wasn't, she wanted to give them a scare, like the one they had given her. She followed them back on to Richmond Avenue and suddenly noticed a radio car coming toward her. Maybe someone had heard her horn!

She flagged down the RMP and identified herself. She told

the cops inside that she wanted to stop the Datsun, that she was sure it had been stolen and described it to them. They made a U-turn and took off with lights and sirens on. Within minutes, they had pulled the Datsun over.

Sally was right behind the radio car and jumped out with the two cops. She was still furious and needed to do something to relieve the tension of the last few minutes. She had her gun out and her badge on a chain around her neck, and waved to the cop making the approach on the passenger's side. He let her go ahead, standing behind her. While his partner asked the driver for his license and registration, Sally moved to the passenger door with her gun in a two-hand grip. The spitter turned around and stared down the barrel of her gun. His face turned white. He looked like someone seeing a dozen fully loaded semis bearing down on him through the Holland Tunnel.

Sally jerked the door open and dragged the kid from the car. She was still so angry she didn't even realize that she was taking physical action against a possible criminal for the first time. She pushed him up against the side of the car, kicking his legs apart. She patted him down, too angry to feel embarrassed as she felt his groin for a possible weapon. His head turned and his eyes widened as he recognized her. He started blubbering, apologizing, saying he was sorry, he didn't know she was a cop, he didn't mean anything by it.

"Oh, it's all right to do that to any passing woman, as long as she isn't a cop? You scared the shit out of me. I thought I was going to get robbed at the very least," Sally practically hissed at him.

She insisted the two cops from the local precinct take the pair in, checking for warrants against them. The stolen car check with Central* turned up nothing on the car but that might be because they had just stolen it. In any case, a look in the backseat revealed several stolen car radios. The car's driver was pulled out, handcuffed and frisked. Both kids gave Bronx addresses. They had probably driven to Staten Island to steal car radios.

Sally let the two uniforms take the collar. She listened to the cops read them the Miranda warning,* finally calm enough to be amazed at her own action. She couldn't believe she had gone after that kid and dragged him out of the car. She had just been so angry at them for scaring her, for spitting at her, for being so selfish and thoughtless of others, that she hadn't stopped to think about it.

The two cops were very nice to her after she said they could take the collar. She didn't want to go back to the precinct and get involved in the arrest procedure. She agreed to testify if needed, but right now she had a lot to think about and she didn't want to be distracted.

Sally realized she wasn't hungry anymore, so she drove to the two-family house she and Jim shared with her parents. She pushed the button to open the garage doors and drove in. Another button brought the doors down again and she unlocked the door to the house. Jim was asleep, but she was too wound up to get into bed. She put her gun in a drawer of the desk she locked, then took off her clothes and put on a nightgown.

Sally was tired but not sleepy. She went into the kitchen and poured herself a glass of white wine from an open bottle in the refrigerator. In the living room, she sat down in an easy chair and lit a couple of candles sitting on a table. She didn't want to put a light on.

Now that she was home safe, she started to shake. Sally could not remember being so angry in her life. She could see the whole thing, hear again the sound of their obscene laughter muffled through the closed car window. Sally remembered the spurt of pure fury when she realized the little punk had spit at her. And the rage she had felt when she pulled him out of the car.

It had felt good to take action. She had been angry, but she still hadn't lost control of the situation. She hadn't shown her anger or her fear. She hadn't been afraid at the time. She had just reacted the way she had been taught. She was grateful she had known what to do, even as small a thing as not opening the windows. Had she still been a civilian, she wasn't sure she would have gotten away safely. Of course, if she had been a civilian, she probably wouldn't be coming home from work at this hour. Still, this was the first time something like this had happened to her and she was pleased with what she had done.

After what happened tonight, Sally felt a lot more confident. She knew she had handled herself well. She had noticed the suspicious car, waited until she had backup to move on them and then acted with authority. She saw again the look on the kid's face when he was staring down her gun barrel. He had been scared and even after she put her gun back in the holster, he had not tried to get away. As soon as he realized he had been spitting at, and making wise-ass comments to, a police officer, he had apologized.

She hadn't wanted a career chasing criminals before she took the test, but now that she was a cop, she ought to be doing what she was trained for. If she couldn't do some of it, it was better that she find out now. She remembered what Geri Casey had said earlier about it taking longer for women to develop confidence on the job. If it was going to take her longer than other cops, it was time she got started.

The next day, Sally decided, she would request patrol assignments. She would tell them she was tired of typing. It would probably mean doing foot posts for a while and working midnights. She would have to explain to Jim. She had just learned that she was as well trained as any other cop. The time had come for her to put that training to use.

# CHAPTER 5

Sophia drove up the Henry Hudson Parkway to the Cross Bronx Expressway, then across the borough to Co-Op City. She didn't like the huge development, but she loved her apartment. It was one of the few good things from her marriage. She and Greg had bought the one-bedroom apartment when they got married and she had kept it. They almost got a two-bedroom, but decided they could always trade up if they needed more room. Now she was glad they had decided on the smaller one.

She thought back on what had happened that day, her confrontation with the woman in the District Attorney's office and her meeting with Mary Frances and Geri. She knew they were right that she shouldn't let those things bother her so much. She had been on the job long enough to know that. But sometimes she just couldn't let go of things. It had been a problem from the very beginning on this job, even when she was still at the Academy.

Sophia Amadetto and Mary Frances Devlin had met on their first day at the Police Academy. Sophia was three years older than Mary Frances, and both of them were older than most of the other recruits. While Mary Frances had worked as a nurse before taking the police test, Sophia had been an executive secretary. She had been bored with the nine-to-five routine and the sameness of her days. Greg was a sergeant then, and had suggested she take the test. It had sounded exciting, a job that wasn't routine, that offered different challenges all the time, so she had done it.

That first day, at the orientation, she and Mary Frances had looked around the auditorium at the apparently beardless boys and giggling girls and seemed to draw together. By chance, they were put in the same company,* so they spent most of the next six months together.

They were both self-conscious at first, but so was everyone else. Everybody looked nervous, wondering what would happen next. The class listened to the instructions about the uniform and where they could buy it. They learned that they would have to purchase their own equipment as well as uniforms throughout their police career, including guns and ammunition. Of course, they were given a yearly uniform allowance and got some ammunition every time they had to go to the firing range to qualify with their guns.

They got a description of the schedule they would be following for the next half year and the details of the curriculum. They learned where to buy the equipment they needed, how to organize the Patrol Guide* and the discipline and restrictions they would be following. They were told that they must use the stairs to get around the Academy. The elevators were for instructors unless a student had a temporary medical excuse.

The next day they felt even more uncomfortable, dressed in the Academy uniform, made up of light blue shirts, dark blue pants, a clip-on tie with a tie clip and black men's shoes. The required black vinyl bags, like old-fashioned gym bags, felt awkward and clumsy to them at first. By the time the six months were over, those bags were like an extension of their arms. The Academy didn't have lockers for the students except during gym for their regular uniforms. As a result, they carried everything with them at all times: books, gym equipment, towels, notebooks and nightsticks. You could always tell a police recruit walking on the street by that black vinyl bag with the wooden baton hanging out.

That half year was probably the toughest they had on the

job. They were due at the Academy by seven-thirty every morning for roll call and inspection. The Police Department was a quasi-military organization and made sure the students knew that from the beginning. The Academy, even more than the precincts, was run like an army base.

Recruits were organized into companies of about forty each. One recruit, usually someone with military experience, was named company sergeant. The company sergeant's job was to give orders during inspections and parades, to report on attendance to the officers and to be general spokesperson for the members of the company. The first week or so was spent learning how to march, to stand at attention, to salute, and all of the other bits and pieces necessary to turn them into a military unit. Orders were given in the peculiar grunts and unintelligible phrases of the military. They were taught how to do about-faces, right and left turns and all the rest.

On the second day Sophia and Mary Frances learned how unprepared the Police Department was for women. Many of the women's bathrooms in the building, which was not yet twenty years old, had urinals. As recently as 1965, when the building was built, no one had expected large numbers of women to be at the Academy. Their class was one of the first in which women and men were going through the Academy together.

It was also one of the first since New York City's fiscal crisis when thousands of cops had been laid off and no new ones had been trained until they were rehired. The layoffs began in July 1975 and the rehirings continued until October 1979.

Just two years before the layoffs began, the status of women in the department had changed drastically. Before 1973 there had been two kinds of police officers, policemen and policewomen. Women were assigned to the Youth Division, as jail matrons or undercover officers. If they wore uniforms, they had skirts, not pants. Most dressed in civilian clothes and they did not patrol in the precincts. That changed in 1973, when the title was changed to police officer and women were put in the precincts. Before that, policewomen got training similar to, but separate from and less thorough than, the men's.

When the recruitment and training program began again

in 1980, women had been patrolling in uniform for several years, although most of them had been laid off, then rehired. There had been a few problems at first because the women sent into the precincts in 1973 had not been trained for patrol duty and most of them had come on the job not expecting to do that kind of work.

Putting women into precincts had created some unexpected problems. At first, the women continued to wear skirts, but that proved unworkable so the regulations were changed to pants like the men's. Of course, the pants for women had to be tailored differently and that took some time to figure out.

The uniform hats for the women were different at first, too. They were also more expensive and shrank every time it rained. After a couple of years of protest, the department changed the hat to the same one the men wore.

Then there were the shirts and tie clips. Somehow, most of the women in their class who had received women's tie clasps had not been able to find a women's uniform shirt, or most of those who had the women's shirt had been given men's tie clasps. There were never enough women's shirts *and* tie clasps for any one class. As a result, almost every woman in the class went around with an upside-down tie clip. After a week or so, the instructors stopped commenting on it. There really wasn't much that could be done until more women's shirts and tie clasps were ordered.

Once the new class had mastered the rudiments of military discipline and marching, the real work began. Every day, the company stood at attention while Academy instructors did a person-by-person inspection, checking for scuffed shoes, wrinkled uniforms, hair that touched shirt collars and other violations of the dress and appearance code.

The curriculum was straightforward: three classes a day (Law, Social Science and Police Science), each class ninety minutes long, plus two hours of Physical Education. Every couple of weeks the schedule changed, so no single company had gym at the end of every day for the duration. That was lucky.

Gym began with a half hour of warm-up exercises, followed by a two-mile run. The rest of the time was devoted to self-defense training. It was exhausting. Geri had warned Mary Frances about it, and she had started jogging as soon as she had learned she was accepted. Still, after gym she was always tired and her muscles ached. Sophia was also in better shape than most of the other recruits, thanks to her gymnastic training, but she, too, felt the strain most days. She and Mary Frances usually stayed together during the run. They often wondered how some of their fatter classmates made that daily run. Of course, by the time they graduated from the Academy, those classmates had lost a lot of weight.

The department preferred that officers approximated the standards set by the Metropolitan Life Insurance Company's weight tables, according to height and frame, but once out of the Academy, weight problems were pretty much left up to individual officers. Occasionally, a commanding officer would lecture his troops about being overweight and require diets or exercising. But, for the most part, if you could do the job, your weight didn't matter. The Phys Ed courses included instruction in aerobics, in hopes the recruits would keep up their own exercise program so they could stay in shape on the job.

They also learned some basic first aid: cardiopulmonary resuscitation, the Heimlich maneuver and the other standard emergency procedures for accident victims or someone suffering from an unexpected illness. They learned to elevate bleeding wounds, not to force liquids on unconscious victims, to cool and cover burns with cloth, not coat them with butter. Mostly, they were told to make the victims as comfortable as possible and to get medical help as quickly as they could.

They were taught what to do about live wires and gas leaks, radioactive materials and toxic chemicals. They also learned how to make rescues from water or ice and how to deliver a baby, although few police officers would have a chance to put that training to use. That instruction made all the men nervous, but the women just laughed when the instructor kept saying, "Let Nature do the work."

Self-defense courses were the most fun. They were taught how to search suspects and how to put on handcuffs. They spent time practicing vehicle stops, learning to split up to approach a car or truck safely, where to stand and how to watch the occupants. Some of the things they were told seemed simplistic, but the instructors always had horror stories about a cop who was killed because he hadn't followed procedures.

They spent days learning how to use their batons: how to hold it while walking down the street, while talking to people, when controlling a crowd. They learned how to use it as a defensive weapon, how to block attackers and how to use it to combat knives and clubs. There were lessons in the various formations used for crowd and riot control, so they could work with large numbers of other cops.

There was training in how to fall safely and how to trip someone. They practiced the rudiments of boxing, judo and other self-defense techniques, learning how much force to use in various situations. The women in their company found those subjects the hardest to learn.

Sophia was better than Mary Frances in most of the gym work. She had been a gymnast in high school and kept up with it, so she was a lot stronger than she looked. They still laughed when they remembered their first boxing lesson. Soph had been in the ring, paired with one of the guys. He was supposed to be a bad guy, and Soph was expected to win, but she wasn't doing too well. She didn't know much about boxing and couldn't seem to land even one punch. Finally, she just got mad and kneed him in the groin. The poor guy doubled over and fell to the mat while the instructor screamed at Sophia that she wasn't fighting fairly.

Sophia had looked at him and said, "I didn't know they used the Marquis of Queensberry rules on the street." The rest of the company broke up, and the instructor admitted that on the street it was best to do what would help you regain control and not necessarily to follow the rules.

Then there had been Inez Miranda. She was the smallest woman in their company, barely five feet tall and not quite a hundred pounds. During the boxing classes an instructor with a sick sense of humor had matched her with one of the biggest guys. The company laughed hysterically when the matchup was announced, and even more when they saw them climb into the ring together. Inez was a sweet kid, from a Puerto Rican family. She was born in New York and spoke fluent Spanish and English without a trace of an accent in either language. She hadn't complained when told who her sparring partner would be, and Soph and Mary Frances figured she would just get in the ring, take a couple of punches and get out.

The match began, and in less than a minute Inez's six-foot partner was on the mat, shaking his head. The instructor looked stunned. The rest of the company was laughing and Inez raised her gloved hands above her head in the traditional victory gesture.

Figuring it was a lucky punch, the instructor sent another guy into the ring. This one was almost as big as the first. Inez waited while he put on the gloves, moved to the center, went into the "on guard" position and started sparring. A minute later, the boxer was on one knee, shaking his head from a solid right to the jaw. Sophia and Mary Frances had watched more carefully this time. Inez, although much smaller, had gone under his arm and, almost on tiptoe, really punched him. A third partner was set up for her. In two minutes he, too, was on the mat.

The instructor congratulated Inez on winning the matches, agreed she didn't need any more practice in boxing, then asked how she had managed her victories. Faking a thick Spanish accent, Inez explained: "My brother Ramon, he was a Golden Gloves champion at seventeen and my brother Jaime at sixteen. Now my little brothers, Carlos and Jesus, they also fight in the Golden Gloves. And they all fight with me, their sister, *si!*"

Sophia and Mary Frances laughed until tears ran down their faces. So did most of the other women in the company. Their company, at least, heard no more jokes about women and boxing.

The classroom courses were even harder than Phys Ed. Each lasted ninety minutes every day. They got a five-minute break and then went back to the same seats. Unlike high school and college, at the Police Academy the students stayed in one place and the instructors moved from classroom to classroom.

It wasn't just sitting in one place all day that was hard. The work was difficult. The Law course went over every possible criminal law in the state, in detail. They learned more about criminal law than law students do, getting more than a hundred hours of lectures. They learned the five subdivisions of harassment, the seven categories of grand larceny, the eight ways to commit theft of service and the legal definitions of all possible sex offenses.

The students were surprised to learn that burglary had nothing to do with stealing. Burglary was a felony committed by unlawfully entering a building with the intent to commit a crime. The theft crimes were larceny—the unlawful taking of property—and robbery—the forcible stealing of property from another person. Most burglaries involved theft, but a person who entered a building illegally to commit a murder, kidnapping, arson or other crime could also be charged with burglary.

They were taught the standards of proof required in court, ways to interrogate suspects and the rules of evidence in a court of law. They learned the importance of keeping memo books accurately and neatly. Police memo books were often used as evidence in criminal cases and the instructors explained if the defense attorney could find one mistake, everything in the memo book could be called into question.

They learned the concepts behind the constitutional protections of suspects and studied the latest Supreme Court decisions on arrest procedure, searches and confessions. They defined probable cause—what any reasonable or prudent person would think under the circumstance.

They were instructed in the legal requirements for Stop, Question and Frisk. Police officers could not just stop anyone on the street to ask questions. They had to have a reasonable suspicion that the person being questioned had committed, or was about to commit, a crime.

One instructor offered an example: A rash of delivery truck robberies had been committed in the area by one tall man and one short man. Two officers noticing a tall man and a short man walking down the street together might have a suspicion that they were the suspects, but they could not be questioned. The officers could, however, follow them. If the pair then acted suspiciously—watching delivery trucks, turning around to look behind them all the time, keeping their hands on something in their pockets—the officers then would have a reasonable suspicion to stop them.

Even then, they could not arrest them just on that suspicion. The officers could question them, and if the answers were unacceptable or raised more questions, they could take them to the precinct for more questions. While questioning the pair, the police officers could search them—pat down their clothes for possible weapons. If a weapon was found, then there would be cause for arrest.

The class practiced giving testimony at moot court sessions, learned how to conduct lineups and memorized the important questions to ask witnesses. They were taught to ask questions that did not lead the witness, but provided information. They were reminded about giving a Miranda warning, informing a suspect of the right to an attorney and to protection against self-incrimination.

Over and over, they were reminded that solid cases against apparently guilty people were lost because police officers had not conducted proper searches or had not asked the right questions of the right people. They heard in detail how important clues were destroyed because the first officer on the scene of a crime had messed up the evidence or allowed others to do so.

They spent days studying the laws and legal decisions about searches—of people, of cars, of homes and workplaces. They studied the important constitutional cases in detail. They explored when to conduct a search before, during and after an arrest. They learned how to apply for a search warrant and when one was not necessary.

They also learned when to arrest a young person as a juvenile and when as an adult, the cases applicable for Family Court, how a police officer might be liable in a civil suit, what charges to bring in a domestic dispute, and how to send people to Civil Court when no criminal charge was involved.

And that was just the Law curriculum.

The Police Science course was almost as bad. They read analyses of police work that were supposed to show the most effective ways to settle domestic disputes, calming both parties and separating them. They learned the causes of riots when police lost control of a situation and the most successful approaches to preventing potentially violent confrontations, and calming responses to emergencies.

Over and over again, they were told to use common sense, to keep cool and remember their position as objective police officers. It seemed to come as a shock to some of the recruits to learn that most police work was service and not running after bad guys. They hadn't realized that, at least while they were on patrol in uniform, they would spend most of their time helping people who were hurt or sick, taking care of lost children, getting people back into their apartments and reassuring crime victims. The work of catching criminals was done mostly by the police officers who worked in civilian clothes. The uniformed officers riding in marked patrol cars were considered deterrents, too obvious to do much good at catching someone in the act of committing a crime.

Much of what they learned in Police Science classes repeated the lessons from Law, but from a different perspective. They went over interviewing and investigation procedures, learned again the importance of accurate recordkeeping, and the techniques for arrests and for giving testimony in court and to the Grand Jury. They practiced taking fingerprints from each other. These classes were more interesting than Law because they used role-playing to teach tactics or watched videotapes or films to illustrate the points being made.

Whole days were spent learning how to fill out the Universal Summons—the form used for traffic violations, parking tickets, misdemeanor crimes that required a court appearance and even violations of the city's environmental protection law. Recruits were taught how to identify explosives, the need to be objective at political demonstrations, and their role as referee in fights, disputes and confrontations. Although all crimes were investigated by detectives, they, as the first police officers to come on the scene in most cases, were taught how to preserve evidence, how to search areas, whom to question and what questions to ask.

There were classes in traffic control and direction, in safety precautions at hazardous locations and in ways to identify accident-prone drivers, that is, people who drove erratically and disregarded lane markers. They learned what to do for accident victims who were injured and for those in shock. They discussed the most often encountered violations of the city traffic regulations and the provisions of the state's Vehicle and Traffic Law; what to do about drivers who ignored a red light and pedestrians who jaywalked. They were taught how to determine if a New York State driver's license was real or fake.

They learned the police alphabet, using words instead of letters. They were taught to give numbers one through ten only, so if something happened at 543 East 172nd Street, it would come out five-four-three east one-seven-two street. That way, the instructor explained, there was less chance of a mixup. Once they got on patrol and used the radio, they understood how important that was.

Sophia and Mary Frances agreed the best classes were Social Science, although they often wondered if someone could be taught to be courteous and friendly. That was the gist of the course—the need for police officers to be helpful, patient and understanding with the public. The Social Science instructor emphasized, even more than the others, that 85 percent of police work does not involve criminals, but the public.

Again and again, they were reminded that police officers most often encounter civilians at moments of great stress, after an accident or crime. Part of their job was to stay calm and help the victim regain composure. They were also reminded that the Police Department was a catchall agency. When people didn't know whom else to call, they called the police for help, regardless of what kind of help they needed. It was incumbent on police, especially in a city the size of New York, to know where to find the most effective help.

Each instructor seemed to have a few pet acronyms to help the students remember what they were learning. There were so many acronyms that Sophia had forgotten most of them. But she remembered a few well, even six years later.

DR. BARKS was the acronym for the serious crimes that a police officer could use Deadly Physical Force to prevent: the use of Deadly Physical Force against oneself or a third person; Robbery; Burglary; Arson; Rape, Forcible; Kidnapping; and Sodomy, Forcible. (That meant a cop was not justified in using a gun to stop Statutory Rape.)

It was permissible to use deadly physical force to arrest a person who was known to have committed the serious crimes represented by MR. & MRS.: Murder, Robbery, Manslaughter (First Degree), Rape (Forcible) and Sodomy (Forcible).

Sophia also found herself thinking SOS when faced with a crisis because one instructor had taught her to think of emergencies as Sudden Overwhelming Stressful Events. And that, it was true, did help her to stay calm and keep other people in order.

First SOS would flash into her mind, then the rest of the techniques explained that day would follow: the ways to use body posture, how to act like the adult, but not like a parent and especially not like a child. Sophia would remember not to point her finger, to reassure those who were upset and to get information from everyone involved in the situation so she could make the most informed decision about what action to take. Most of all, thinking SOS would remind her to stay in control, not to let her emotions dictate her actions.

Sophia got off the expressway, drove along the road that circled most of the Co-Op City site and into the garage near her building. She hated the idea of so many people living so close together—there were five hundred apartments in the high-rise she lived in and more than fifteen thousand in the entire complex. But it was convenient to have shopping so close, and a safe place to park.

She walked from the garage to her building, thinking over her memories of the Academy. Why had she been thinking about that? Sophia laughed. She should have remembered SOS today, when that damn ADA made her so angry. It seemed that she could recognize Sudden Overwhelming Stressful Events for others, but not for herself. Had she thought SOS, she would probably not have lost her temper.

As she took the elevator to her apartment and unlocked the door, Sophia decided to try to put some of that police professionalism to work in her personal life. She had learned to control herself on the street, to keep the tears out of her eyes and the tremor from her voice. After everything was over and she was alone with her partners or at home, sometimes she would cry. But she never did so in public. She had learned that while still in uniform—maybe being in uniform had helped.

Soon after they started working together, she and Irv had come across a dog that had been run over. The driver had not even bothered to stop and some kids in the neighborhood had flagged their patrol car down. Sophia could see there was no way to save the poor thing. It was in pain and she really wanted to take her gun and put it out of its misery, but the City of New York frowned on that.

She had sat there, holding its head in her lap, looking into brown eyes that seemed to ask her for mercy, waiting for the ASPCA to show up. Sophia petted the dog on its head, hoping that would help and biting back her tears. She kept hearing the neighborhood kids whispering about the lady cop and the dead dog. It wasn't dead yet, but that was only a matter of time.

She didn't cry then, at least not until the dog was taken away and she and Irv were back in the car. Irv didn't say anything at first, but when Sophia reached for a Kleenex, he patted her hand and muttered, "You were all right out there. You didn't embarrass me." She looked at him and he shifted his eyes. "I thought you were going to start crying," he said. "I like working with you. It's a lot better than I thought it would be, but I won't work with a partner who cries on the job."

Sophia had laughed at that, but it stuck in her memory. She had learned to control the tears—and the other emotions. She had learned that Irv was right. Her fellow cops and the public would accept women in uniform, but they wouldn't accept uniformed cops who cried.

# CHAPTER 6

Sophia got to the precinct about one the next afternoon, Wednesday. Her court appearance was postponed to another day, a delay requested by the defense attorney. It took a couple of hours for that to happen, and by then it was time for lunch. She ate downtown with a couple of friends who worked at One Police Plaza, the police headquarters building behind City Hall.

Afterward, she drove to the precinct, planning to do some long-put-off paperwork: monthly reports, requests for commendations and vacation days. She hated the self-congratulatory attitude needed to write up Requests for Departmental Recognition, but it was expected. No one else was going to recommend her for medals unless the case was spectacular, and a cop was lucky to get one really good case in a career. Until that one came along, she had to follow custom and make her own reports of her good police work. She would have preferred to ignore the whole thing, but if she wanted to make detective or get into a special unit, she had to have more than marksmanship medals. That was just one of the little odd jogs in the career path of the Police Department.

There were others. Sophia had discovered them one by one: the need to stay in touch with previous supervisors, the imperative of getting out from under personal conflicts with bosses, the stories that trailed along with job changes, the hook* from headquarters. The politics of promotions in the Police Department came easily for some, but to Sophia, they smacked of favoritism, nepotism and sexism, and she had had many problems adjusting to their necessity.

Fortunately, she didn't want a position of power. She would be perfectly happy to make detective in a year or two and work at that level. Of course, she wanted interesting assignments as a detective, but she had no desire to become a boss. Sophia knew some women who wanted to make police commissioner, but she liked the challenge of police work, not administration and power. It was a good thing, because she had made some mistakes and some enemies. She also impressed some bosses, so she thought she came out about even, as long as she kept her sights on a gold shield and not a command.

But that didn't mean Sophia could ignore the need for recognition of her work, which meant she had to write up her best collars, explaining the circumstances and why they represented good police work. It meant going back to the original crime complaints and checking the details. Most of her write-ups were almost duplicates of the original complaints, but she added a few adjectives to point out careful police work, extra bravery or smart instincts she might have used. It was like patting herself on the back, hoping the action would attract someone's attention and they would take over.

She sat down at her desk, automatically kicking the bottom drawer so it would open. Like most of the furnishings in the room, it had seen better days. She had gotten used to its idiosyncrasies. She kept her purse in the drawer that had to be kicked open, thinking if a thief ever got this far in the precinct, he would never figure out how to open the drawer. So far, no one had.

Sophia picked up a typewriter from another desk. She still found it hard to believe the Police Department had so many old manual typewriters. But then she had watched some of her colleagues typing up 61's—the reports filed by victims with the first police officers when a crime has been committed—with two fingers, a wing and a prayer. Obviously, anything more complicated would slow them down even more. As a secretary, she had used an electric for years before she came on the job and found it hard to adjust at first to the old-fashioned manuals again. Now she was used to them.

Her partners, Norm and Van, came in before roll call. They were both surprised to see her. Sophia explained about the case being postponed again. They asked if she was going out on patrol with them, but she said no. She was working a day shift* because of the court appearance and going on patrol would mean overtime. They seemed none the worse for the cuts they had received from the nut with the broken bottle. They left, saying they would be waiting for her tomorrow.

She was sorry to be stuck in the office. Sophia had liked being on patrol in uniform, but she liked the Anti-Crime work she did now even better. It was much more rewarding. They worked in plainclothes and often caught criminals immediately after they had committed a crime. The victims were usually right there and were always grateful.

The three of them rode in an unmarked car, driving around the precinct, looking for suspicious people, people who appeared to be getting ready to grab a purse, commit a robbery or steal a car. Spotting potential trouble was easier than most people thought. Sophia had learned to recognize the telltale signs almost subconsciously. A little bell went off whenever she spotted two or three people, usually teenagers or young men, all wearing sneakers (known as "Felony-Flyers"), and walking against traffic on a one-way street. One kid would be a few yards ahead of the group as a lookout, another a few yards behind them. They all looked around constantly and kept their hands in their pockets, usually holding whatever weapons they had. They would walk around for hours, eyeing potential victims. If an Anti-Crime team in the precinct spotted such a group, they would start to follow, two people on foot, the third staying as close as possible in a car. That's how they caught them so quickly.

Sophia sighed, thinking she would be back with Norm and Van tomorrow, and went back to her paperwork. The lieutenant stopped by and she gave the Requests for Departmental Recognition she had completed to him to sign. She told him about her run-in with the ADA the day before, and he just looked at her and shook his head. He didn't even bother with a comment. He left and Sophia was alone in the Anti-Crime squad room. Everyone else was out on patrol or had the day off.

The phone on her desk rang and Sophia answered it. The caller was one of the new young women in the precinct who had been on the job only about eighteen months. Sophia didn't know her very well, but was her contact as the representative for the Policewomen's Endowment Association. She often got calls from the other women because she held that position.

Her name was Kate Delano and she was calling Sophia to complain. Earlier in the week she had gotten a call from the administrative lieutenant in the house telling her to come in and work a sixth day, just before her regular weekend. She was furious because it was her regular day off and she had other plans.

Kate said she had told the lieutenant that she didn't want to work and he explained that they had a special detail because of a block fair at one of the local churches in the precinct; they were short of uniformed officers and she was being ordered in on a sixth day. Then she told the lieutenant that she had a sore throat and didn't feel good. He said in that case she should call in sick the next morning, just as if it were a regular day. He told her that was the only way she could avoid working the sixth day.

Instead, Kate explained to Sophia, she called the next morning and asked the desk sergeant for an emergency 28*—the request for a day off. The sergeant, not knowing about the call from the lieutenant, had given her an okay. Then the lieutenant found out about it and called her at home, telling her to come in. He told her the day off had been canceled the night before, when he first called, and she couldn't get it back with a 28. If she could not come in, the only way to get out of it was to take a sick day. So that was what she did.

Now she was calling Sophia to complain because she was angry about losing her two-day weekend and having to give up a sick day to get it back.

Sophia found it difficult to keep her temper. "Don't you

understand that your day off was canceled when the lieutenant called? You can't just get it back by requesting a 28."

Kate couldn't seem to grasp that. "They can't do that. It's my weekend. I'm entitled to a two-day weekend."

"Not when they call you in," Sophia answered. She tried again. "You are given days off at the expense of the Police Department, if there's nothing going on. They can cancel both days if they want to. You're given your meal* if your service is not needed. But if it is, you work."

Kate just didn't want to listen to that. She said she was going to call the PBA* and complain. Sophia explained it one more time.

"Look, remember the time last summer when there were two big street fairs and an event in Central Park and a couple of other things all on the same Sunday? Everyone worked that weekend and they brought cops in from all over the city to handle the crowds in Manhattan. When they need the people, you have to work. It's just that simple."

But Kate still wasn't buying it. She didn't think it was fair that she could lose a day off like that. She remembered the weekend Sophia was talking about, but she had been scheduled to work anyway and hadn't paid any attention to how many cops were called in on a sixth day. Kate repeated her plans to call the PBA and Sophia told her to go ahead.

After hanging up the phone, Sophia sat staring at it in amazement. She wondered about some of the new kids on the job. How could anyone join the Police Department and not know that sometimes you would have to work overtime or extra days? But when she thought about it, Sophia remembered other rookies who complained about midnight tours and holidays. At least Kate seemed to understand that she was not going to get Saturday and Sunday off on a regular basis.

Sophia went back to her paperwork, finishing most of it. She was putting the papers away when the phone rang. It was Kate again.

"I called the PBA. They said they could cancel my day off like that."

"I told you that an hour ago," Sophia said. Kate still didn't accept the reason she had been forced to take a sick day on what was supposed to be a day off, but Sophia decided that further explanation would not accomplish anything.

She remembered another young woman who had been equally stubborn about accepting the quirks of the department. Sophia had been assigned to headquarters for a few months with Bobbi, and they had been sent to attend the funeral of a retired detective. They had run into several acquaintances who had the day off and decided to go to lunch with them. Sophia had called up their CO and asked for the rest of the tour off, but he had not been too accommodating. She didn't tell him that they had met friends, saying instead that the car broke down. She kept talking and finally the lieutenant said to call back after the mechanic looked at the car.

Sophia waited half an hour and called him back, saying the mechanic didn't know what was wrong and couldn't tell how long it would take to fix it. By then, she could tell he knew she was lying. He told her he would put her on meal as of twelve-thirty and she agreed.

Sophia went back to her friends and told Bobbi that the lieutenant was putting them on meal. Bobbi was pleased. "Good, we'll call him back in an hour and tell him the car still isn't fixed."

"You don't understand," Sophia said. "He's giving us the time we've already taken and an hour to get back to work."

"That's not what he said," Bobbi replied.

Sophia tried again. "He's being nice about it. We have an hour to get back to the city and he won't say anything about the time we've already taken."

"I don't know how you can make that interpretation when that's not what he said," Bobbi answered.

"Well, you're a jerk," Sophia said. "I'm going back. You can either come back with me or stay here. But I know this guy and he's being nice about it. I don't think you should press him." Bobbi went with Sophia, but she argued about it all the way back to headquarters.

When they got back to the office, Sophia greeted the lieutenant and thanked him. He just grunted and walked away.

Bobbi still wasn't convinced that Sophia was right. Sophia figured she would learn the ropes soon enough. She didn't bother arguing anymore.

Kate and Bobbi seemed to have the same outlook about the job. Sophia had met other young cops who also had a problem with the discipline required. She thought they had learned to be on time at the Academy, but some forgot very quickly and were always late for roll call. Sophia had her own problems about discipline, but mostly they involved other people's attitudes and the bureaucracy. She didn't object to the dress code or the scheduling demands of the job.

But she was older than most rookies when she had come on the job. She was married at the time. She had been working for several years and knew what the world was like. Most of the new kids seemed to be right out of high school or college. The minimum age to join the Police Department was nineteen, and when the drinking age in New York State was raised to twenty-one Sophia heard one CO complaining that he had some guys on the street who couldn't get into a bar. She laughed, but knew it was true.

Sophia remembered riding with a very young rookie one night while she was still in uniform. Irv had been on vacation or at court or something, and the kid had been put in her car for the day. After the tour, Sophia asked the sergeant to give her an older partner next time. "Someone who's gotten laid at least once, Sarge, so we'll have something to talk about." The sergeant laughed and promised not to give her the real young ones again.

The kid had been okay, as long as she did the driving. After one hour with him behind the wheel, Sophia took over. She had heard about how the new young men on the job were driving, but she didn't believe it until that day. He wanted to turn on the lights and sirens and go after anything and everything. He wasn't the only one apparently. A few days after that tour, a directive came down from headquarters limiting car chases to two cars and requiring a sergeant to call it off. She heard later that rookies had been cracking up one RMP a day, chasing people who had run red lights.

Sophia and Mary Frances had laughed about it. They could just see the bosses downtown looking at the statistics: eight-thousand-dollar cars smashed up chasing someone for a sixty-dollar traffic violation; civilians and cops hurt in chases that started with someone going through a stop sign.

Mary Frances told her that the newest classes of rookies didn't show much improvement. Sophia didn't ride with rookies anymore, but Mary Frances still did when Paul was out.

"These guys seem to think they have carte blanche to go through a red light just because they wear a uniform," Mary Frances had told Sophia, shaking her head. "I just can't see it, driving like a raving lunatic with people around. Some of these guys will jump a sidewalk to get someone who went through a red light, not realizing the danger to people around them."

They had talked about the subject a few times, going back to the Academy. The guys in their class seemed so young and immature. They discussed it once with Geri, who had noticed the same thing.

"A twenty-year-old today is more like a seventeen-year-old of ten years ago," she had said. "I see it all over, but it seems particularly obvious on the job. I guess it's because most of the guys who came on with me served in the Army. Many of them had been in Vietnam. These kids have never been in the service. They don't understand discipline. They're just immature."

Geri told them about working with a rookie one night about six years before, when she was still in uniform. He was right out of the Academy and still lived at home with his parents on Long Island. He barely knew his way to the precinct and had never really been on the streets of New York.

"He started complaining to me about the people who hang out in the street drinking," she said. "He was upset that they were just going to sit on the stoops, get drunk and make trouble for us. He couldn't understand why they didn't go to a club to do their drinking.

"I tried to explain to him that these were laborers, unemployed people, poor people who couldn't afford a club. To them, a six-pack of beer was a party. They sat on the stoop with their friends and talked and joked. Most of them weren't looking for trouble and didn't want it."

Sophia and Mary Frances, both of whom had grown up in the city, didn't believe a cop could be that naïve until they ran into the same attitude themselves. A lot of the younger men coming on the job seemed to be from the suburbs. Some of the dinosaurs* in the precinct teased them about living in East Cupcake or North Nowhere. In the last half-dozen years, Mary Frances and Sophia had both run into many of them—kids who still lived at home, who had rarely been in any of the five boroughs of New York City until they started at the Academy, who really didn't understand the streets. Neither of the two women had been a real street kid, but they understood the dynamics of the street just from riding the subways all their lives better than those cops who had not grown up in the city.

There wasn't much point to thinking about that. Sophia couldn't do anything about it anyway. She looked up at the clock on the wall, noticed it was a few minutes after three and decided to see if Mary Frances was in the locker room, changing for her tour. Sophia didn't feel like starting anything new.

She walked up a flight of stairs, trying to ignore the big chunks of paint peeling from the walls. The One-Six was in an old precinct house; the building was four stories without an elevator and barely habitable. A new building was planned, but given the City of New York's usual procedures, Sophia didn't expect it to be built for years.

The women's locker room was on the third floor. About ten years before, it had been created from a couple of old storerooms and part of the male detectives' locker room. The bathroom was down the hall, but the women of the One-Six were lucky. In some houses, the women's bathroom was on a different floor from the lockers. In at least one precinct, Sophia knew the only way into the women's lockers was through the CO's office. The New York Police Department had really not been prepared for women in the stationhouses.

Sophia pushed the door open and found Mary Frances putting on her uniform. Like the rest of the precinct, the locker room had seen better days, even when it was used for storage.

The walls were covered with NYPD green paint, which was filthy after years of neglect. The floor tiles were worn and the concrete was visible where tiles had come off. The room was cramped, filled with metal lockers of all shapes and sizes, all bearing a "Police Don't Move" decal. Some lockers also had more personal decorations: NRA* bumper stickers, cartoons, even some male pinups. The lockers were in four rows, two facing each other with a rickety picnic bench between. A cracked mirror sat on a wobbly chair at the end of one row.

Mary Frances was the only one in the room when Sophia walked in.

"Hi, things better today?" she asked.

"I guess so," Sophia answered. "I was too furious yesterday to think straight. I'll take some time to think about things more calmly." She straddled the bench and watched Mary Frances put on her bulletproof vest, then a long-sleeved uniform shirt and a blue turtleneck dickey. "My court case was postponed again. And I spent the rest of the day telling the CO what a good cop I've been."

"Writing up your collars for medals, huh?" Mary Frances laughed as she strapped on an ankle holster and put her off-duty gun in it. It was much smaller and lighter than the regulation service revolver, which was a .38 calibre with a four-inch barrel. Most cops wore their off-duty gun while in uniform. It was extra protection, in case someone managed to get the service revolver. "I know how much you like doing those."

"How about you?" Sophia asked. "You didn't sound too enthusiastic about the job last night."

"Oh, I guess I'm okay," Mary Frances replied. "I thought about it on the way home. I think I've got some ideas that might help." By the time she had explained it all to Sophia, she had finished dressing. It was nearly three-thirty and time for roll call.

They walked down one flight of stairs together, then Sophia went back to her office to collect her purse while Mary Frances headed to the first floor for inspection.

# CHAPTER 7

The muster room* was full of cops talking with each other. Some held Styrofoam cups of coffee. Paul spotted Mary Frances and waved. She walked over to the automatic shoe shiner and gave her shoes a quick buff. The sergeant came in and everyone lined up for roll call and inspection. Then the sergeant started with the usual warnings to avoid corruption-prone locations, mostly construction sites. The warnings were repeated frequently. In addition, every room in every precinct house and police office that Mary Frances had ever seen also had a sign reminding everyone that corruption could be reported to the Internal Affairs Division. The warnings and signs were a legacy of the Knapp Commission's* findings on police corruption in the early 1970's in New York.

The sergeant gave them notice that the Narcotics Squad was going to be concentrating in the One-Six for the next few days. It was part of the new offensive against street-corner drug dealers. Anyone who spotted a new drug-buying location while on patrol was told to notify the squad.

The One-Six was on the West Side of Manhattan, a rapidly changing neighborhood that only a few years earlier had been a high-crime precinct. A combination of federal housing projects and private developments had changed the area's profile from one of low-income residents living in tenements to that of young professional people in new high-rises or renovated brownstones. The area was often described as "Yuppie headquarters," the neighborhood of choice for people in their twenties and thirties who worked on Wall Street or Madison Avenue, or as doctors, lawyers or bankers. They were well-educated, high-income people and many of them considered drugs a form of recreation.

The sergeant reported the weather forecast—cold drizzle with periodic showers—and recommended that everyone have a raincoat in the car if they were driving. He told those on foot posts to wear slickers all the time. He read off the meal hours for everyone on the tour. Mary Frances and Paul would have to wait until eight. Then roll call was over and they were dismissed to go on patrol.

Mary Frances got the car keys while Paul picked up the radios. As usual, she would drive for the first half of the tour and he would take over after their meal. Mary Frances knew some men who never let their women partners drive, but neither Paul nor Doug had ever cared.

They went out to their regular car, glad it was back from the garage after a routine maintenance. They both did a radio check before starting the motor. The radios were okay, but the car, as usual, was dirty. Mary Frances went back into the stationhouse to get a paper bag. She filled it with the old coffee cups and cigarette packs that littered the backseat. She also brought along a can of Lysol and sprayed the car. Paul waited patiently for her to finish her housecleaning.

"I just can't sit in this filth for eight hours," she said, smiling at him self-consciously.

"Hey, I don't mind," he answered. "I wouldn't do it myself, but I sure don't care if you want to do it."

"I know. I feel funny doing it sometimes, but I just can't stand the dirt," Mary Frances said.

"You really don't have to apologize. Most of the guys would be glad if you'd clean their cars, too." Paul smiled.

"Not on your life," she answered. "Most of those creeps are the ones who get them dirty. If they can't be bothered cleaning up after themselves, I'm sure not going to do it for them. I'll never understand how so many of the guys can just ride around for eight hours in a car that looks like a garbage dump. I don't like cleaning up after whoever used this car before us, but it's that or sit with the dirt and I'm not willing to do that."

"Come on, MF, I was just teasing," Paul said.

"I know," she replied. "I just get so aggravated at having to do this every tour. Come on, let's get going."

All New York precincts are divided into sectors, usually ten or twelve, but sometimes more, depending on the size of the precinct. Sector cars patrolled the assigned area, looking for signs of trouble, responding to calls from the 911 dispatcher known as Central and backing up other sector cars when needed.

In 1974, after the corruption scandal rocked the Police Department, it was decided that the neighborhood cop who patrolled a specific area on foot was too available for bribes. Foot patrols were ended and all uniformed officers were assigned to patrol cars. That created a new set of problems, mostly a greater distance between the police and the civilian population they were supposed to be protecting.

Foot patrols for specific high-crimes areas were reintroduced on a temporary basis. In 1984 the Community Patrol Officer Program (CPOP) was begun as an experiment in Brooklyn and expanded to other precincts on a test basis. A uniformed officer was again assigned to patrol a specific beat regularly, to get to know the merchants, residents, building employees and other people. Only a few officers in a few precincts are assigned to CPOP; the vast majority still cruise sectors in marked patrol cars.

Paul and Mary Frances usually got Sector H, Henry, at the south end of the precinct. It was one Mary Frances liked because it combined residential areas—in Manhattan that meant apartment houses and brownstones—several commercial streets like Broadway and Columbus, and Riverside Park. The mixture meant the jobs they were called for were just as varied—lost kids, robberies, sudden illness, lost keys, the whole gamut.

They made one wide tour through the sector and a call came from Central, a 10-20—past robbery—at a small hardware store only a couple of blocks away. The store was on the corner of a block known for heavy drug dealing and they notified Central they were on the way. When they arrived they parked at a fire hydrant. Police cars often used fire hydrant spaces to park. If a fire occurred while they were there, they would simply move the car to block traffic for the Fire Department and allow access to the hydrant.

Mary Frances and Paul picked up their uniform hats from the seat and got out, not bothering with raincoats for the few seconds they would be outside. They went inside the store and found the owner. He didn't know anything about a call to police, had not been robbed that day and wasn't sure who had called. He was concerned that the false report would be held against him if something happened, but they assured him it would not. He thanked them for coming and they went back to the car, notifying the dispatcher that the call had been unfounded. Paul as the recorder made an entry in his memo book and they resumed patrol.

The drizzle made it seem like night, although it was barely four-thirty in the afternoon. Paul was hungry but they had nearly four hours until their meal, so they decided to stop for coffee. Paul went in to a nearby coffee shop and came out with two cups of coffee and donuts, and they sat in the parked car.

"It looks like this is going to be as boring as yesterday," Mary Frances said. "I am so tired of driving around like this. We just circle the same blocks over and over again, rarely seeing anything criminal or even suspicious. I'm thinking about asking for something else."

"What else?" Paul asked.

"I don't know yet," she answered. "Maybe Mounted, or Highway. I'll probably apply for OCCB, but I haven't given it much thought. Anything that will get me off round-the-clock schedules and uniformed patrol. I'm bored with patrol and these crazy schedules are ruining my marriage."

"I'd sure hate to lose you as a partner," Paul said.

"You can request a transfer, too," she suggested.

"Sure, but the chances of us getting to the same place are almost nil. Besides, I like patrol. It's always different. I never know what's going to happen and I'm on my own. I'm outside

and I only have to answer to bosses a couple of times a tour."
Paul grinned. "You know that's one of the few things we disagree
on, partner."

"Yeah, I don't understand that," Mary Frances said. "You
see this as always different and freeing, and I see it as basically
boring and with too much supervision. Mostly, we seem to answer car alarm complaints, but when we do get something interesting, a boss shows up. I just can't figure out why you think
you have so much freedom in an RMP when there's always a
boss second-guessing you. I sometimes feel I might as well have
stayed in nursing."

"If you're inside, handling the paperwork, it's the same
routine every day," he countered. "Out here, I'm my own boss.
If I want to really work, I can. If I'm tired one day, or have my
share of collars for the week, I do what I have to do and relax.
Nobody's standing behind me. Inside, there's so much work that
has to be done every day and someone watching to be sure it
gets done."

The radio crackled, calling for one-six Henry. Mary Frances
replied and they were told to report to the precinct for a job.
They drove back and found the sergeant standing outside with
an elderly, heavyset black woman with a cane.

"Mrs. Washington has to see her sister about a family problem. The sister doesn't have a phone and Mrs. Washington is
afraid to go there by herself. Says she got robbed the last time
she went to visit her sister. You two give her a ride over there,
stay with her and then take her home. It's only a couple of blocks
altogether," the sergeant explained.

"Yes, sir," Paul said, getting out to open the back door for
the woman. She sat on the seat, dragging her feet in and pulling
the cane after. Paul closed the door and got in the front seat,
trying not to look at Mary Frances, knowing she would be biting
her lip to keep from laughing. This kind of job was hardly the
kind of routine thing she had been complaining about. On the
other hand, it was even less exciting than a car alarm.

They drove the few blocks to the address Mrs. Washington
gave them, listening to her explain over and over how she had
been robbed and was afraid of the hoodlums who lived near her

sister. She spoke with the dialect of the street, what educators call Black English, and repeated herself continually. Mary Frances pulled up at the address, behind a beat-up green Chevy double-parked on the narrow side street. It was not one of the better blocks in the precinct, still filled with tenements and brown-stones that had been divided up into tiny apartments.

Paul got out to help Mrs. Washington and Mary Frances opened her door. The owner of the double-parked car in front of them was crossing the street and she recognized him.

"Paul, you go with her. I want to talk to my friend Willy North," she said. She walked up to the man putting the keys to the front door of the beat-up Chevy. "Hey Willy, what are you doing here?"

The short black man turned to see who was calling him. He was wearing filthy dungarees, spotted with grease and oil and other things that could not be identified. He wore a tattered jacket and a wool cap pulled down over his short kinky hair. Paul and Mrs. Washington disappeared into the building and Mary Frances neared the man she called Willy.

"I'm just here working," he said in a nasal whine, with a Southern accent. "I'm a handyman and someone called me about leaking gas."

"That's okay, Willy," she said. "But what about your driver's license? When I picked you up a month ago it was suspended. It still is. And this isn't the car you had then. Is this one registered? Let me see your papers."

"Nah, this one belongs to my uncle," he answered. "I got rid of that other one. I just borrowed this to come on this job. I'm getting the registration. I sent in for it and they're supposed to mail it back to me. I should be getting it any day."

"Come on, Willy," Mary Frances said. "You know better than that. You can't just drive around without a driver's license in a car that's not registered or insured. I'm going to have to write up a ticket. Let me see what you do have."

"It's coming in the mail," Willy repeated. "They're supposed to send it to me any day. I wrote away for that stuff, but they ain't sent it yet. I just came here because I got this call about the gas leak. I did some shopping for my old lady. I got a couple of chickens at the store. They're in the backseat and I came to do this job."

"It doesn't matter why you're driving," Mary Frances told him. "You don't have a license. I'll have to run a check on these plates, too. Do you have registration papers for the car?" Mary Frances called Central on the radio, requesting a check on the license plates. She read off the numbers and turned back to Willy.

"They're in the mail," Willy said again. "It's my uncle's car. He said everything is okay with it. I ain't got the papers with me. He's got them. He lives way up in the Bronx. I just borrowed the car to do this job. They told me they had a gas leak and I came out here to fix it."

"Willy, when I stopped you last time and gave you a ticket for not having a license or registration, I told you not to drive again until you got them." Mary Frances was getting tired of the conversation. "And I saw you two weeks after that at another precinct for the same thing, driving without a license or registration. I'm going to have to give you a Desk Appearance Ticket* this time."

"It's in the mail," Willy repeated. "I sent for them and they're mailing all that back to me. I got that stuff. They just ain't mailed it to me yet."

"This isn't getting us anywhere, Willy," Mary Frances stated. "I know you. Your license has been suspended for more than ten years. You know you're not supposed to be driving." The radio called for one-six Henry, reporting the car was not stolen. Just then, Paul and Mrs. Washington came out of the building. Paul had a disgusted look on his face. Mary Frances wondered what had happened inside.

"Come on, Willy," she said. "You'll have to go back with us. You've got too many problems for just a summons. You have the right to remain silent and to refuse to answer any questions without a lawyer present. If you can't afford a lawyer, one will be provided for you without cost. Do you understand what I just said?" Mary Frances repeated the Miranda warning from memory, enough to remind Willy that he could get a lawyer and did not have to answer any more questions. She doubted he would fight the charges on the grounds of a Miranda warning, but she wanted to be sure there was no chance for him to do so.

"Yes, I know about that, but what about my car? I can't leave it here," Willy said.

Mary Frances looked around. By luck, there was a parking space up the block. If there hadn't been, she or Paul would have had to drive his car back to the precinct to park it in the lot behind the building. "Put your car there. When we get to the stationhouse, you can call your wife or someone to get it. We'll hold the keys and they can come get them there."

Willy agreed. He got in and started the engine with some difficulty, then pulled into the parking space. He got out, locked the doors and came back to the patrol car. He sat in the backseat, next to Mrs. Washington. Paul looked at Mary Frances. "No handcuffs?"

Mary Frances hesitated for a second. The Patrol Guide called for handcuffing prisoners, but Willy wasn't dangerous. She had patted him down for weapons, but he had never, to her knowledge, carried any. He had just moved his car without showing the slightest inclination to try escaping. He would be all right without handcuffs. He wasn't really violent, just dumb. She shook her head.

"No, Willy's not a bad guy," she stated. "I've picked him up before. He just doesn't have a license or insurance. He won't give us any trouble. We'll drop you off, Mrs. Washington. Where do you live?"

She told them and Mary Frances drove away. On the way, Willy whined about being out to fix the gas leak and expecting his registration in the mail. Mrs. Washington mumbled about her sister and the hoodlums who lived around her. Paul and Mary Frances sat in the front seat, listening to both of them and trying to keep straight faces. Mrs. Washington lived only two blocks away, so they reached her apartment house in no time. The elderly lady pulled herself out of the car and trudged up to the door.

The car pulled away with Willy muttering in the backseat. Mary Frances looked over at Paul, who still seemed disgusted. "What's wrong?" she asked.

"That was an unnecessary trip," he said. "There wasn't a family problem. The sister owed her money and she went there to collect. I don't even think she was robbed there. She just wanted a cop with her to scare her sister." He shook his head again in disgust. "I'm just glad we don't have to do things like that too often. I felt like a bodyguard and that's not my job." He turned back to glance at Willy, who was still mumbling to himself. "What's with him?"

"Oh, Willy and I are old friends," Mary Frances answered with a smile. "I've picked him up a couple of times in the past year. No license, no registration, no insurance, nothing. I guess you've missed him each time, but I know he's been arrested a few times in the neighboring precincts as well."

By that time, they had reached the stationhouse and Mary Frances double-parked behind another RMP. She, Paul and Willy got out and walked into the building. She put handcuffs on Willy as they approached the desk so the sergeant wouldn't bawl her out. She patted him down again while they waited for the sergeant to look up. The sergeant was seated in the middle of the desk, which was actually a big counter that stretched halfway across the room and was a step higher than the ground level. Putting the desk officers above anyone standing in front of them was a typical police station trick.

"What you got?" the sergeant asked.

"Willy North, no license, no registration, no insurance. I've picked him up a couple of times and I brought him in on a DAT and to check if he has any outstanding warrants," Mary Frances answered.

"Okay, go ahead. Willy, you go sit down over there." The sergeant pointed to some folding chairs at the back of the muster room. Paul sat next to Willy to make notations in his memo book about Mrs. Washington, then headed upstairs to the men's lockers.

"Willy, when's your birthday?" Mary Frances asked, standing by a computer screen next to the desk. He told her and she typed his name and birthday into the computer. Within a minute, information started appearing on the screen. She watched as it came up. Willy had an outstanding robbery warrant and another for failing to appear in court on a DWI* charge. She printed that and typed in the license plate of the car. The screen filled up again. She called out to ask him his uncle's name and address. He gave her the information and that matched the computer. Not a stolen car, but no record of insurance.

She pushed a button to print up the rest of the data on the screen, then walked over to where Willy sat waiting. He was still mumbling about getting his papers in the mail and just being out to fix the gas leak.

"Willy, I'm afraid I'll have to take you downtown. I can't just write a ticket. You've got an outstanding robbery warrant. And you got picked up for drunk driving and didn't show up in court. Were you due in court last month and didn't go?" she asked.

Willy looked up. "I was there, but I couldn't find where I was supposed to be, so I just left." He looked resigned to spending the night in jail.

"Come on, Willy, you'll have to go back until I fill out the papers. Then I'll have to fingerprint you," Mary Frances said. She was beginning to get angry. He wasn't a bad guy, but he just didn't seem to understand about needing a driver's license or showing up for court. She would have a lot of paperwork to do: forms for the warrants, for the tickets she was giving him tonight and the fingerprint sheets.

She took him to the small bare cell and removed the hand-cuffs. The cell, about ten by six feet, was empty and had no seats. A bench, wide enough for one person to lay down on, was attached to one wall, but Willy sat down on the floor in a corner, leaning his back against a wall. He took a crumpled pack of cigarettes out of a pocket and asked for a light. The desk sergeant gave Mary Frances a book of matches, which she handed to Willy.

Paul came downstairs. "Well, what's the story?" he asked.

"He's got an outstanding robbery warrant and one for non-appearance on a DWI," Mary Frances answered. "I'll have to take him downtown. You don't have to stay. Ask the sergeant if there's anyone to ride with you for the rest of the tour. No reason you have to stay inside while I do this.

"Do me a favor and do a thorough search on Willy before you go. I patted him down, but I didn't go in his pockets. I doubt if he has anything, but no sense not doing it," Mary Frances said. Paul brought Willy out of the cell, and while he was searching him Mary Frances reminded him to tell the sergeant about the useless trip for Mrs. Washington. He ought to know so they weren't caught again.

Paul agreed and went to the desk sergeant. He told him about Mrs. Washington, then explained about Mary Frances's collar.

"You got an extra body tonight, sarge?" Paul asked. "I'd sure hate to have to spend the next six hours sitting around doing nothing."

"Well, Sally Weston wants to start going on patrol," the sergeant said. "See if she's caught up with the typing. If she is, take her with you."

Paul went down the hallway next to the desk. Sally was looking over some papers in one of the offices that opened on the hall. She looked up when he came in.

"Mary Frances has a collar she has to take downtown," he said. "Do you have work to do? The sergeant said if you're not busy, you can take her seat for the rest of the tour."

"I just finished the last of it," Sally replied. "I was wondering what I was going to do until midnight."

"Looks like you're going to be my partner." Paul smiled at her. "You'll need your jacket and a vest. And don't forget your raincoat. It's pretty miserable out there. I'll wait for you at the desk."

Sally ran up to the locker room for her vest, jacket and raincoat, and put her off-duty gun in an ankle holster. She picked up her nightstick and went downstairs and into the back room where Mary Frances was filling out the forms for her arrest.

"You sure you don't mind my taking your partner?" she asked.

Mary Frances looked up and smiled. "No, you go ahead. Don't worry about Paul. He'll help you. He's not like some of these guys. I remember what you were saying last night. Just ask Paul what to do and he'll tell you. Take my radio. Good luck."

Sally thanked her and walked out of the stationhouse with Paul.

# CHAPTER 8

**D**o you want to drive or you want me to?" Paul asked.

Sally was surprised. She knew that patrol teams were divided into an operator—the driver—and a recorder—the one responsible for keeping a memo book up-to-date. The few other times she had been on patrol with men, they had insisted on doing the driving. She hadn't expected to be given a choice. She smiled hesitantly and said she didn't mind being the recorder. She got in the passenger seat and Paul slid behind the wheel.

"You haven't been here long, have you?" he asked.

"Only a couple of months," Sally replied. "I've been inside, on clerical most of the time. I haven't been on patrol too often."

"I didn't think I'd seen you very much," he said. "Are you friends with my partner?"

"I know Mary Frances," Sally answered. "But mostly from being in the locker room. I haven't really been here long enough to make friends with anyone. There isn't much time to talk while we're changing and after work everyone is anxious to get home."

"Yeah, I know what you mean," Paul said. "But you'll get to know people. Don't worry."

He headed back to the original sector assignment and called Central to report that they were back on patrol. Sally just sat quietly for a few minutes, looking out the window. Then she turned and asked him why he worked with Mary Frances when most of the men in the precinct seemed not to like women.

"I think they're dumb," Paul said. "The other guys, not women. I've been on the job for fifteen years and I can think of maybe two times when brute strength made a difference. I'm willing to take my chances on that, especially now that we have radios and can get backup so quickly. I think women are more levelheaded. When someone really wants to fight, women are often able to calm them down. Men will aggravate them."

"That's not the way most guys feel," Sally observed, somewhat surprised at his answer.

"I know. Most cops don't like the idea of women. I can understand that, but times change. That doesn't mean I'll work with just any woman. But there are some men I won't get into a car with either. It depends on the individual." Paul smiled at her.

"I hope you'll like working with me," Sally said. "I haven't done too much real patrol, but I was getting tired of being inside all the time. I decided last night to ask to be let out of the paperwork and to go on patrol. The sergeant said he'd try to get me out in another week or so, when the next schedule is made up. I didn't expect it this soon."

There was constant chatter on the radio, mostly for other precincts in the division. New York City was so large and had so many police precincts that the communications system had to be divided up, especially after 1970 when all police officers began using walkie-talkies. Four or five precincts that are geographic neighbors are assigned to the same radio frequency and handled by a single dispatcher. There are also special frequencies that cover all five boroughs of the city, for the specialized units.

A few of the calls were for the One-Six, but in other sectors. None of them sounded serious enough to require a backup. The dispatcher and the cops who called used codes to describe their actions, and Sally strained to hear what was being said and to understand it.

"How long did it take to learn how to use the radio?" she asked. "It sounds like gibberish to me. I can make out some of the sectors and the numbers, but I don't know the codes yet. They went over them at the Academy, but I just can't remember what they all mean."

"Don't worry," Paul said. "You'll learn them. Until you do, there's a card on the sun visor. And until you get them down, you can just tell Central what the situation is. If you can't remember that a vehicle accident is a 10-53, just tell them you have two cars crashed or whatever. They'll figure it out. Just say it as clearly and succinctly as possible. But you'll be surprised how fast you'll learn the codes once you start hearing them every day."

Sally nodded, but didn't feel as confident as Paul sounded. He asked her how she liked the job so far. She explained again that she hadn't really seen too much of it. She had liked NSU, except for making mistakes.

"What kind of mistakes?"

She told him about the first day, when she and another rookie had almost caused an accident while they were directing traffic. Paul laughed.

"Then there was the time we were ordered to the South African embassy, the one on Park Avenue," Sally recalled. "There was a big anti-apartheid demonstration and the barricades were up. We were told not to let anyone into the building for any reason. I was assigned to the door with another rookie. We were determined no one was going to get past us.

"These two men came up. They were wearing suits and ties and started to walk in the doors. We said: 'No, sorry, no one's allowed in.' They pulled out plastic ID cards that said Federal Bureau of Investigation, but we just said: 'Sorry, our orders are not to let anyone in the building.' A sergeant came over and said: 'You two are doing a remarkable job, but you can let them in. They have passes.' "

Paul laughed again and Sally grinned sheepishly. "They didn't tell us not to let anyone but the FBI in. They just said don't let anyone in. We were so nervous it never occurred to us that they were okay."

"Well, no one can say you don't follow orders," Paul said,

still laughing. "If those are the worst mistakes you've made so far, I wouldn't worry."

The radio called for one-six Henry. Paul answered and Central reported a group of teenagers being disorderly at a subway entrance at Seventy-second Street and Central Park West.

That was the corner of the Dakota Apartment, one of the most famous buildings in the city. John Lennon had been killed at the entrance to the Dakota and his widow, Yoko Ono, still lived there. Central Park West was like that, filled with huge old apartment buildings with expensive apartments. A lot of show business people lived on the street and a group of rowdy kids could mean trouble. Paul acknowledged the call and they were on their way.

He drove quickly through the streets, getting most of the lights with him. Sally felt a little apprehensive and was glad to hear a second one-six sector car telling Central they would back them up. The drizzle had stopped for the time being, but it was still cold and damp.

They got to the corner and found a half-dozen teenagers on the sidewalk, break-dancing to the music coming from an enormous portable radio, the kind known as a ghetto-blaster. A crowd had gathered to watch and the kids had put out a hat in hopes of picking up some money.

Paul stopped the car and got out, carrying his nightstick. Sally picked up hers as she followed him. The second RMP pulled up. Sally was nervous, but with three other cops there, she figured she would just go along with them. Paul approached the dancers, who stopped when they saw him.

"Sorry, kids," he said. "You'll have to break it up. There's been a complaint that you're too noisy. This isn't a great place to do this anyway." Street entertainers were common in New York, but they usually chose to work in midtown or in less congested areas. Central Park West and Seventy-second Street was not a wide corner, and the dancers plus the spectators blocked the sidewalk for pedestrians who wanted to keep moving.

Sally stood behind Paul, next to the two other cops. They seemed surprised to see her, but nodded hello. The teenagers agreed to move, picked up the hat and the radio, and walked down Seventy-second Street toward Broadway. The spectators went into the subway or continued on their way home.

Paul turned around and said hello to the backups.

"Where's Mary Frances?" one of them asked. Sally remembered his name was Frank Gordon. He was one of the worst when it came to making comments about women.

"She made a collar and I didn't feel like staying in for the rest of the night," Paul answered.

"So you got stuck with another empty suit?"* Gordon laughed. "When're you going to work with a real cop again, Randall?"

"I always work with real cops," Paul said pleasantly. "Let's go, Sally." He waved to the other two and got back in the patrol car. Sally followed him, unsure if she should do or say anything. Paul called Central to report the teens had moved on. Sally made a notation in her memo book.

They drove off and Paul turned to look at her. "Don't let him get to you," he advised. "Hasn't Mary Frances or one of the other girls talked to you about these guys? Just ignore them. They're the ones who don't do anything themselves."

"Yeah, I guess I know that," Sally said. "I just can't help wondering why they dislike us though."

"Like I said, just ignore them." Paul smiled again. "I told you, I feel safer working with a woman. You girls aren't so willing to start trouble. You walk into a situation and want to talk. Most of the guys, they want to start a fight, to prove something. They probably don't like the idea that you girls can do the job without starting a fight all the time. I've been on this job too long to want to fight. I just want to do my job and go home every night."

They continued driving. The radio called again for one-six Henry. Paul answered and they were sent to a brownstone on West Seventieth Street. A woman had called to complain about someone in the apartment who would not leave when asked. It was a typical job, one that they got frequently.

Paul drove across Seventy-second and turned down West End. At Seventieth, they found the address and double-parked the RMP. Paul and Sally picked up their nightsticks and caps and walked into the building. At the intercom, Paul rang the apartment and asked if someone had called the police. The buzzer sounded and he pushed the door open. They looked up the stairs and saw a woman standing in the open door of an apartment.

As they got to the head of the stairs, Paul recognized the woman. "We were here a couple of weeks ago, weren't we?" he asked.

The woman nodded. She was in her forties, with short dark hair. She was wearing slacks, a sweater and several heavy gold chains around her neck. She invited Paul and Sally inside.

They found themselves in a brownstone apartment typical of the newer, wealthier residents of the area. An entry hall about five feet square opened to a living room barely ten by twelve. A narrow stairway just off the entry led down a flight, probably to a couple of bedrooms. Behind it was a kitchen no bigger than a closet. In the living room, a card table was set for two and a man dressed in a suit sat at one place, in front of a half-eaten meal.

A second man stood silently in front of a small loveseat, on the wall opposite the fireplace. He was wearing Levi's and a sweatshirt and still had on a heavy outer jacket. He looked angry. The other man looked worried.

"What's the trouble?" Paul asked.

"I was having dinner with my friend when this guy showed up," the woman said. "I want him to leave and he won't."

"Did you let him in?" Paul asked.

"Yes," the woman replied.

"Well, if you invited him in, we can't force him to leave," Paul said. "He's not guilty of trespass and there's no cause for us to take action. We can ask him, though. Sir, you've been asked to leave this apartment. It would make things easier for everyone if you did."

"I just want to talk to her for a few minutes alone," the man said. "I'll leave after we talk. I have some business things to discuss and I don't want him to hear about them," he added, pointing to the first man.

"We have nothing to discuss," the woman stated. "Our

business is over. I don't want to talk to you and I'm certainly not going to ask my dinner guest to leave because you want me to."

"What's your relationship to each other?" Paul asked.

"We were friends and had some business together, nothing more," the woman answered quickly. "I don't want to be in business with him any longer. I don't want to talk to him and I do want him to leave."

The first man sat silently, watching the conversation, his head turning back and forth like a spectator at a tennis game. Finally, he spoke up: "If it will settle this, I'll leave."

"No," said the woman. "You're my guest. He's not. I don't want to talk to him."

"Look," Paul suggested, turning to the intruder. "Why don't you just leave with us now and call her tomorrow on the phone? You can talk to her in private then and we can settle this without a problem."

"I've tried," the man told him. "She won't talk to me on the phone. That's why I had to come here."

Paul turned to the woman. "Ma'am, this would be a lot easier if you'd agree to speak with him tomorrow."

"Okay, if he leaves now, I'll talk to him on the phone," the woman answered, none too graciously.

The man walked toward the door, then stopped, waiting for Paul and Sally. Paul turned to the woman.

"In the future, remember that if you let someone in, we can't make them leave," he said. "We're not here to act as bouncers. We can only remove someone who has entered unlawfully. If you don't want him here, don't invite him in." The woman nodded, and thanked Paul and Sally for their help.

They walked back down the steps, with the man following. On the sidewalk, he stopped and apologized for the trouble, trying again to explain the situation.

"It doesn't matter," Paul answered. "Just don't do that again. A gentleman would leave when he's asked."

The man walked off without responding and Paul and Sally headed for the car.

"You didn't say very much," Paul commented.

"I didn't know what to say," she replied. "You seemed to have the situation in hand."

"Yeah, but you really should try to do more," he said. "You can't let your partner do everything, even in a situation like this." He called Central to report on the incident while Sally made entries in her memo book and they resumed patrol.

"This is going to be one of those nights," he said. "A lot of nothing calls. It doesn't look like you'll get much experience tonight."

Sally smiled. "I'm just glad to be out of the office. Besides, at the Academy they told us this is what most of the job is like."

"That's true," he said. "Mary Frances and I spend most of the time riding around and answering calls that are about nothing. You'd be amazed at some of the things people call the police about."

"Not anymore," Sally said. "I was on the TS* one night when a woman called because her basement was flooded. You should have heard the sergeant cussing. Or the time a woman called to say she had two mice caught in a trap and they were still alive and could a police officer come and put them out of their misery."

Paul laughed. "Did the sergeant send someone with a shotgun?"

Sally grinned at him. "He told her someone would come, but it wasn't top priority. Then he waited a couple of hours before sending a car.

"When I was really bored, I would let the crazies ramble on. There was one woman who called regularly to report alien invaders in her bathroom. She claimed they were in the sewer system and came up through the drain pipes," Sally told him.

Paul laughed, but then pointed to an Olds Cutlass with Florida plates parked on West Seventieth just east of Broadway. "That car has been there for more than an hour," he said. "I noticed the plates before. I let it go last time, but it should have been moved by now. You want to write the ticket?"

"Sure," Sally replied. Paul parked the car and she started

writing in her summons book. As she did, a man charged out of the building across the street, yelling that he was just about to move the car.

"Sorry, I've already started writing it," Sally said, not looking up. The Universal Summons forms contained several carbons and once begun were an annoyance to tear up. Besides, she had to keep track of every ticket written. "You've been here a long time. We let it go once, but you should have moved the car." The man argued, but Sally kept writing the ticket. She finished and handed it to him, got in the patrol car with Paul and they drove off as she made the memo book notation.

"Welcome to the club," Paul said. "I don't know why people think it's okay to park illegally, complain about everyone else who does and then get angry when we write up a ticket for them. There's the sergeant. Got your memo book up-to-date?"

Sally nodded as the patrol sergeant's car pulled up next to them. Paul handed both books through the window for a scratch.* Sergeant Bailey handed them back, noticed Sally and asked where Mary Frances was. Paul explained again about the collar and Sally filling in.

"Well, it's a surprise to see you out of that office," the sergeant said. "Just take it easy. You can learn a lot from Paul. He's an old-timer." The sergeant's driver pulled away and Paul and Sally resumed patrol.

By now it was a few minutes after eight. They agreed to go to a nearby coffee shop for dinner and Paul reported to Central that they were going on meal. They talked some more while they ate, with Paul emphasizing again the need for Sally to speak up and not let her partner do everything.

"The first time I worked with a woman partner was about ten years ago," he said. "I'd been on the job awhile. So had she, but she was transferred from another precinct. The first night we went out I was the operator. Every time we had to stop, I'd run around the car and open the door for her. I felt like I was on a date or something. She didn't say a word, just let me do it.

"When we changed after our meal, she really taught me a lesson." He grinned at the memory. "We got a call and drove to the location. She parked the car and ran around and opened the door for me! I couldn't believe it. I asked her why. She just looked up and said, 'Oh, you were doing it for me, I thought it was one of the operator's responsibilities.' "

Sally laughed with him. "I get the picture. Don't just talk about problems. Do something about them."

"That's right," he said. "Some of the older guys, the real hairbags, are never going to accept you. You'll just have to learn to live with that. But the others, they're just waiting to see what kind of cop you are. If you're a good cop, they'll leave you alone."

They finished eating and called for the check. The waiter told them the meal was on the house. Paul refused, insisting they pay. He explained that they were not allowed to accept such offers and the waiter finally produced the bill.

"You've got to watch out for this kind of thing," he cautioned Sally as they returned to the RMP. "People are always trying to give you something for nothing in this job. But it's not really for nothing. If you accept a meal or even a cup of coffee, the owner figures you owe him. Besides being against department regulations and a very serious offense, you end up making more enemies than friends. If there's trouble in this place, the guy will expect you to be his bouncer. It's just not a good idea."

Sally nodded as they got into the car. Paul called Central to report they had ended their meal and were back on patrol while Sally made the memo book notation of their meal. The rest of the tour was quiet, just riding through the sector. They went to a few complaints about car alarms, but most had turned themselves off by the time they arrived.

Car alarms are low priority for patrol cars. They often go off when a car is jostled or from some other outside cause, like a radio transmission in the area or even a high wind. If the alarm is particularly loud and prolonged, the police will try to locate the owner through the license plate. If that is not possible, they can break in themselves or call in an Emergency Service Unit to break into the car and turn it off. When that happens, the officers involved must fill out a form reporting their action to file with the desk sergeant.

The department does not encourage officers to break into

cars to turn off alarms because of the bad feeling it creates with the car owner. On the other hand, the residents who are awakened by the alarm in the middle of the night may be just as unhappy.

"Some nights I swear that all we do is answer noise complaints," Paul grumbled after one. "Used to be you could count on a couple of good fights a night in this precinct. Now, it's car alarms and trucks on West End and radios on the street. I'm not sure if I'm glad that it's safer or annoyed because it can be so boring."

About eleven, near the end of their tour, Central called them about a man reported running down Central Park West with a big stick. Paul answered the call and they were off. A second one-six sector car also responded, coming from farther north in the precinct. They spotted the man on the corner of Seventy-seventh Street and Central Park West. He wasn't hard to pick out. He was waving what looked like a small tree and civilians were walking in the street to avoid him.

Carrying their nightsticks, Paul and Sally got out of the car. Paul had his hand on his gun, but Sally just held the baton in the "on guard" position and walked up to the man.

"What's the matter, mister?" she asked. "Why do you need the stick?"

The man had trouble focusing his eyes, but finally succeeded. He stopped waving the stick, but didn't let go of it. The rest of him kept moving, swaying precariously as he tried to take a step backward.

"They want to hurt me," he declared. "I can't let them hurt me. They've been trying to get me all night."

"They won't hurt you," Sally said softly. She wasn't sure whom he was talking about, but at least he wasn't waving the stick anymore. She didn't notice that Paul had slowed down to let her talk to the guy. She concentrated on what she had been taught at the Academy, to stay calm and speak quietly and not to incite him further.

"You're a nice lady," the man said. His straight gray hair was long and scraggly, sticking out all over his head. His clothes seemed to have been picked out of garbage cans from all over, and were covered with stains, ragged at the cuffs and ill-fitting. They hadn't been cleaned in months at least. And neither had he, from the smell. He was very drunk, and the smell of cheap booze and vomit hung over him. He had several days' growth of beard and his hands were more black than any other color, the dirt ground into the nails and cuticles.

"Where do you live?" she asked him.

"Over there." He waved vaguely toward Central Park across the street. "Do you want to take me home? I'd like to marry you. You're a nice lady."

"Well, we can talk about it if you'll put down the stick," Sally said. The wild look seemed to be leaving his eyes. Then the second patrol car pulled up and he raised the stick again.

"Come on, now," she continued. "I thought you were going to put that down. I won't let anyone hurt you, so you don't need your stick."

He looked at her again, then past her. She didn't bother to turn around. Whatever was behind her, Paul would handle. She kept looking at the man. The training seemed to be working. He was not waving the stick and he seemed to be considering what she was saying to him.

"Put the stick down and we'll talk," she said again. His glance came back to her and his hand came down. The stick was resting on the ground and she breathed a sigh of relief.

"I'd like to marry you," he mumbled. "You're a pretty lady. You won't let them hurt me, will you?"

"No, I told you I wouldn't," Sally promised. "Who is trying to hurt you?"

"Those people, the ones with the arms coming out of their stomachs," he answered. "They're from Mars and I can recognize them. Most people think they're just fat because they keep their arms folded up, but I know who they are. They know I do and they want to keep me quiet."

"Well, I won't let them get to you," Sally reassured him. "Give me the stick and I'll make sure they don't hurt you."

"Will you marry me?" he asked again. Sally could hear Paul behind her on the radio, requesting an ambulance for a drunk.

"Why don't you give me that stick? We'll consider it an

engagement present," she suggested. She could see the man liked that idea.

He handed her the stick. Sally put it behind her, then let it drop to the pavement.

"I thought that was a present," he said, looking hurt.

"I'm just leaving it there for safekeeping," she said in a comforting tone. He was much calmer now. She stepped nearer and could smell the odor of his unwashed body combined with alcohol and the ammonia-like stink of dried urine and God knew what else. She didn't like the idea of touching him, but knew she had no choice.

"What's your name?" she asked.

"Billy."

"Well, Billy, we're going to see that you have a warm place to sleep tonight, even a place to get cleaned up," Sally told him.

"No, I don't want to go anywhere." Billy backed away several steps.

"Now, come on, Billy," Sally said. "If you want me to marry you, you'll have to get cleaned up. I think you ought to go. You can take a bath, have a good meal, get a good night's sleep and we can talk again."

"Okay, if you say so," Billy agreed. Sally edged closer, handcuffs in one hand.

"Just put your hands behind your back, Billy. I'm not going to hurt you and I won't let anyone else hurt you either," she said. Sally was breathing through her mouth, but she could still smell him. She thought she could see lice moving in his hair and wished she had a pair of rubber gloves, but it was too late for that.

Billy did as she asked and she put handcuffs on him just as the ambulance pulled up. "Don't worry, Billy, they won't hurt you," she reassured him. "They're just going to take you someplace to get warm and clean. You'll have some hot food and a bed for the night."

The attendants came up quietly, took Billy by the arms and led him to the back of the ambulance. They opened the door and helped him climb inside. Sally watched him as he sat down.

"Good-bye, Billy," she said. "Be good. I'll try to stop by tomorrow."

One of the attendants turned to her. "You're new. I don't remember seeing you before. You don't have to if you don't want to," he said. "Billy's an old friend. He's too drunk to remember any of this. Once he gets sober and clean, he'll be okay. We've dealt with him before." He got in the ambulance and drove off.

Sally just stood there. She was still holding her nightstick in one hand. Paul came up behind her and she turned as she heard him. The two cops from the other RMP were next to their car, holding their nightsticks.

"Hey, partner, you did pretty good," Paul said. Sally smiled shakily. Frank Gordon was one of the other cops and he smiled at her, too, and nodded. He didn't say anything, but his partner also complimented Sally for calming the drunk down so quickly.

"I just didn't stop to think about it," she said. "I was concentrating on getting that stick away from him before he hit anyone and it just sort of happened after that."

"Well, you did real good, whether you meant to or not," Paul teased. "Come on, partner. It's the end of the day."

He called Central to report the ambulance had picked up the man with the stick and that they were going back to the precinct. Sally wrote up the incident in her memo book while the other RMP drove off.

"You got more than I expected tonight, thanks to the nut with the stick," he said.

The tour was over and they headed back to the precinct. Sally thanked Paul for his advice and his company.

"You'll be okay, Sally," he commented. "You just need some experience, but you handled the drunk real well. You kept your head. That's all this job is, just common sense. And you've got enough. Maybe you can ride with me when Mary Frances goes on vacation. I'll mention it to the sergeant. I've got so much time in this car, they give me all the rookies to train." He smiled at her as they drove up to the precinct.

# CHAPTER 9

Geri Casey's day began shortly before noon on Wednesday. She woke up without the alarm and climbed out of bed to be greeted furiously, as usual, by Mac. He seemed anxious to go out, so she washed quickly, threw on a pair of jeans and a sweatshirt, and grabbed his leash. They were back in minutes and she began her morning ritual, putting the coffee on to brew while she showered, then read the paper as she ate a bowl of cold cereal. She thought about going to her health club for a swim, but decided the run the night before had been enough exercise.

She went into the bedroom to dress. She had to pick up a suspect in the afternoon and had a dinner date after work with her old partner from Brooklyn, Alex Grandey. She wouldn't be off until nearly midnight, even later if the arrest got complicated, but the date wasn't romantic, and a fellow cop like Alex would understand. It looked like rain again later. She decided on slacks and a sweater, a wool jacket and leather boots. She would have her trenchcoat if it did rain. The boots had heels, but she could run in them if necessary. She didn't expect it to be necessary.

Sometimes, Geri thought she most resented the job when she got dressed every day. When she had worked in uniform, it was a lot easier. She had just tossed on jeans or whatever, worn a gun in a shoulder holster or a bellyband and gone to work. She had only needed civilian clothes for getting to and from work and on weekends. The money she saved on clothes she spent on vacations.

Now that she was working plainclothes, though, dressing was a problem. Buying clothes was difficult when she had to think about hiding a gun. Some of the women on the job kept their gun in their handbags, but Geri preferred not to. The Patrol Guide said to keep it on your person. It was easy to lose a purse, or forget it or have it stolen. Geri agreed with the rule, but it made choosing clothes difficult. Most of the men she knew used shoulder holsters with a jacket and wore an ankle holster if they were more casually dressed.

The choices for women were not as easy. Women's slacks had tighter cuffs—except in those rare years when bell bottoms were popular—which made it hard to wear an ankle holster. While Geri often wore a suit or jacket over a blouse, a shoulder holster was uncomfortable if she also carried a shoulder bag. She usually wore her gun in a bellyband, but that also caused a problem. She had to buy slacks that were larger than she really needed in the waist, which meant they didn't fit if she wasn't wearing the bellyband.

Still, she had been facing the problem for several years, and although she had yet to find the perfect solution she had several acceptable alternatives. Today she would be wearing a jacket so she could use the shoulder holster. She would just carry her purse on her left side.

Geri dressed, took Mac out one more time and left for work. She was somewhat early, but she wanted to talk with the captain about the suspect they were picking up. If she had enough time, she would call Sophia before she left.

This was the best part of being a detective, finally having enough evidence on someone to get a warrant for their arrest. Most of the time she spent in the office, going through new crime complaints or reviewing old ones, looking for patterns or clues that had been missed. She spent a lot of time on the phone and even more time interviewing people who had already talked to several cops and didn't want to see anyone else. Or she convinced victims to come in and look at mug shots, hoping they would be able to identify the person who attacked them.

She walked into the office more than an hour early. About half of the dozen or so desks were full. The Sex Crimes Unit had offices on the upper floor of one of the newer precinct houses in Manhattan, so they had not yet acquired a layer of grime.

Someone along the way had realized the difficulty of keeping a police precinct in the middle of Manhattan clean, so the new houses had tiled walls. That helped, although the tile was the same peculiar green as the painted walls in the older stationhouses—a mixture of olive drab and chartreuse. The tile also made it more difficult to hang the wanted posters, departmental bulletins and calendars that covered the walls of every police office Geri had ever seen.

A few years before, when Geri first got her gold shield, she had been working with a Robbery Task Force. She was assigned to the group in one of the oldest precincts still in use in the city. The windows of that building were so grimy it was impossible to tell if it was raining or sunny. Geri had taken a lot of teasing from the men when she came in one day with a bottle of Windex and a roll of paper towels. Once she got the windows cleaner, she brought in some plants. There was a lot more teasing about that, but she noticed the plants were always well-watered whenever she went on vacation.

"Who's catching* today?" Geri asked as she sat down.

"Joe and I," answered Mike Belton.

"Anything good?"

"Not a fucking thing so far," he replied. "What are you doing here early?"

"Danny and I are picking up a suspect later," Geri explained. "I wanted to read his rap sheet* again and look at some old cases. There may be a pattern we've missed until now."

"Which one?"

"That case in Chelsea two weeks ago," Geri said. "The girl gave us an ID from mug shots—one Joey Johnson. He served some time for a rape a few years ago. We have him placed at the scene; he was making a delivery and his truck got a ticket.

And she remembers seeing him in the neighborhood before he attacked her. He's the regular deliveryman who brings produce to the Korean fruit stand on her corner. The Korean remembers that he didn't leave right away, so we got the warrant."

Just then Captain Evans, the commanding officer of the Sex Crimes Unit, came out of his office and spotted Geri.

"Danny just called in sick," he announced.

"What's wrong?"

"Just an upset stomach, but he's been sick all day. He said he was sorry he would miss going with you to get Johnson," Captain Evans reported.

"You want to wait on picking up Johnson, then?" Geri asked. "I really want to get that guy up here to answer some questions. And we do have a positive ID on him from one complainant."

"You'll have to take Alice with you. Try to pick him up at work," the captain said. "I've got the file with his working address inside on my desk. He should be back from his deliveries by four."

Geri nodded in agreement and turned to talk to Alice Sanders. They were old friends, going back to their first days on the job. They had lost touch with each other through the years, then met up again when Geri was assigned to Sex Crimes a year and a half before. Alice had been working in the unit for nearly a year by then.

Geri liked Alice, but often wondered why she had let herself get so out-of-condition. Alice was at least fifty pounds overweight, although it didn't seem that much on her big frame. Still, Geri knew if the mutt* they were after tried to run, she would be chasing him alone.

"Well, it's you and me," she said as she sat on the corner of Alice's desk. "How do you want to handle this?"

"We've got a picture of the guy, don't we?"

"Yeah."

"Let's go up there and see if we can just wait outside where he works and pick him up when he leaves. I'd rather not have to bother his boss or anyone else," Alice suggested. "I know the area. If we get up there before he gets back, we can pick him up as he gets out of his truck. He probably parks in the lot nearest the stall. I'll call right now and make sure he's at work today. We can leave as soon as we're sure he's there."

"Okay." Geri went back to her desk and checked to be sure her gun was loaded. Deciding not to carry her purse with her, she slipped her wallet with her driver's license and police ID in a pocket of her jacket. Alice came up and they left the office.

"What did you tell his boss?" Geri asked as they walked out of the building.

"Nothing. I just asked if Joey was at work today. When he said yes and offered to take a message, I told him never mind, that I was Joey's wife and was checking to see if he really was at work. I told the boss I didn't want Joey to know I was checking up on him." Alice smiled.

Geri laughed.

They got into an unmarked car and drove through Central Park, taking the FDR Drive to the Triborough Bridge. They took the Bruckner Expressway to the Hunt's Point exit.

Geri hadn't been in the area for a few years. Hunt's Point was the main produce market for the City of New York. From midnight on, the area was a beehive of activity. Huge trailer trucks delivered the fresh fruits and vegetables shipped from all over the world to the wholesalers who rented space in the market. They, in turn, dealt with supermarkets, sidewalk vendors, restaurant chefs and anyone else who wanted to buy what they were selling.

Beginning in those predawn hours, the bustle in the sprawling market and the streets around it built to a peak until 6 A.M., then slowly eased off. The late-morning streets were filled with the paneled vans of the small produce sellers found in all the shopping areas of the residential neighborhoods in the city.

It was now late afternoon and the streets were almost deserted of moving vehicles. Geri and Alice saw only an occasional gypsy cab, a few delivery vans from one of the Hunt's Point wholesalers and trucks making pickups at one of the hundreds of small manufacturers who filled the blocks of one-story brick buildings. Other blocks were filled with junkyards and auto parts stores.

"The last time I was up here, it was early in the morning. I was working Narcotics," Geri remarked to Alice. "Even after my time on the job, I was shocked."

"Yeah, the hookers who hang out around here are really something, aren't they?" Alice said. "Have you been here when it's warm and the trucks are coming in? I swear I've seen some of them standing in the middle of the street, bare to the waist and not much on below."

"At least it's quiet now," Geri said.

They followed the signs through the local streets to the enormous twelve-foot fence that circled the massive produce market. Alice showed her police ID to the guard at the gate and they were waved through. Next to the fence on the inside was a row of parked cars. On the other side of the narrow passage allowed for moving vehicles were the big semitrailers, angled into the loading docks that made up the facade of the first building in the complex.

Alice drove down the row until she came to a road that led under the second story of the market. They passed another row of unloading trucks, then a row of parked trailers, stopped apparently at random, more angled trucks and a second market building. They drove through two more passageways before they came to the building that housed Joey Johnson's employer. On a few loading docks, the trucks were replaced by railroad cars, pulled up on the tracks that paralleled the wider roads through the huge complex.

They were on the outside of the market area, where an empty field filled several acres. There were two lines of trucks parked on the edge, mostly pickups and the trailers for the big semis. There were apparently random empty spots in the lines, but there was also a hint of order. Trucks belonging to the same company were parked close together.

"It would be a lot easier if we knew for sure where he was going to park," Geri suggested. "If I go talk to his boss, he might be able to tell me what his regular parking spot is. And he probably follows some kind of pattern when he comes back from his deliveries."

"Yeah, you might as well talk to him," Alice agreed. "He

can't call him now, unless he's got a car phone or something. And I don't think he would. His boss may know when this joker is due back."

Alice found the right stall number and Geri went inside. She came out in a few minutes. "He's got a spot, right over there. He should be back any minute now. After he parks the truck, he comes in to give the boss the bills of lading and the rest of the forms."

"We might as well sit in the car, wait until he gets out of his truck and pick him up after he gets to the office," Alice said. "I'll park here, across the street. We can see when the truck pulls in and get out then. He won't suspect anything, seeing two women sitting in a car. He'll think we're here to shop."

They sat quietly together, smoking. A van pulled into the lot across the street. Geri recognized the driver as the man they wanted. "That's him. Let's go." They both reached for their guns and got out of the car. The driver crossed the road and went into the building. He stopped at the office next to the third stall in, knocked and went inside. Geri and Alice moved in and stood on either side of the door. It opened and the suspect walked out.

"Hold it. Police." Geri raised her gun. "You're under arrest."

The man, nearly six feet two and more than two hundred pounds, turned around, his eyes widening as he spotted Geri. She could see his muscles tensing as if he were trying to decide whether to surrender or run.

"Don't even think about it," she said. "Put your hands up, spread-eagled against the wall. Let's go, Joey. You know the routine. You've done this before."

"I ain't done nothing. What do you want me for?" he asked, but he followed Geri's orders. She patted him down, feeling his back, waist, legs and groin for weapons. He was clean and she pulled his hands behind his back for the handcuffs.

"I have a warrant for your arrest on charges of rape and sodomy," Geri said. "You have the right to remain silent and not to answer any questions. Anything you say may be used against you in a court of law. You have the right to consult an attorney before answering any questions and to have an attorney present during any questioning. If you cannot afford an attorney, one will be provided for you without cost. Do you understand?"

Joey nodded his head.

Alice was standing to one side, her gun still aimed at Joey, while Geri holstered hers and took him by one arm. He looked at both women again, and again she could see the hesitation in his eyes, the feeling that maybe he could shake loose and escape.

"If you take off on me, I'm not going to chase you," Geri warned him. "I've got a date after work and I'm not going to work up a sweat. But I'm not going to lose you either. You take off and you're going to get one, right in the back." Geri didn't turn around to see how Alice was taking that.

"You can't shoot me in the back." Joey was outraged.

"Trust me. I'm not going to get in trouble with my boss for losing a prisoner. You'll get shot in the back and I'll deal with them later," she said.

"You wouldn't do that," he countered.

"All right, try it and you'll see," Geri replied. "I'm allowed to shoot if I'm in fear of my life and if a guy your size tries anything, believe me, I'll be in fear for my life. Don't do it."

Joey gave up the argument and walked quietly to the car with them. Geri smiled to herself. She wouldn't have shot him; she would not have been able to justify it under NYPD guidelines. But he didn't have to know that. She sure wasn't going to tempt him to get into a fight with her. As long as he thought she would shoot first, he wouldn't take a chance.

Joey got into the backseat and Geri sat next to him, following procedures. She hated this part of an arrest, sitting next to one of these creeps for the ride to the stationhouse, but that's the way the book said to do it. They waited while Alice searched the truck. She found an ice pick under the front seat. Geri was pleased. The rapist in several open cases had used an ice pick to keep his victims quiet.

Alice drove back the way they had come and returned to the Bruckner. From the expressway, Geri could see the neighborhood called the South Bronx. It was the part of the city Geri hated the most, a breeding ground for drugs and lowlifes.

There were blocks of rubbled lots, boarded-up buildings and fire-blackened tenements. Fire hydrants dribbled continuously. Geri knew that for some people living in the area, that was the only running water they had. There were a lot of addicts and alcoholics who cared little about running water, but there were also many families, usually unwed teenage girls on welfare with a couple of children.

They passed one street of tenements with windows that seemed to have curtains, flowerpots, even an occasional cat. Geri realized they were the decals the city put on the plywood that covered the windows of burned-out buildings, in hopes of making the neighborhood look more cheerful. When she first read about the idea, she thought it was dumb. Now that she had seen the decals, she knew her original reaction had been correct.

They were passing some buildings that still had tenants. Geri could see the window shades, mostly blue or green. Every once in a while she spotted a red shade or a white one. One of the little mysteries of the city, as far as Geri was concerned, was why poor people preferred blue and green window shades. No one had ever been able to explain it to her, but then, she didn't spend a whole lot of time worrying about it.

They were going back to Manhattan, to the Sex Crimes Unit office. Joey sat quietly in the car. He seemed to have given up thoughts of escaping. Geri wondered what Alice would say to her later, when they were alone, about her threat to shoot him in the back. Alice had been on the job as long as Geri and knew there were times you had to say what was necessary to make a point. One of the first things you learned was how to bluff and how to tell when someone else was bluffing.

It was still fairly early, only a little after five. That gave Geri several hours to question Joey, process him at Central Booking and still make her date. Alex was working at headquarters and they were meeting at a restaurant near there. She shouldn't be too late, depending on how long it took to get Joey's lawyer. He would probably want Legal Aid so that shouldn't be a problem.

Geri and Alice walked Joey up the stairs to the Sex Crimes office. Geri pushed him into a chair by her desk, then walked to the back of the room with Alice.

"We could do a lineup if we could get in some other complainants," she said. "We hadn't been thinking about the fruit stand angle, but there have been a series of rapes using an ice pick. I think they go back a couple of years and they're mostly in Manhattan."

"I remember some of those cases," Alice said, nodding. "You think you can tie this guy into some of those?"

Captain Evans came out of his office, looked at Joey sitting handcuffed at Geri's desk and walked over to where the two women were talking.

Geri liked Captain Evans. He had been CO of the Sex Crimes Unit a couple of years when she got there. He was a good cop, an even better detective and a decent boss. Evans had turned an unproductive unit into a model of efficiency. Sex Crimes used to be a dead-end; now it was considered a good career move and that was all Evans's doing. He had gotten rid of some deadwood, recruited good people and set up procedures that reduced the workload by making it easier to find the patterns that often led to suspects.

"You got him. Good work."

"Captain, remember those ice pick rapes over the last two years?" Geri asked. "They're spread all over Manhattan, so we never really tied them together except that the attacker used an ice pick and was described as a large black man. I'd like to bring some of those victims in for a lineup with Johnson."

"Okay, if you think you've got something." The captain looked pensive. "Check out the vegetable stands near those sites. Maybe they all used this guy to make deliveries. If we can tie him to the locations, we may not need any more ID's. Has he called a lawyer yet?"

"No, we just got in," Geri answered.

"Casey, you take care of him. Sanders, you see if you can get some of those complainants to come down here this evening for a lineup. Tomorrow one of you or Danny, if he's back, can start checking on the produce stores." Captain Evans·walked back to his office.

Geri went to her desk. "Do you have a lawyer, Joey, or should I call Legal Aid? We have a lot of questions to ask you about some attacks on women. I have a feeling you know a lot about them."

"I need Legal Aid," Joey replied. "I'm not going to answer anything until I get a lawyer."

"Okay, I'll call." Geri dialed the number for Legal Aid, told them about the case and the suspect, then asked how long it would be before someone got there.

"It'll be a couple of hours, Joey," Geri told him as she hung up the phone. "Come on. I guess we're stuck with you for a while. You'll have to go sit in the cell until your lawyer gets here. Then we'll ask you some questions. If you need anything, let me know."

She walked him to the small barred cell, barely ten feet square, in the corner of the room. She unlocked the door, opened his handcuffs and gave him a light push inside. The door clanged shut as Joey went to the back of the cell and sat on the floor, his back against the wall. He lit a cigarette. Geri walked back to her desk and began filling out the forms for an arrest.

# CHAPTER 10

**N**ot too long after midnight, Geri finished up the paperwork and processing on Joey. They had had to wait a few hours at the office for a Legal Aid lawyer to show up before Joey could be questioned. She asked him about the other cases and where he was on those dates. As she expected, the lawyer wouldn't let him answer. They tried to set up a lineup, but none of the other victims were home.

Joey might feel more like talking after he had been arraigned and spent a few days at Riker's Island in the Men's House of Detention. Geri had been told that rapists got rough treatment from the other prisoners—what was called hard time. She hoped so. She really wanted to clear up those other cases and she was sure Joey was the creep she wanted. The descriptions were similar and the attacker had used an ice pick in all of them.

The captain was right. If those stands bought from Joey's employer, she could tie him in that way. If they could get enough circumstantial evidence on him for the other attacks and good witnesses in at least one, there was a good chance he would just come clean even without witnesses in every case.

That was for the next day. For now she was meeting Alex across the street. He was probably there already. The place was a hangout for cops and Geri was really hoping to be able to talk to him. She worried that they might not have enough privacy, but few restaurants were open at that hour in lower Manhattan.

Geri walked into the restaurant, nodded hello to a couple of acquaintances and spotted Alex at the bar. He greeted her with a hug and a kiss. They had been friends for years. Alex had worked in the first precinct Geri had been assigned to after the Academy. They had been partners for a while, until Geri got laid off during the fiscal crisis. Alex had more seniority, so he stayed on the job. When she was rehired almost three years later, she was assigned to a different precinct.

They talked on the phone all the time, but Geri hadn't seen him in months. He looked the same if a bit grayer; he was forty now, but still thin. He always looked good in uniform, and he looked even better in civilian clothes. When he worked plainclothes, he wore jeans a lot. She always thought he could have modeled for cowboy ads because he looked so good in them and had a weathered kind of face. He was married when she first knew him, but was divorced now. Still, they had never been more than pals. Or maybe they were such good pals neither wanted to mess up the friendship with a more intimate, but less lasting relationship.

A couple of months after they started working as partners, he had come on hot and heavy to her. Geri convinced him that he was confusing his feelings. She had explained that he felt the same closeness with her that he had experienced with male partners, but because she was a woman he was thinking of it as something more, something physical. He thought about it for a couple of weeks, then agreed she was right. Geri knew lots of other women who had the same problem with their male partners. Some guys resented being told that, but Alex had been great.

"What have you been doing?" Alex asked. "And what do you want to drink?"

"Dewar's and water, and I've been booking a creep on rape and sodomy charges," she answered.

"That's my Geri, first things first." He grinned. "You hungry? Want to sit down?"

"Yes, I'm starved," Geri said. "I haven't eaten since I woke up. We picked up this guy this afternoon after work and I haven't had time for more than a couple of cups of coffee."

Alex led her into the next room where only a few tables were occupied. They chose a table near the fireplace. A waitress came with menus, and they both ordered the prime rib. She took their orders for side dishes, then left only to return in less than a minute with Geri's drink and the second round for Alex. Geri lit a cigarette and Alex shook his finger at her.

"When are you going to give those things up?" he asked. "It's been two years for me."

"And there's nothing worse than a reformed smoker," she answered. "I never smoked as much as you did and I still don't. And I'm probably in better condition than you are. I swim or run almost every day."

"You're right," Alex said. "My big exercise is walking to the car. Since I started working down here, I don't even climb stairs anymore."

"I don't know how you stay thin," she observed. "I know people who would sell their souls for your metabolism. Remember Alice Sanders? She was with me on the collar today. Have you seen her lately? She's about fifty pounds overweight."

"I haven't seen her in years, but I know she's been in Sex Crimes even longer than you have," he said. "By the way, when are you going to get out of there?"

"I don't know," Geri answered, frowning. "I don't know where I want to go. I don't really dislike it. Since I got my gold shield, the only assignment I really loved was Robbery. And the most fun I ever had was working undercover in Narcotics."

"That was fun?" Alex gave her a questioning look.

"Yeah. That first time, when they asked me to work on a temporary basis to get into the building in the South Bronx, I was scared shitless. But after it was over, I couldn't wait to do it again." Geri smiled at the memory.

"I remember that," Alex said. "They dressed you up as a hooker and sent you in to make a buy. They had been trying to get into that building for weeks to get evidence and build a case but all their regular people were known in the neighborhood, so they brought you in."

"Yep. None of the guys could get near the place and even the black girls were made, so they decided to try for a white prostitute." Geri was smiling as she remembered. "Everyone knew there were narcotics sales in that building. Word on the street was you could get anything you wanted there: heroin, cocaine, marijuana, uppers, downers. It was a regular drugstore, but without proof, nothing could be done about it.

"They sent me in with this little teeny person, one of the first Puerto Rican girls on the job. She did a real chitchat thing, kind of like a Hispanic Betty Boop. We got in with no problems, no threats, nothing.

"It was a typical run-down tenement—broken stairs, peeling paint, no light. They had a lookout at the front door and another at the door of the apartment where the sales were made. A hole had been drilled through the door and the seller stayed behind the locked door so we couldn't see him. We told him what we wanted, shoved the money through the hole in the door and the dope came back the same way." She grinned at Alex.

"But you had a big argument with someone." Alex frowned. "I remember you calling me and being upset."

"Two weeks later, after my Spanish pal had left, they decided they needed more evidence to build the case. They told me I'd have to go in again." Geri took a drag on her cigarette.

"Only this time, they gave me details about the building, how bad it was, how many dealers worked there, the whole bit. And instead of Betty Boop, they wanted this guy, Evan, to go with me."

"That was Evan Danson? Tall black guy with a thick mustache?" Alex asked.

"Yeah, I remember telling you about that part of it," Geri recalled. "He looked too much like a cop, and I didn't want him with me. I asked them to use a Spanish guy or an undercover who looked dirty, someone who could fit in. They said not to worry, Evan would fit in. He was posing as a pimp."

Alex laughed. "He might pass for a disco deejay, but not a pimp."

"That's what I said," Geri agreed. "They insisted and I

began to get nervous. That's when I called you. I ended up going with him, though. We got to the door, it was one of those heavy wooden ones with steel plate nailed on, and I started banging on it and no one answered. The lookout was a junkie on the stairway, not that he could see much of anything because there was only one bulb about two flights up.

"He just kept saying: 'We ain't got nothin', man. Go away. There's nothin' here.' I kept insisting, telling him I'd bought some coke there a week earlier and I knew they were selling and I wanted to buy more, and if he didn't have what I wanted, I wanted to talk to the guy behind the door," she continued.

"And all the time there are people behind me, lining up to make their buys and getting pissed off because nothing's happening. The junkie knew he couldn't turn us all away, that was too much business to lose. So he finally let us all in. I gave the guy a ten and he handed me a packet of coke.

"Now everyone decided I'm okay, because I'd just made a buy and suddenly everyone wants to sell me junk. I tried to remember what each one looked like, but they all looked like mopes.* We finally got out of there and Evan didn't say a word the whole time." Geri looked up with a grin.

"And that's what you call fun?" Alex shook his head.

"Well, it was the first time on the job that I could be creative," Geri replied. "I didn't know what I was going to find there and I had to worry about Evan with me and not blowing the whole thing. I think they got five good collars on that, not just the lookout and the guy who sold to me, but three of the people who were offering me stuff afterward."

"Yeah, that's the reason you got to Narcotics in the first place, I remember that," Alex said.

The waitress appeared with their dinner and as they ate, Alex continued. "I remember how pissed some guys were when you got Narcotics. I heard from guys all over the city who had worked with us in Brooklyn. Most of them were saying it was just because you were a girl and you'd never have gotten it if it hadn't been for that."

"They may have been right," Geri said facetiously. She thought he was probably trying to tease her, but she was on to his tricks. Narcotics was a plum assignment. It was part of the Organized Crime Control Bureau and one of the sure ways of making detective after a couple of years.

"I decided early on in this job that no matter what I got, someone would say I got it because I was a woman. So I figured I might as well take advantage of whatever I'm offered, because it's not going to stop that kind of thing. It's the same thing for the black guys," she went on.

"Don't get upset with me, I'm on your side, remember?"

"I know," Geri said. She heard herself getting defensive as she tried to explain. "It's just so damn aggravating to still be fighting the same battles. I thought we'd be over this in a couple of years, that the men would see that women could do the job and they'd stop all this bullshit. But it's been more than a dozen years now, and if anything, it seems to be getting worse.

"Remember what it was like when we started working together?" she asked. "All the guys in the precinct were always looking for me to make a mistake. They were just waiting for me to do something wrong or to chicken out on something."

"I remember the night we chased that mope who was beating up on cabbies," Alex recalled. "We ran after him for about two blocks and he ran straight into the hospital emergency room and you jumped on his back."

"The two of us were rolling around on the floor, with people screaming and gurneys flying in all directions," Geri continued, laughing at the memory. "You were right behind me and threw yourself on top of us. All three of us were rolling around on the floor. We were trying to get his hands behind his back, and he's knocking us around and kicking and slugging.

"I could see blue pants and black shoes standing around us in a circle. I thought I was in a wrestling match with an audience watching." She smiled. "When we finally got him cuffed and stood up, it turned out all those blue pants and black shoes belonged to cops and one of them belted the mope in the mouth."

"Yeah, that pissed you off," Alex said, chuckling. "You turned to that guy and said, 'Don't you touch my prisoner.' I think you were angrier at that cop than at the prisoner. We were both all bruised and scratched and our uniforms were torn."

"I was pissed at that guy. He stands around watching us fight with him, then comes up to hit him after we have him in custody," she said. "And when we got back to the precinct, I saw those guys from the hospital talking to the desk sergeant and I was sure they were accusing me of starting the whole thing. I got really mad then.

"I went up to the desk and started to explain and the sergeant said, 'Wait a minute, Casey. These guys are apologizing. They said they couldn't believe what they were seeing, you rolling around on the floor with that bruiser. They were so stunned to see a woman fighting like that, they didn't help and they're really sorry.'

"I told the sergeant I accepted the apology, but they should let my prisoner alone." Geri laughed again. "I didn't have any more problems in that precinct, but it didn't stop the attitude in general. Other women had problems there and I've had problems elsewhere."

Alex had finished eating and leaned back in his chair to look at Geri. "What prompted this? Something happen to set you off on women's lib again?"

"Don't start with me, Alex." Geri scowled at him. She knew he was only teasing, but that didn't matter. "You know I don't like jokes about this. I don't think it's funny that after all the time I've got on the job, I still have to prove myself every day. The guys I work with know I'm a good cop, but if I go to a new detail, it would be the same thing all over again."

"I'm not trying to start an argument, Geri. Like I said, I'm on your side. I've worked with women and always got along well with them," Alex said calmly. "Maybe there just aren't enough of you yet. Most of the guys I know would probably change their attitude once they worked with a woman and got to know her as an individual.

"Don't forget, you girls are still only about ten percent of the force. There are twenty-eight thousand cops out there and fewer than three thousand of them are women. Most guys haven't worked with a woman partner, so they can still be selective and stupid. When they do ride with a girl for eight hours, they're more accepting—unless she's a lousy cop," he pointed out.

"And if she's a lousy cop, a real do-nothing, it's not that that particular woman is a lousy cop and the next one probably won't be, but that all women are lousy cops with a few exceptions," Geri replied with more than a hint of resentment. The waitress came to collect their plates and they ordered another round of drinks.

"That's just men." Alex resumed the conversation. "We've talked about this before. The Police Department is a lot like the Marines, a bunch of guys working together, sitting around swapping stories afterward, cursing and drinking. When a girl shows up, they don't know how to act."

"Oh, they know how to act—like real shitheads," Geri answered, teasingly.

"Some guys," Alex said, grinning. "Didn't I stand up for you when you got transferred to Narcotics? I remember some of the guys really pitching a bitch about it. They were screaming and yelling that they would never get anywhere with all the special treatment for the blacks and the women. When I asked some of them, it turned out none of them had even requested a transfer for themselves, so they weren't even in the running for the assignment. That didn't stop them from complaining, though. You ought to be able to ignore that kind of stuff by now."

"Yeah, you're right," Geri said. "In fact, that's exactly what I told a new girl who works with Mary Frances. We had pizza last night and this kid joined us. She wasn't expecting me and I thought she was going to run out of the place when she saw me. She's only been in the One-Six a couple of months and the guys there are really riding her. I told her to just ignore them. I guess I ought to follow my own advice."

The waitress brought the drinks and put the bill next to Alex. Geri made a grab for it, but he got it first. "The last time you paid. This one's on me." He took a credit card from his wallet and put it down.

"Let's change the subject," Alex said. "Tell me about the guy you arrested today."

"He's a nothing, a real mutt," she replied. "Convicted once before on a rape charge, ID'd by the victim and other witnesses to put him at the scene. We picked him up at work; he's a deliveryman for a wholesaler at the Hunt's Point Market. He looked like he was going to make a break and I told him if he tried it, I'd shoot him in the back, so he stayed put."

"You can't do that." Alex looked shocked.

"I know I can't shoot him in the back." Geri nodded. "But I can tell him I'm going to. I use that all the time. Some of these guys would really try to get over on me if they didn't think I'd use my gun on them. It's one of the tricks we girls use to make things easier."

"I don't understand," Alex said.

"I'm sure I've told you about this before," Geri explained. "Some of these mutts wouldn't hesitate to hit a cop and if they tried to hit me, I'd be out cold. But they won't even lift a finger if they think I'm going to shoot if they move wrong. I tell them that's what will happen up front. So they're good little boys.

"In fact, sometimes I wonder if women cops don't have an advantage rather than a disadvantage," Geri said thoughtfully. "All of these guys, no matter how bad they are, all had mothers. And for at least a few years, they did what their mothers told them to. When we come along, they kind of react like they're kids again and Mommy is shaking a finger at them. There have been some collars when I wanted to call the mutt's mother and thank her for teaching her boy it's not nice to hit a woman," she added.

"But that doesn't work all the time," Alex noted.

"More often than you'd think," Geri responded. "One time, when I was still in uniform, on a foot post, there was a fight on the street about a block from where I was. Suddenly, a bunch of people came running up to me, yelling, 'Officer, officer, there's a fight down the block.'

"I ran to see what was happening and there are these two big gorillas swinging at each other. It was a minor fender bender, but these two huge Italians were really punching each other out. They were enormous: tattoos on their noses, hairy arms, the whole bit."

Alex laughed at her exaggerated description, and Geri went on. "I'm there all alone and I edge closer, trying to stay out of their way and not get hit. I get a little closer and say, 'Excuse me, what's the trouble?' One of them turns around, his hands up, ready to throw another punch." Geri demonstrated graphically.

"He sees me and the other guy sees me and they both drop their fists, just like that," Geri continued. "I said, 'Listen, we've got a problem. You two are blocking traffic. Why don't you pull your trucks to the side and we'll talk about what happened?'

"The two of them say, 'Yes, ma'am,' meek as little mice. I couldn't believe it. They move the trucks to the curb and we stand there, and they exchange names and license plates and everything. They each give me their version of what happened, like two little boys accused of fighting at recess. I fill out the accident report and they go on their way." Geri laughed. "I said novenas to their mothers for a week."

"You're really something, Casey," Alex said, laughing. After a minute, he asked, "You mentioned Mary Frances, how's she doing?"

"Oh, she's fine," Geri answered. She didn't think Alex would be interested in Mary Frances's worries about her marriage.

"And her friend, the Italian girl. What was her name, Sophie?"

"You mean Sophia," Geri said. She told him about Sophia's run-in with an assistant district attorney.

"That's a bitch, but I'm not surprised," he remarked.

"I know," Geri agreed. "That's what I told Soph. She's been on the job long enough to learn to accept that kind of thing, but she was really pissed off yesterday. I haven't had a chance to call her today to see if she's calmed down."

"She's a real looker," Alex said. "I remember meeting her and Mary Frances with you years ago, when they first came on. I was still married at the time but she made an impression. Now that I'm free again, maybe I'll give her a call. She's divorced, right? Is she seeing anyone?"

"I don't know," Geri answered. "I can ask. If she's available, we can all go out for a drink or something."

"That's a good idea," Alex said. "I'll hold you to that."

The waitress picked up the credit card and Alex and Geri drained their drinks.

"You going home?" Alex asked. "I've got the car. I can drop you off."

"I accept," Geri said. They picked up their coats and walked toward the bar. They both stopped to chat briefly with some acquaintances, then left the restaurant.

"I'm not kidding," Alex said. "I'd like to meet Sophia again."

"I told you, I'll see if she's available," Geri told him. "But you'll owe me one."

"It's a deal," he said, sticking out his hand. They shook hands, laughing, and walked to the garage under the police headquarters building.

On the way home, Alex asked whom she was dating. Geri just looked at him and laughed. She knew if he found out she was dating a doctor, a gynecologist, he would laugh himself silly while making every joke he could think of about a detective from Sex Crimes going out with an OB/GYN specialist. There was no way she was going to open herself up for Alex's sarcasm.

"No one you know, love," she answered. "And if it were, I wouldn't tell you. In fact, if you start going out with Sophia, don't tell me about it. I don't want to get involved with anybody's personal problems, especially not between two good friends."

"Come on, when have I ever involved you?" Alex was indignant.

"I can remember a few too many nights listening to you bitch and moan while you were getting your divorce." Geri looked over at him. "All I did then was listen, but when it involves a friend of mine, I won't even listen. I don't want to hear about any problems."

"I swear," Alex said. "I'm not asking you to arrange a marriage, for God's sake. I just remembered that she was something of a knockout. I found her attractive while I was married, and now that I'm free, I thought I'd try to get to know her.

"I'm always surprised to find good-looking women on the job." His eyes squinted and Geri knew he was going to say something outrageous.

"Why is that?" Geri knew what was expected of her.

"It's like the women in the Army," he answered. "Most of them are girls who don't stand a chance of getting a date with even odds, so they put themselves in an environment where the men are ten to one or even better. Sooner or later, they get someone."

He looked over to see how she was taking that. "I remember when I was in the service and stationed in a military town, the kind that exists just to serve the base. You would find girls there who were beaten to death with an ugly stick." Alex bit his lips to keep from laughing, then continued his comment, watching Geri's reactions.

"Everybody would criticize them, rank them out, look down on them because they weren't attractive or were too fat. But somewhere along the line, there came a time for each of them when all the criticism stopped, because some guy fell in love with her.

"I think it's the same type of thing with a lot of women who come on the job. There are men here and they don't have a chance on the outside," Alex concluded with a flourish. He glanced again at Geri.

"I just can't see that." She looked as if she had been biting her tongue, waiting for him to finish. "If that were the case, then these women would be finding guys, getting married and quitting the job. How many women do you see who do that?" Geri asked indignantly.

"How many women on the job are married to cops?" He was incredulous.

"Okay, a lot, but that's normal in any place. People meet people where they work." Geri backed off a bit, then attacked again. "People in the private sector marry people they meet at work, too. But how many women on the job quit just because they get married, whether to a cop or a civilian?"

"I'm not saying that all the women who come on this job do so to meet husbands, but I am saying that a lot of women come on the job because there are twenty-five thousand men," Alex said, unable to resist a final jab. Geri was getting annoyed, he could tell, so he decided to stop tormenting her. "But I also know a lot of good women cops who are on the job for the same reason most men are, because they want to be cops."

He had stopped in front of her building. Geri leaned over and kissed him on the cheek.

"I'll forgive your sexist remarks, Grandey, but I'm going to tell Soph about them," she threatened.

Alex groaned. "Come on, Geri," he said, pleading. "You know I was only teasing you. I'm not really a sexist. You know that. Just see if she remembers me."

"No, you're not a sexist at work, but you're a real male chauvinist in your personal life. Maybe Sophia can raise your consciousness more than I could. I'll call you," Geri promised. She waved him good-bye and started up the steps. He waited until she got inside the locked door before driving off.

# CHAPTER 11

Thursday, Mary Frances and Paul were assigned to Sector H, as usual. Almost immediately, the dispatcher had a job for them: a man hurt, apparently in a fight, at the Off-Track Betting (OTB) parlor on Seventy-second Street. Paul acknowledged the call and made a U-turn. They drove south on West End, then turned on to Seventy-second Street. A crowd was gathered in front of the OTB windows. They could see a man lying on the sidewalk and a couple of people kneeling down next to him.

Paul and Mary Frances got out of the car and pushed their way through the crowd. Most of the onlookers left when they saw the patrol car arrive. Those who remained were mostly OTB regulars and a couple of the Good Samaritan types found everywhere on the West Side. Remnants of the 1960's radicals, such people took it upon themselves to watch the police whenever they could. They were often the source of brutality charges at the Civilian Complaint Review Board.* Mary Frances thought they were a pain in the ass; Paul usually had a stronger reaction.

The man on the sidewalk had a cut on his scalp that was bleeding heavily, but didn't look too serious. Mary Frances called Central to request an ambulance while Paul moved the crowd back. The injured man tried to sit up, his hand to his head. He seemed surprised to see blood.

"What happened?" Paul directed the questions to men he recognized from previous jobs at the OTB parlor. Something was always happening there, usually drunks getting hurt, but occasionally a real fight broke out or someone with a big winner got robbed.

"He fell and hit his head on the corner of the window," one of the regulars explained. The man offering the explanation spoke with a Spanish accent slurred by alcohol. "He's my friend. We were just standing there and he fell down."

Paul nodded and turned to Mary Frances, who was kneeling next to the injured man. "How is he?"

"He looks okay," she said. She had taken out a couple of the individually wrapped wet tissues she always carried and was wiping the blood from his face. A lot of dirt came off, too. "It's still bleeding a little, but it doesn't look like it's too serious."

"What's his name?" Paul asked the man who seemed to have taken over the situation. He was still repeating his explanation of what happened to his pal in between sips from a small bottle of Bacardi he kept in his back pocket. The other regulars had backed off, most of them returning to the serious work of picking their horses for the next race.

"Enrique," the friend said. "But everyone calls him Hank."

"Okay, Hank, how do you feel?" Paul looked down at the injured man, who was still trying to push himself up. "Don't try to get up. There'll be an ambulance here in a few minutes."

The man was apparently too drunk and dizzy from bumping his head to move much at all. He would lift his head, then let it fall back on *The New York Times* someone had put down to keep him from hitting the back of his head on the sidewalk.

"I'm okay," Hank mumbled, trying again to get up. He was wearing several layers of shirts under a thin, dirty windbreaker. His pants were grimy and the smell of previous drunks hovered around him like an awful aura.

Paul asked Hank's friend for his last name and his address.

The friend told him Hank lived in an SRO, one of the ubiquitous West Side hotels that rented rooms by the week and offered bathroom and kitchen facilities on each floor, but he didn't know Hank's last name. They were, it appeared, drinking buddies, one of any number of men who hung out on the same street corners, sharing whatever alcoholic beverage any of them could afford.

The ambulance arrived and the two technicians climbed out, nodding to Paul and Mary Frances. "What have we got?" one attendant asked.

"Hank, here, fell down and hit his head," Mary Frances answered. "It's almost stopped bleeding, but he's a bit the worse for the wear."

"We'll take him to the emergency room to at least get that cut cleaned up," the attendant said. "With these guys, even a small cut like that can get infected and mean big trouble." They took down a lightweight, collapsible wheelchair, opened it up and set it down on the sidewalk next to Hank.

"Come on, buddy, let's get you out of here." The attendant tried to lift Hank from under his arms, but Hank didn't want to be moved and went limp. Paul and Mary Frances went to help, as did the other attendant.

"Let's go, Hank, get in the chair so they can take care of your cut," Mary Frances said, trying to win Hank's cooperation. Hank shook his head.

"I'm okay, just leave me alone, I don't want to go," he said from the sidewalk, squinting up at the four people who stood around him. He was a small man, but stocky and overweight enough to be hard to lift.

Hank's friend tried to help. "Come on, *amigo*. Get in the chair. Your head is still bleeding. You need to go to the hospital."

It took the combined efforts of the two EMS technicians and Paul and Mary Frances to heave the injured man into the wheelchair. One of the technicians braced his foot against the chair to keep it from rolling as Hank sank down, while the other moved quickly to fasten the straps to keep him there. Hank thrashed feebly, looking close to tears at being taken to the hospital.

"You go with them," his friend said. "They'll take care of you. Don't worry. They'll let you go after they clean up the cut."

Hank was wheeled to the back of the ambulance, then lifted into it. One technician climbed in with him while the other moved to the driver's seat. They thanked Paul and Mary Frances for their help and drove off.

Paul called Central to report that the injured man had been taken to a hospital and they were resuming patrol. Mary Frances made the entry in her memo book, then filled out the aided card.*

"Looks like it's going to be another one of those days," she said with an unhappy expression on her face. "I'd better get my rubber gloves out of the trunk. I have a feeling we'll be needing them tonight."

"Come on, partner, it's no different than any other day," Paul assured her, trying to cheer her up.

"I know," Mary Frances answered. "I just hate dealing with the drunks so early in the tour. They're always so dirty and smelly and they never want our help. They'd be perfectly happy sleeping it off in the street. You know I hate dealing with these skells.* Why can't they just take a bath once in a while?"

Paul listened to Mary Frances complain. He felt the same way, but part of the job was dealing with the alcoholics and junkies, the mental cases and the homeless people who wandered the streets. Civilians seemed to think that the police spent all their time chasing criminals or sleeping. But most cops, those who worked in uniform anyway, went days without dealing with a lawbreaker. Mary Frances liked helping people, but the street people they were most often called on to help frequently resisted their efforts and frustrated her.

Paul and Mary Frances drove around the streets again. The dispatcher from Central called to everyone on the frequency, asking for a female officer to go to the 22nd precinct. Paul turned to Mary Frances to see if she wanted to answer it.

"No way," she said. "They need someone to make a search. It's bad enough doing my own collars. I'm not going to volunteer. If they need someone badly enough, they can use one of the girls on clerical."

He nodded his agreement and kept going. They were driving west on Seventy-fifth Street when Mary Frances noticed someone waving to them. "Stop the car, Paul," she told him. "Looks like someone is trying to flag us down."

He pulled over and they got out, walking back to the woman who had been motioning. Standing next to her were an older Chinese man and woman, both of whom seemed upset.

"What's the trouble?" Mary Frances asked as she neared the trio. Paul lagged behind, calling Central to report they had been flagged down and would not be on patrol until he called back. A few doors down was a Chinese hand laundry and shards of broken window glass littered the sidewalk. The Chinese woman held a broom in her hand.

"Someone threw a rock through their door," the Caucasian woman explained. "I was inside, picking up my husband's shirts, when all of a sudden this rock came through the door. I saw the guy who threw it. He ran up Amsterdam."

At this point the Chinese man offered his explanation. He spoke with a thick accent and a limited English vocabulary, making it difficult to understand him. The Caucasian woman had walked away, apparently feeling she had done her civic duty by waving the patrol car down.

Eventually, Paul and Mary Frances figured out that the rock thrower was a disgruntled customer, someone who had picked up his laundry and believed some of his shirts were missing. The owner had disagreed, explaining that every shirt was marked and none could have been lost. The customer had become angry, accusing the laundry of stealing his shirts.

He had left the store about ten minutes earlier, then returned with two big chunks of concrete. Without warning, he had thrown them through the glass panel on the front door. Mary Frances asked the laundry owner for a description. He said the man was tall and thin, black, with a mustache and short beard. He was wearing jeans and sneakers and a blue windbreaker. The laundry owner repeated the story of what happened, apparently hoping that the police could explain to him why the angry customer did not believe that all of his shirts were in the package.

Mary Frances made a notation of the incident and filled out a report on it. She explained to the Chinese man that searching for the rock thrower now would be a waste of time—he had probably disappeared into an apartment—but if he was a regular customer who lived in the neighborhood, there was a possibility of getting him in the future.

"If you see him again, call nine-one-one," she said. "This complaint will have a number on it. Give them the number of the complaint. They'll send a patrol car to look for the guy. If he's in the neighborhood, they may be able to get him. You'll have to call the precinct later today to get the number on the complaint."

Paul was helping the Chinese woman pick up the larger pieces of glass, putting them in an empty cardboard box. He suggested she take the shards still stuck in the door frame out before they fell.

Mary Frances questioned the laundryman to see if he understood her instructions. He seemed confused, so she explained again about calling 911 if he saw the rock thrower in the neighborhood. She emphasized the need to get the number of the complaint and to give that number to the operator when he called. It took a few more tries, but at last she was convinced the man understood what to do. They left the Chinese couple cleaning up the glass and muttering to each other in Chinese.

"You have to be a linguist on this job," Mary Frances remarked as they got back in the car. "First the Spanish guy, then the Chinese, next we'll probably have to deal with a Haitian and in between are the drunks. Doesn't anybody speak English anymore?"

Paul laughed. Her complaint was one he had heard before and not just from Mary Frances. He called Central to report one-six Henry was resuming patrol. It was nearly six by now and they were scheduled to take their meal at seven, so their conversation turned to what and where they would eat. It didn't take long. They both felt like Chinese food and decided to go to one of the fast-food places and bring it back to the station-house.

Going to a restaurant in uniform was often uncomfortable. The other customers kept watching them, apparently wondering why they were not on patrol. Civilians never seemed to understand the job and believed the TV cop shows portrayed reality. Mary Frances hardly ever watched them; it was too frustrating knowing what police work really was and watching the version offered by Hollywood.

Sophia had told her once about going before a grand jury only to find that the jurors apparently thought T. J. Hooker worked for the NYPD. Sophia and her partners had been chasing a suspect who had pulled a gun. Several shots were exchanged, and Van had managed to hit the guy. The mutt had died of his wound and Soph, Van and Norm were all called to testify before the grand jury. After they each explained what had happened, one member of the jury had asked Van if he was wearing a bulletproof vest. He said he was and the juror wanted to know why, in that case, he didn't shoot to disarm.

Mary Frances told Paul the story and he wasn't surprised. "They see it on TV all the time," Paul pointed out. "I'd like to see someone try to hit a target as small as a gun after running three or four blocks at top speed. Your heart is pounding so fast, your arm shakes. But on TV, they do it every time.

"Of course, the TV cops never have to answer to Internal Affairs either," he went on. "They shoot some guy one week, and the next they're back on patrol, shooting someone else. I don't know a police department in any big city in this country that would allow that anymore.

"And they always have those long drawn-out gun battles when all the studies show that most shoot-outs involving police last only a few seconds and are at distances of seven yards or less," Paul finished with disgust. "That's what they tell us at the firing range, anyway."

The dispatcher from Central called again for a female officer and Mary Frances again shook her head. They continued their random cruising of the sector until their meal and then drove back to the precinct after picking up the Chinese food.

Paul, as usual, decided to eat in the lounge, but Mary Frances went to the women's locker room. She rarely sat in the lounge. Most of the guys took their meals there and they were always watching some sports event. No one ever said anything, but she always had the sense that she was invading their turf, so she usually stayed away.

Besides, it wasn't all that pleasant. The room was always filled with cigar and cigarette smoke. There were a couple of sofas with broken springs and some rickety armchairs with torn and tattered upholstery. During a family day at the precinct, the wife of one of the guys had looked at the lounge and remarked that she understood why prisoners complained about being treated badly. Her husband had explained the lounge was not for prisoners, but for cops.

A few minutes before eight, Mary Frances was reading a magazine when she heard a knock on the locker room door. She picked up her jacket and went out to find Paul waiting for her. "I wasn't sure if you were asleep or not," he said. "The bosses are always coming in to make sure we're not asleep, but they never check on you girls."

"Are you kidding? I wouldn't even lie down on that mattress," Mary Frances responded with a shudder. "I'm not willing to risk picking up whatever lives in it for a few minutes' rest. Neither are any of the others. The bosses don't check on us because they know we won't sleep on that filthy cot. I don't know why they even bothered to put it in there."

Paul laughed. "You girls are just too finicky, partner." They went downstairs and out to the car. Mary Frances got behind the wheel and Paul called Central to report they were resuming patrol after their meal.

It was dark out and cold. The last of the evening rush-hour crowds were heading home from the subways. Fewer cars were double-parked on the side streets and the delivery trucks had disappeared from Broadway, Columbus and Amsterdam. Chinese kids on bicycles raced through the streets, delivering food to apartment houses and brownstones. Some nights it seemed that everyone on the West Side was eating Chinese. The cyclists ignored red lights, wove in between cars and sometimes brushed pedestrians waiting at crosswalks. A couple of the delivery boys had been hit by cars, but that didn't seem to slow down the rest of them.

Mary Frances drove randomly through the sector, concentrating on the busier side streets and trying to circle the intersection of Seventy-second, Broadway and Amsterdam as frequently as possible. The tiny triangular plot of trees and grass, lined with benches that divided Broadway and Amsterdam, was no longer known as Needle Park, but it was still a prime drug-selling location.

The drugs of choice these days were marijuana and cocaine, not heroin, and most of the buyers were the white newcomers to the gentrified neighborhood. When the patrol car was spotted, the people standing close to each other would move away, trying to appear casual. Mary Frances often wondered if they knew how obvious they looked.

It was easy to spot a drug sale: A guy in a suit and Burberry raincoat shaking hands with someone in dirty, tattered clothes could be doing little else. But most of the buyers had so little contact with cops or street people they didn't realize how out of place they looked.

Ever since the Knapp Commission hearings in the early 1970's revealed widespread corruption in the Police Department, especially connected with narcotics arrests, the procedure had been changed. Uniformed cops weren't even supposed to try to arrest drug dealers. When they noticed street sales, they were supposed to notify the sergeant or lieutenant, who would pass the information on to the Narcotics Unit. When the plainclothes cops made arrests, bosses were always present and a careful accounting was made of the drugs found to avoid any charges of corruption.

Uniformed officers trying to bust the sellers did little good, anyway. The dealers all knew that less than an ounce of marijuana was only a misdemeanor, so they made sure they had less, even if they had to keep going back to replenish their supply. The coke dealers also kept only small amounts and would drop what they had in the street if uniformed cops came too near. So the radio cars drove past just to keep them on the alert and left the arrests to the plainclothes people in unmarked cars.

Paul and Mary Frances were driving north on Amsterdam, past one of the blocks of boarded-up storefronts. A developer had bought the site and was getting ready to demolish the old buildings and put up another high-rise condominium. Mary Frances saw a man standing with his back to the street, where two buildings met and the corner of one jutted out slightly. She stopped the car quickly and Paul turned, asking, "What's wrong?"

"That guy, peeing on the street," she answered, taking her nightstick and getting out of the car. She walked over to the man, who was still facing away from the street and didn't hear her coming up behind him.

"Hey, mister, that's a violation of the Health Code," she said. The man continued to urinate, but looked around, still holding his penis in his hand. He was wearing paint-spattered dungarees and shoes. His hands and face were dotted with white paint and he looked surprised to see her.

"You can't go to the bathroom on the street," Mary Frances continued. "It's a violation of the city laws, besides being disgusting. Haven't you heard of bathrooms? What's wrong with you?"

The painter had finished and turned to face her, zipping his pants as he did so. He was somewhat embarrassed at being seen by a woman, but still didn't understand what she was upset about.

"I had to go," he explained. "I had a couple of beers after work and just couldn't wait until I got home."

Mary Frances wasn't buying that. "I don't care what your reason is," she said. "This is New York City, not the farm. There are bathrooms in bars, restaurants, even on the subway. If you have to go that badly, you can find a toilet. Now you're going to clean that up. I'm not going to let you go and leave that on the sidewalk."

The painter was shocked. "How can I clean it up, lady? What are you making such a big deal about?" He spotted Paul leaning against the patrol car and turned to him for help. "Hey, tell your partner what it's like. I just couldn't wait."

Paul didn't answer. This was Mary Frances's pet cause and he had gone through this often since they had become partners. He found it funny most of the time. He left it to her to do as she wanted. Most cops didn't bother taking action, but Mary Frances almost always did something.

"I told you I don't care why you did it," Mary Frances said, getting angry. "You're an adult and you don't have an accent, so I assume you were born in this country. You know about indoor plumbing and there's no excuse for using the streets of New York as a public toilet. So you're going to clean this up."

"Hey, lady, come on." The painter was beginning to sound annoyed. "How can I clean this up? What are you talking about?"

"You're either going to clean this up or I'm going to give you a ticket," Mary Frances replied. "And if I have to write a ticket, it will be for something more than urinating in public. Get some water and wash the sidewalk down."

"Where should I get water?" the painter finally asked, giving up the argument.

"There's a grocery store," she said, pointing across the street. "Go buy some bottled water and bring it back. Better get a big bottle so you can wash it all away."

The man shrugged and walked to the store while Paul and Mary Frances waited by the patrol car. He was back in less than five minutes, carrying a quart bottle of Perrier in a brown paper bag. Mary Frances watched as he poured the water into the corner where he had urinated, then carefully washed the stream down the sidewalk and into the gutter.

"Maybe the next time, you'll remember and find a bathroom," Mary Frances said to him. "And don't throw that bottle on the street. If you're not going to take it back for the deposit, there's a litter basket on the corner." She watched as he walked to the litter basket and carefully placed the empty bottle and the bag inside. He walked away, shaking his head and muttering to himself as she and Paul got back in the car.

"You're really something, Mary Frances," Paul said. "I know cops that pee in the street all the time. I can't believe you made that guy buy Perrier to wash the sidewalk down."

Mary Frances laughed. "I just think it's disgusting. I'm not going to arrest anyone for it—and get laughed out of the precinct—or even bother with the paperwork of writing a ticket, but making him wash it away will cause him to think twice the next time. And if you know cops that do it, they shouldn't. If I saw one of them, I'd make him wash it down, too. That guy's lucky it was me that caught him. When Sophia was on patrol, she used to spray those guys with Mace!"

"You girls are just jealous 'cause you can't go wherever you happen to be," Paul said.

Mary Frances didn't bother to reply. Paul noted the incident in his memo book as she drove off. He wasn't sure if she was angry or not and decided to let the subject drop.

"Have you made any decision about a transfer?" he asked.

"No, not yet," Mary Frances answered. "As soon as I can talk to Neal, I'm going to suggest that he try to change his schedule a little."

"He should be able to do that," Paul said. "I don't think there's any special shift for that job, just whatever works out best. It depends on the area. But it would mean losing some overtime money."

"That's not all that important," Mary Frances responded. "It would make my life a lot easier. We could switch Stevie to the afternoon session at the day-care center. Neal's mother is always willing to take care of him in the evening if both of us are working and we would save on baby-sitters."

A call came over the radio for one-six Henry. Paul answered and the dispatcher said there was a report of a man with a gun in a fifth-floor apartment at 200 Amsterdam Avenue. Mary Frances turned the car and Paul reported they were on the way. They heard another sector car from the precinct respond that they would be on backup.

Mary Frances parked the car in front of the building and she and Paul walked quickly inside carrying their nightsticks. Both of them unsnapped their holsters. They took the elevator to the fifth floor and found the apartment. The sound of reggae and the smell of incense filled the hallway. Paul stood on one side of the door and Mary Frances on the other. She reached over and banged loudly with her nightstick, yelling, "Police, open the door."

Paul had his gun in his hand. Mary Frances took hers out as the door opened. A man, about six feet tall and wearing the twisted braids that marked a Rastafarian, stood in the open doorway. She reached over, grabbed him by his shirtfront, pulled him into the hallway, then pushed him up against the wall next to the door.

"Hands on the wall, feet spread," Mary Frances ordered. She patted him down, but found no weapons. Paul stood behind them and to one side of the door, looking into the apartment. He couldn't see anyone else inside. It was only one room with a mattress on the floor in one corner, a tattered couch in the other. The door to the bathroom was open. A very messy Pullman kitchen was next to it. A couple of bare bulbs lit the room. Bob Marley and the Wailers blasted from a stereo.

"Who else is in the apartment?" Mary Frances asked.

"No one," the Rastafarian said. "My roommate was here, but he left a few minutes ago to pick up a pizza."

Four more cops came off the elevator as the doors of several other apartments on the floor opened. One of the residents approached them. "That damn stereo has been blasting for hours," he told Mary Frances. "I'm glad you finally showed up. Maybe now we can get some peace and quiet around here."

Mary Frances turned to him. "Are you the one who called the police?"

"Uh, no, I didn't call anyone," the man said, his eyes looking past Mary Frances. She knew he was lying, but couldn't prove it. If she could, she would arrest him for filing a false report. She turned to the other residents. "Okay, folks, it's all over. Nothing's happening. Everyone go back inside."

The other police officers, who had been standing silently near Paul, got back on the elevator. The apartment doors closed and Mary Frances turned again to the Rastafarian, who was looking extremely angry and upset.

"We got a call about a man of your description with a gun in this apartment," she said to him. "That's why I pulled you out so fast. I'll have to fill out a report on this and it will be on file at the precinct. You can see it anytime you want. I guess your neighbors don't like the music and just wanted to get us here. If I knew for sure which one had called in the report of someone with a gun, I'd make an arrest for filing a false report. Why don't you turn the music down a little and save us all more trouble?"

"Hey, man, thanks," the Rastafarian said. "No other cop ever bothered to explain to me before when they frisked me. They usually just treat me like a criminal because I'm a Rasta. I appreciate it. No hard feelings. You were just doing what you had to do." He went back inside his apartment and closed the door.

Paul had pushed the button for the elevator and it arrived as the sound of the music faded. Mary Frances and Paul got in.

"Why did you apologize to that guy?" Paul asked.

"I didn't apologize, I explained," Mary Frances answered. "Did you hear me apologize? I explained what happened because I wanted to avoid another complaint with the CCRB. It doesn't cost anything to explain. I just told him why we did what we did. You heard him. He understood. And I bet he stops by the house to see if that report is filed."

"I see your point," Paul admitted. "But I'm not sure I would have bothered with a mope like that."

"Come on, you know I don't do it all the time," Mary Frances said. "It's just this time I thought the guy deserved an explanation. We were called on an unfounded gun run and he took the brunt of it." Paul nodded as they got back in the car.

They reported the disposition of the job as unfounded and Paul wrote it up in his memo book while Mary Frances filled out the Stop, Question and Frisk paperwork. Sergeant Bailey's car pulled up next to them and he asked about the gun run. Paul told him what had happened, then passed their memo books for a scratch.

They reported to Central that they were back on patrol and immediately were sent to a reported fight at a fruit and vegetable stand on Broadway and Seventy-first Street.

They arrived to find the Korean owner standing with an empty bucket in his hand, cursing in his native language. A thin black woman, missing a few front teeth, was standing nearby, her clothes sopping wet and cursing him back in English.

"What happened?" Paul asked as he got out of the car. The Korean began shouting that the woman had tried to steal an apple. The woman denied it and accused the Korean of throwing water on her as she walked past the stand.

By this time, Mary Frances was out of the car. She moved between the shouting pair, then turned. She tried to calm down the Korean while Paul took on the angry woman. The two combatants stood with their backs to each other, as Paul and Mary Frances listened to their stories.

The store owner agreed to put down the bucket and go inside, letting the incident drop. The woman talking to Paul was getting angrier, however. He tried to convince her to go home, but she wanted to bring charges against the Korean.

"You honky cops, you're all alike," she screamed. "You're just protecting your own. You don't pay no attention to me just because I'm black."

Paul tried again to calm her down and convince her to leave. He knew if she insisted on filing a charge against the store owner, the Korean would probably file an attempted theft charge against her. Since neither person was hurt and nothing had been taken, both cases would probably be dropped by the District Attorney's office or the judge. It would save a lot of paperwork if they both just forgot the whole thing. Another sector car pulled up and the two cops got out, nodding to Mary Frances. They stood leaning on their car, not interfering.

"No, I want to bring charges against the son of a bitch," she yelled. "Just because he's yellow and I'm black, you think it's my fault. That little gook just threw the water on me. Look at me, I'm all wet just for walking down the street."

Paul nodded sympathetically, but didn't answer. The woman continued to rave about the racism of the Police Department.

"You ask anyone here," she said, waving at the spectators who had gathered. "I live in this neighborhood. I walk down this street all the time. You honkies are always picking on me. You never bother that motherfucking little bastard. I want to bring charges against him. Look what he did to me."

"Come on, just forget it," Paul said. "It's not worth the trouble."

"Not worth the trouble!" She was screaming again. "I'm all wet and I want the little bastard locked up." The Korean was standing in the doorway of his store, his face impassive as he listened to the woman. He started to move closer to Paul and Mary Frances motioned him back.

"You're all racists!" The woman was still yelling at the top of her lungs. "You'll protect him just because he's nearly white. I've been here all my life. He's probably one of those Moonies taking over the country and you're letting them get away with it."

Paul was getting bored with the whole thing. He looked at Mary Frances and the two cops who had arrived as backup. None of them offered to intervene and he realized that further discussion would not accomplish anything.

"Lady, I think you're the racist," he said, walking toward the car. "I'm not going to write up charges against the guy. If you want to do something, file a suit against him in Civil Court. Next time, walk on the other side of the street. Now go home, dry off and go to sleep."

He opened the car door and got in. The backup team got into their car and drove away. Mary Frances started the patrol car and Paul made the notation in his memo book. The woman walked away, pulling at the wet blouse that was clinging to her bra. She was muttering to herself as she went.

"Just another ordinary night on patrol in the One-Six," Mary Frances said with a smile. She looked at her watch. "Less than a half hour to go. Maybe the rest of the night will be quiet."

Paul called Central to report the job and that they were back on patrol. Mary Frances made one more circle through the sector, then headed back to the precinct.

# CHAPTER 12

Geri was working a later shift on Thursday and arrived at her office after stopping for a swim at her health club. She and Danny were scheduled to catch—go through the new complaints of rapes and sodomies and make arrangements to interview the victims. That usually meant a day spent at her desk, making phone calls and reading the 61's—forms filled out by the first cops called to the scene of a crime. She also wanted to call the man who employed Joey Johnson.

Danny Thomson was already at his desk. "How are you feeling?" she asked.

"I'm fine," he answered. "I must have had a twenty-four-hour flu or something. I was sick as a dog the night before last and yesterday, but I woke up today feeling great.

"How did the collar go yesterday?" he asked. "I'm sorry I missed that. The captain told me you got Johnson."

"Yeah, he's at Riker's now," Geri replied. "I think he's the one in all those ice pick cases over the past two years. Evans wants us to check the fruit stands closest to those cases, see if Johnson's boss supplied them and if our boy made the deliveries."

"Good point," Danny answered. "I remember we were trying

to find a common denominator in those cases. The fruit stand angle may be the answer. It makes sense and it would explain why they were so scattered."

"I told Evans we'd get on it right away," Geri said. "We're stuck inside today, but we could call Johnson's boss and get a list of his Manhattan customers. We might be able to make some matchups from that, without going out. We got anything today?"

"Not yet," Danny replied. "There were a couple of things, but the guys on the early tour cleaned them up."

"Nice of them." Geri picked up the folder containing Joey Johnson's file and found the number for the Hunt's Point wholesaler where he worked. She lit a cigarette, then picked up the telephone receiver and dialed.

Danny listened to her explain to the person at the other end. She apparently was getting cooperation, because he heard her spell out her name and the address of the Sex Crimes Unit. She hung up and turned to him. "They'll send us a list of all their regular customers in Manhattan. He promised to have it in the mail tonight."

Danny nodded and Geri picked up a *Daily News* lying on the desk next to hers. She leafed through the paper, stopping occasionally to read some article.

"Oh, no, that's too bad," she murmured. Danny looked over at her desk. He could see that Geri was looking at the obituary notices.

"Who died?"

"Oh, a nice old guy I helped out once when I was in the Senior Citizens Robbery Unit."* Geri put out her cigarette. "He lived in a real bad section of the Bronx; he had lived there all his life and he didn't want to leave. He owned his house and it was all he had, so even though the neighborhood had changed, he stayed on.

"Anyway, someone broke into his house, roughed him up and took his TV, radio, stuff like that. I got the case and went up to talk to him," she went on. "He was living there all alone. He didn't have any family and most of his friends had died or moved away. He knew a few people in the neighborhood and some of the women would stop by and talk to him, but he was really by himself. I guess I got more involved than necessary with him," Geri said sheepishly.

"What happened?"

"Oh, I convinced him he would really be better off if he left the area. He wasn't all that well and he really didn't leave the house too often, except to shop. He'd had a dog, but it had died a few years before the robbery and he didn't want to get another one because he figured he would die before the dog did," she said.

"Anyway, I talked to him and he agreed to go look at some of the nursing homes. I managed to get some time to take him around to a couple. He seemed resigned to selling his house and moving into one," she continued.

"We were just about ready to make a decision when he called me one day and said he had a better offer. An old friend, a woman he knew from church whose husband was dying of cancer, wanted him to come live with them. The couple had a big house and plenty of room, they liked Mr. Gower and he liked them. It worked out well. I called him a few more times after he moved, to make sure everything was all right. He managed to sell his house, so he could pay them a little rent. He was a real nice old guy," Geri concluded.

Danny nodded absently and went back to the paperwork he was doing.

Geri sat with her elbows on her desk, her head propped up in her hands. She had really liked working with the Senior Citizens Unit, which had been her first assignment after getting her gold shield four years before. She had gotten very involved with several of the cases, not just Mr. Gower.

One she remembered well was Mr. Liffey. He was another nice old guy, a real gentleman, who lived by himself in Harlem. He had saved his money and had thousands of dollars in his checking account. He reported a robbery when he got back a bank statement one day and saw the balance was almost nothing.

Geri had been sent up to talk to him. It wasn't a robbery, it was larceny. The people who lived next door had done it. Mr. Liffey had mentioned to them that he needed someone to help him clean the house and they said they knew a girl who needed work. So he hired their friend to be his housekeeper. She was there when Geri arrived and Geri had questioned her briefly.

A couple of days later, the girl had called Geri, asking to see her. They met at a coffee shop a few blocks from Mr. Liffey's home. The girl told her the family next door had two teenage sons who were stealing blank checks from Mr. Liffey and writing checks on his account. Geri took the girl's name and address and left to see Mr. Liffey.

When she got to the house, she asked to see his canceled checks. The girl had told the truth about the boys next door; she just hadn't admitted that she was also part of the scheme. Geri went through the checks with Mr. Liffey, asking him about each one. He didn't remember most of them and didn't recognize the signatures. There was one for five hundred dollars with the housekeeper's name on it that he had written himself.

"What was this for, Mr. Liffey?" Geri asked him.

"Oh, she said she wanted to open up a luncheonette," he answered. "I was giving her the money, she would do the cooking and I would get some of the profits."

Geri had sorted through the other checks.

"Mr. Liffey, do you realize what was happening?" she asked him. He was confused and unsure about the checks. He didn't remember writing them, but was obviously upset to think that his nice neighbors could have been responsible. Geri promised to clear up everything and left him after putting the checkbook away and telling him to keep it out of sight.

Luckily Mr. Liffey had a son who lived in Florida. Geri called him and contacted the priest in Mr. Liffey's parish. The priest helped her find the old man a place in a Catholic nursing home and the son came up to sell the house. The teenagers pleaded guilty to grand larceny, but were given a suspended sentence because it was their first offense.

Geri made arrangements for Mr. Liffey to get involved with several community groups. She went to visit him at the nursing home a few times. He was still very active even after he developed a kidney problem. Once his sister-in-law came by while she was there. The sister-in-law told Geri that Mr. Liffey just smiled whenever her name was mentioned. He claimed she was his girlfriend.

He had died a couple of years ago and she had gone to his funeral. That was the last time she had seen Mr. Liffey's sister-in-law and son, but they had both taken the time to thank her for helping him. Mr. Liffey and Mr. Gower were among the reasons she stayed on the job when things got bad, even though she took a lot of teasing from the men in the unit about mothering her cases. None of them seemed to get as involved with the victims as she did.

She had really liked working with the Senior Citizens Robbery Unit, although many people in the department joked about it because the initials spelled out the acronym SCRU. Some of the bosses downtown had tried to change the name when they realized that, but nothing else seemed right, so it stayed SCRU.

SCRU wasn't as exciting or creative as Narcotics, but she found the cases challenging, like trying to put a puzzle together. Somehow, the Sex Crimes Unit wasn't the same thing. She hadn't been able to get as involved with the victims, perhaps because the crimes were so vicious and violating that they were threatening to her personally.

She also found her inability to help the victims, immediately or later, very frustrating. With robbery, she always had a chance of getting back whatever was stolen. Or, with luck, there was insurance to replace it. But nothing could replace what was taken from a woman who had been raped or a child who had been abused.

Geri also disliked the way the Sex Crimes Unit worked. The day-to-day procedures were all right, but she hated the necessity of getting information from complainants. The victims she questioned were often in the hospital, having been badly beaten. There was nothing she could do for them.

She would try to comfort them, but she had to ask questions, too. She had to ask women and girls who had been badly beaten and violated to go over and over every grimy detail of the whole horrible thing; she didn't want to do it. She didn't want to talk to them about it anymore. She could see they were physically hurt; how could they not be emotionally hurt as well?

Geri often wondered how the victims held up under the repetitive questioning. They had to tell the story to the first cops on the scene. Then they would go to the hospital and the nurse would ask more questions, then a doctor. A police supervisor would show up and the victim would have to tell the whole thing again and finally, the detectives from Sex Crimes would come and demand another telling.

Usually, the victims were sick and tired of it by then. They would tell Geri and her colleagues to get the details from some other cops. They couldn't understand why they had to keep remembering and repeating it. A rape victim's counselor from the hospital would come in and explain why retelling the details would help the woman recover and maybe bring to light a forgotten but important detail. Most women just wanted to be alone and not think about what had happened to them.

At least, Geri thought, rape victims had it a little better now than they did when the detectives interrogating them were mostly men, who often showed very little sympathy. Of course, some victims refused to talk to a woman. They were usually the elderly ones, especially Hispanic or Jewish women. They seemed to feel that a nice girl like her shouldn't have to listen to such a dirty story. They felt more comfortable, if that was the word, telling it to a man, who wouldn't be shocked. She would usually reassure them by telling them she had been married. That seemed to make it better; they felt she would be less horrified or something.

Geri remembered a sergeant at the Brooklyn precinct, when she first came on the job, who insisted that a male cop should be the first to interview a rape victim. He believed that the woman should know that not all men were like the one who had attacked her. That was a great idea in theory, but it assumed that all male cops would show some sensitivity and understanding. She knew that wasn't necessarily the case.

When she started working in Narcotics, there had been a boss who was really a bastard. He hadn't liked her at all and Geri was never sure if it was just her or all women on the job. His dislike was obvious to everyone in the squad and some of the guys talked about it with her. One of the other women suggested it was because Geri wasn't married, as he seemed less hostile to the married women. Geri supported herself and wasn't actively looking for a man to take care of her. The boss apparently believed that if a woman worked, she should do so only on a part-time basis. Geri often wondered what his home life was like.

One day she had taken a long lunch hour and he noticed. When she got back to the office he started screaming at her. He was furious, his face bright red and his eyes looking as if they were popping out of his head. The veins on his forehead stood out. He yelled at her for nearly half an hour about taking so much time for lunch. She had tried to explain that she spent part of that time at headquarters, but he didn't want to hear it; he just wanted an excuse to get on her back.

After a while she realized he was just trying to get to her, to make her react. She finally said, "Sir, you're right. I was half an hour late. Do whatever you have to do about it."

That got him even crazier. He screamed at her some more, then asked, "Don't you have any explanation?"

She didn't feel like explaining the whole thing again and didn't think he would listen any more than he had before, so she just said, "No. You feel there's a half hour unaccounted for, then take whatever action you feel you have to. Is that all, sir?"

She got up and left his office. She thought she could see steam coming out of his ears as she left, but he didn't write her up. Geri was sure he had been trying to make her cry. He left her pretty much alone after that. Luckily, he was transferred a short time later.

Thinking about jerks like that reminded her of Sophia's anger at the ADA, and she remembered she was going to call her for Alex. They would make a good pair. Geri picked up the phone and called the One-Six Anti-Crime Unit. She knew it was unlikely Sophia would be in the office, but she could leave a message. The cop who answered the phone said Sophia was off that day, so Geri tried her at home. There was no answer.

Two guys from the squad came in, Mike Belton and Joe Hauptman. She liked Joe, but Mike could be a pain in the ass. He was one of those guys who thought using four-letter words constantly made him sound tough. Every other word out of his mouth was "motherfucking."

Geri had commented on it at first, but now she usually just ignored it. Sometimes she would tease him about it, telling him he had the vilest mouth in the office and he should be glad he was number one in something. He would just look at her and say, "You're a cop, you should be used to it."

Once, she asked him if he talked that way in front of his wife or daughter and he was insulted. Of course he didn't, he told her. So Geri pointed out that she was somebody's girlfriend and someone's daughter and really didn't want to hear his foul mouth all the time. That seemed to make an impression. He didn't stop cursing, but now he would apologize occasionally.

She wasn't embarrassed or even offended by his language; she used it herself sometimes. With some of the mutts she dealt with, that kind of language was the only way to get through to them. Geri just didn't feel it was necessary all of the time. Most of the guys agreed. When she first came on the job, some of the old-timers in the precinct would apologize to her every time they said "damn." That didn't last too long, but it was better than someone like Mike, who just called everyone "mother-fucker."

The phone on the desk rang and Geri picked it up. "Sex Crimes, Detective Casey."

The woman at the other end said, "This is April Gibbons. Do you remember me?"

Geri couldn't place the name for a few seconds, and then she remembered. April had been an unwed teenage mother when Geri met her a few years before. She was involved with a guy who was part of a gang that had robbed old people. April's boyfriend made her part of their nasty little scheme.

April would approach an elderly person with a heavy shopping bag and offer to carry it home for them. Usually, because she was a girl, the old person wouldn't be afraid and would gratefully agree. The gang would follow behind them. As April waited in the open apartment door while the elderly victim fumbled for change to tip her, the gang would force their way in.

Geri had been part of the team that investigated the cases and finally caught the gang. She felt sorry for April, who had no record, and had talked to the judge for the girl. April had been released on low bail because of her baby, but had failed to show up at court for a hearing.

She wrote a panicky letter to Geri a few days later about missing the court date and being afraid the cops were going to come after her. She said that nobody cared what happened to her and she was very depressed and didn't know what to do. Geri went to her apartment and talked her into surrendering and trying to straighten out the mess she was in. Geri had realized that April was just afraid of going to jail and worried about having a record.

April had been given a suspended sentence because it was her first offense. Geri helped her apply for food stamps and find a part-time job. She was able to get the baby in a day-care center for welfare recipients.

That had been more than four years ago. It was one of the first cases Geri had worked on as a detective. She hadn't thought about April since.

"Sure, I remember you, April. How are you doing?"

"Just great, Detective Casey," April said. "I called because I wanted to invite you to my wedding. I'm getting married in two weeks."

"That's great, April," Geri answered. "Who's the lucky guy?"

"He's a construction worker," she said. "I met him when he was working on a building near my job. We've been going together six months and decided to get married. He likes my daughter and we have an apartment in Queens.

"And I'm back in school. I go nights and I want to keep going after I get my diploma. I learned to work on a computer at my job and I want to stay with it." April sounded excited, and Geri was happy for her.

"That's terrific, April," she said. "I'm sure you will. I'm glad to hear everything turned out well for you."

"Yeah, that's why I called," April told her. "It took me a while to find you, but I wanted to let you know that I've really changed. It's all because of you. If you hadn't helped me, showed me that there were people who cared what happened to me, I'd probably be in jail right now and my baby would be in a foster home. I can't tell you how much you've meant to me."

She gave Geri the details of where and when the wedding would be held. Geri promised to try to make it. April thanked her again and hung up.

The day seemed to be one for remembering the past, first Mr. Gower's obituary, then April. Geri wondered if any other ghosts would show up, but the rest of the tour was quiet.

# CHAPTER 13

**T**wo days after her night on patrol with Paul Randall, Sally drove to work, hoping she would get another chance to get out. Yesterday, she had been back at her desk, but the sergeant promised she would be able to get out in a couple of weeks. He said the next schedule would take her off clerical, although the CO was upset about it, complaining he was losing his fastest typist. Captain DiMilano had stopped by her desk the day before to ask if she was sure she wanted to go on patrol. She told him she did and he agreed she could.

She had told Jim about her decision. He didn't like the idea of her working midnight tours, but he seemed to understand that she wanted to go on patrol, to see what the job was like on the streets. He said he would be worried about her, but she had reassured him. As she came into the precinct now, Sergeant Bailey called to her.

"How would you like to drive for me today, Sally?" he asked.

She was stunned. "Sure, sarge. Anything to get away from the typewriter." She smiled to show him she was joking, then turned to go upstairs and change. "I'll be right down."

Sally came back to the desk fifteen minutes later. "What happened to Bill?" she asked. The sergeant's usual driver was one of the nicest guys in the precinct.

"Nothing. He asked for a 28 because he had to take his wife to the doctor. She's expecting a kid and he wanted to go with her," Bailey explained. "You'll have to stand roll call and I have some paperwork to do, but we'll leave about five. If you want to do some work until then, that's okay."

Sally sighed and agreed she would do some typing after roll call until he was ready to leave. Even when she got away from her desk, she couldn't get away.

During inspection Sally was standing next to Mary Frances, who turned and smiled at her when Bailey announced Sally would be his driver. A couple of the men frowned. After they were dismissed, Mary Frances stopped to talk to her.

"Don't worry about the rest of those jokers," she advised. "They're just jealous that you're driving the sergeant. And don't worry about Bailey. He's an old-timer, but he's a great guy. Just remember, you're the one who has to answer when Central calls and be sure to say you're on your way to a job. That way, the cops on the scene know the sergeant's coming."

"Thanks, Mary Frances." Sally smiled. "I've never driven a patrol car before except for the course at the Academy, let alone with a sergeant. I'm a little nervous."

"Don't worry," Mary Frances reassured her. "Like I said, Bailey is a good guy. He'll tell you what to do and where to go and if you aren't sure, ask him. He knows you haven't been out in the precinct much and you're new on the job. Have a good time and good luck." Mary Frances left to join Paul, and Sally went to her desk until the sergeant called.

She managed to type up a few reports before he came to get her. She stood and saluted when he walked into the office and he waved his hand. "You don't have to bother with that," he said. "If you're going to salute me all night, we'll waste a lot of time. Come on, let's get moving."

Sergeant Bailey had the keys for the RMP and handed them to Sally. She checked to make sure he had a radio as well. As they walked out of the precinct, he turned to her and said, "Don't worry. This will probably be an easy night. And if you're not sure what to do, just ask."

"Thanks, sarge," Sally replied. "I am a little nervous. I

haven't had too much patrol experience, and I'm really grateful for this chance to get out."

They had just finished checking to be sure the radio worked when Central called for the one-six patrol sergeant. An RMP was involved in a minor accident at Seventy-ninth and Broadway. NYPD procedure required a sergeant to go to the scene of any accident involving a departmental vehicle to fill out the accident report.

"Okay, let's go," Sergeant Bailey told Sally. "You know you have to call Central and tell them we're on our way." Sally started the car, then picked up the radio to make the call.

At the intersection, they found the RMP with a dented bumper. Danny Strada and Vic White were standing next to it, talking to a civilian. They saluted when Sergeant Bailey got out and explained to him what happened. The civilian admitted the accident was his fault. His car also had some minor dents and scratches. Bailey took his name and address and the name of his insurance company, then went back to the car for the NYPD accident forms.

"You don't have to wait in the car, Sally." She got out and went to talk to Danny and Vic while the sergeant filled out the forms. He stood with his foot on the bumper, writing on a clipboard. They had been there only a few minutes when a crowd surged out of the subway exit on the corner. A few passersby stopped to see what had happened, but most just kept on going.

"I don't know what the hell is going on here, but I don't like the idea that it takes four cops to write a summons." The voice they suddenly heard was loud and strident. Sally, Vic and Danny looked up to see a man with a tan overcoat and briefcase approaching the sergeant. The three of them edged closer, surrounding the angry man.

Sergeant Bailey looked up, nodded and said, "Can I help you, sir?"

"Yeah, you can tell me why four cops are wasting their time on this corner when you should be out chasing muggers." The civilian's voice had gone up another decibel.

"This is police business and really doesn't involve you, sir."

Bailey was trying to be courteous, but Sally could see he was irritated.

"Don't give me any of your crap." The loudmouth was not the least bit polite. "I'm a taxpayer and I'm not paying your salary to stand around and chitchat when there are murderers and rapists walking around the city. You should be out patrolling the streets, protecting the citizens of this city, not standing on a corner gossiping."

Sally was just staring at the man, trying not to let her mouth hang open in amazement. Vic and Danny, she could see, were biting their lips to keep from laughing, but Sergeant Bailey was struggling hard to keep his temper. The man was still yelling at the top of his lungs about lazy cops who were making too much money for doing nothing to keep the streets safe for decent people.

He wound down after a few minutes and Vic, seeing that Bailey was still ready to explode, tried to diffuse the situation.

"Sir, there's been an accident and we have a procedure to follow. We're not just standing here to talk." Vic spoke in a soft, soothing voice, but it didn't help.

"I don't care what happened," the civilian said, off again. "It doesn't take four police officers to fill out a form. There's nothing life-threatening because none of you have your guns out. There's no reason for all of you to be standing here doing nothing."

Sergeant Bailey had had enough. He looked the man up and down and said, "Sir, we are following the procedure laid down by the police commissioner. If you disagree with the policy, you can write to him. If you have a complaint about our actions, you can report us to the One-Six precinct desk officer. My name is Sergeant Sheldon Bailey.

"Now, if you don't leave and continue on your way, I will be forced to arrest you for interfering with government administration, disorderly conduct and anything else I can think of. If you will excuse me, I still have some work to do." Bailey returned to the forms on the clipboard.

Sally struggled to keep a straight face until the man walked away. She could tell he was still angry by the way he marched off, but apparently he had decided to drop the subject. She looked at Vic and Danny, who were both laughing silently.

Bailey finished the paperwork, ordered Vic and Danny back on patrol and got in the car with Sally. He didn't mention the nutty civilian and she didn't either.

They drove around the precinct, stopping whenever they saw a patrol car so Bailey could sign memo books. He asked her how she liked the job and she told him she was too new to patrol to be sure, but she had enjoyed riding with Paul Randall the other night.

"He told me about it," Bailey said. "He said you handled a drunk really well. He thought you were very effective in calming him down. He also said he would be willing to ride with you when Mary Frances goes on vacation. That's quite a compliment. Paul Randall is very choosy about his partners."

Sally was happy to hear the praise. She wondered if that was why the sergeant had asked her to drive him tonight. She finally got up the nerve to ask him.

"That was one reason," Bailey answered, smiling at her. "But I also like to have women drivers. They're more interesting to talk to. Most of the men can only talk about sex, sports and the job. Eight hours a day, five days a week, that can get boring."

"Well, what do you want to talk about?" Sally grinned back at him. He asked her about her background and why she had joined and she told him. He knew she was married to a civilian and asked what her husband thought of her being on the job.

Sally explained that Jim wasn't happy about her working midnight tours, but was proud of her job and so far hadn't complained.

"Some of the women who are married to civilians find their husbands are upset that their wives are carrying a gun all the time," Bailey remarked. "There have been a few cases where civilian husbands hid their wives' guns and shields."

"Jim was in the Army," Sally explained. "He says he's just glad he doesn't have to carry one anymore."

Bailey nodded, then returned to their earlier conversation. "I've had a couple of women drivers. Some of them were real surprises. I remember one I worked with when I was in Queens. She was a tiny little thing. She came on the job right after they ended the height requirement and probably didn't weigh a hundred pounds, but she was feisty." The sergeant smiled at the memory.

"She had just started as my driver when we passed a group of kids hanging out on the corner." Bailey was clearly enjoying telling the story. "One of them made an obscene gesture as we passed and called out something about pigs. I turned to the girl and asked if she was going to stand for that.

"She looked at me and said, 'You mean I don't have to?' She made a U-turn and jumped out. Most of those kids started to run when she stopped the car, but two of them stayed there. I guess they saw how small she was and figured she couldn't do anything to them." Bailey grinned.

"We walked up and started questioning them, asking for their ID. One kid said he didn't have any and we told him to keep moving.

"The other one, a tall skinny kid, gave us a smart-mouth answer. We put him in the backseat and asked him where he lived, what school he went to, who his friends were. He wouldn't answer, just gave us sassy replies," Bailey continued.

"This girl, she just wasn't taking that from him," he went on. "She opened the back door, grabbed the kid by the scruff of the neck, pulled him out and threw him up against the trunk of the car. I couldn't believe it and I don't think the kid could either. She didn't look strong enough to lift a piece of paper, but I guess she was mad.

"She made him spread for a frisk, then started in on him: 'Who the hell do you think you are? That's a sergeant asking you questions and you're going to show him some respect. He's my boss and I have to respect him for eight and a half hours a day and you're going to do the same for eight and a half minutes. The next time he asks you a question, you are going to answer it and you are going to say "Sir." Do you understand?'

"She threw him back in the backseat and turned to me. 'He's all yours, sarge.' I had a hard time keeping a straight face, but I went through the questions again and got the answers this

time. We let the kid go finally and he flew down the street."
Bailey laughed.

"After he left, I told her I'd never had a driver do that
before and that was true. Ever since then, I've taken women
drivers whenever I can."

Sally joined in the sergeant's laughter at the end of the
story. "Well, if anyone calls you a name or gets too smart, I'll
know what to do," she said.

"Yeah, women drivers are a lot more fun than men," Bailey
finished with a chuckle. "I know some bosses don't like them,
but I think those guys are making a mistake."

He had another story, this one about a reported DOA. He
and his driver, another woman, had met two patrolmen from
the sector car at the location and they had gone to the apartment
and tried the door. It was locked, so Bailey sent one of the cops
up the fire escape in back to see if he could look into the apartment. After a few minutes the cop came back and reported he
could see what looked like a body lying under a bed, the legs
sticking out.

Bailey found the building super and had him unlock the
door and they went in. The smell of rotting flesh was nauseating
and they opened the windows to air the place out while they
searched for valuables to voucher for relatives. One of the cops
called the dispatcher for a meat wagon while the rest of them
went through the apartment. There were maggots eating the
flesh on the legs under the bed and all four cops tried not to
look at them.

Suddenly, Bailey thought he noticed one of the legs move.
He asked another patrolman in the apartment, "Is that leg moving?" All four of them turned to look. They all saw both legs
moving, and simultaneously turned to run for the door, trying
to get through at the same time.

Bailey told Sally that it turned out the guy wasn't dead,
obviously. He was a diabetic and hadn't taken care of some cuts
on his leg, so gangrene had set in. They canceled the request
for the morgue wagon and changed it to a bus.*

Sally shuddered at the story. She couldn't imagine having
to see something like that or not getting sick if she did. The

sergeant could see she was upset by his story and remarked, "It's not pleasant, but unfortunately, you get used to it. It's just part of the job."

They had been driving around for a couple of hours and Bailey suggested they eat. Sally wasn't sure she could after the story he had just told, but agreed. He wanted to go back to the precinct, so they picked up some pizza and drove back to the stationhouse.

As they walked in, Frank Gordon, who was working the switchboard because he had sprained his ankle the night before, looked up and said, "Here comes the sergeant and the empty suit."

Sergeant Bailey didn't hear the comment, but Sally did. She was so angry she didn't know how to answer and then it was too late to say anything. She just ignored him, going upstairs to the women's locker to eat after checking to see when the sergeant wanted to leave again. Gordon's comment infuriated her, but she wasn't sure what, if anything, she could do about it.

About twenty minutes after she finished eating, there was a knock on the door. When she opened it, Jeff McMichaels, one of the better young cops in the precinct; greeted her. "The sergeant sent me to ask if you're through with your meal," he said. "We picked up a couple of girls trying to pass bad checks at a supermarket and they have to be searched."

Sally grimaced, then promised she would be right down. She hated doing searches and went to her locker for a pair of rubber gloves. They were minimal protection if the women were really disgusting. Most cops wore gloves to search prisoners, especially since the AIDS epidemic.

When she walked into the muster room, she saw the two women standing at the desk, their hands cuffed behind them. One was only a teenager, maybe fifteen, wearing overalls and a sweatshirt. She looked scared. The other one was much older and had obviously been arrested before. She had on a shabby wool coat and a terrible red wig that didn't fit her at all. She stood calmly, not looking around.

Jeff was emptying their purses on the desk. Five or six wallets fell out of one.

"Why do you have so many wallets?" he asked.

"I got all kinds of things in them," the older woman said. "Women always carry more than one wallet."

Jeff looked skeptical and spotted Sally. He saw her smiling, raised a quizzical eyebrow and she shook her head. He started to go through one of the wallets and turned to the woman with the wig. "So you're a friend of the New York Philharmonic?" he asked in a sarcastic tone. The woman didn't bother to answer and Jeff motioned Sally nearer. "Do you mind searching them?"

She just shrugged and walked over to the pair. She felt through their clothes, being careful to search their breasts and groin, knowing the arresting officers had not patted them down there. They had no weapons and nothing in their pockets. She stepped back, telling them to take off their shoes. Both did and she checked those. The younger one wanted to go to the bathroom, so Sally had to go with her.

When they returned, Jeff and Larry Holland led the two prisoners back to the precinct holding cell, where they removed the handcuffs. The women asked for their cigarettes and were handed a pack from one of the purses. The younger one looked ready to cry, but her companion seemed unconcerned. Sally felt sorry for the girl, but knew she had brought her troubles on herself.

Sergeant Bailey came out from behind the desk and said he would be ready to leave in a few minutes, so Sally went upstairs for her jacket and gun. She had taken off her equipment belt while she was eating and hadn't bothered to put it back on to search the women. By the time she returned to the first floor of the precinct, Bailey was waiting for her.

Sally felt more confident getting into the car this time. The first half of the tour hadn't been too bad. Mary Frances had been right about the sergeant. He was a nice guy and she was less nervous about making a mistake or doing something wrong.

They followed the same procedure as before, driving around the precinct and stopping whenever they saw another RMP. When they came across Paul and Mary Frances, Sally was able to signal that everything was okay. Central called for the sergeant to go to a family dispute and Bailey told her to answer. They got the address and she turned the car.

She double-parked behind an ambulance, picked up her nightstick and followed Sergeant Bailey into the building, a four-story walk-up tenement on Amsterdam. Tom Neville and Linda Brandt were already there.

Sally had been expecting a husband and wife fight, but this didn't look like that. The man and wife were sitting together on a plastic-covered sofa. The ambulance attendants were kneeling on the floor, giving first aid to an elderly woman. A hulking young man in his early twenties, well over six feet and two hundred pounds, was standing in one corner with his hands behind him, apparently in handcuffs.

Tom explained what happened to Sergeant Bailey: "The guy in handcuffs is the couple's son, the old lady's grandson. He had an argument with his grandmother, slapped her a few times and she collapsed. The parents called an ambulance and the EMS guys say she may have had a heart attack. The father says the kid has been in trouble before and has been violent. Everyone in the family is afraid of him, apparently.

"The father wants us to arrest his son. He says he'll press charges. He thinks the old lady wouldn't have had the attack if his son hadn't slapped her," Tom told him.

Bailey nodded and turned to the couple on the sofa. "Don't worry. We'll take care of him."

Sally watched as the sergeant stood quietly for a few minutes, apparently making up his mind. She thought he was angry, but didn't know him well enough yet to be sure. He walked over to the prisoner, handcuffed in the corner.

"You like slapping your grandmother around?" Sergeant Bailey's right fist shot out and the hulking bully doubled over. When he was able to stand up again, the sergeant was still in front of him.

"I guess you think it's fun hitting someone who can't hit back?" This time, Bailey's knee connected with the prisoner's groin and he went down again. The boy's mother turned away, but her husband was watching it all. He didn't say anything and

Sally figured the father was glad to see someone finally giving his son a taste of his own medicine.

Bailey left the prisoner writhing on the floor, trying to regain his breath, and walked over to the EMS technicians. "How's the old lady?"

"She ought to be okay, sarge," one of them said. "We'll take her to the hospital and they can run some tests. I don't think it was too bad. She looks like she's a pretty strong old dame."

"Okay, tell the family where she'll be and when they can come to visit," he said. He turned to Tom and Linda. "You two, get this creep back to the stationhouse. Book him on everything you can think of." They nodded, picked up the handcuffed man by his elbows, threw a coat over his shoulders and led him out of the apartment.

"Sir, if you want to come to the One-Six precinct and fill out a complaint tonight, that will help," Sergeant Bailey said to the father as if nothing had happened. The man agreed to file a formal complaint at the precinct and went to get his coat. The mother hadn't moved and Bailey leaned down and said softly, "Sorry, ma'am."

He motioned to Sally and they left the apartment. On their way downstairs, Sally thought about what happened. She really couldn't blame the sergeant; a man who would hit an old lady was bad enough—someone who would do it to his own grandmother seemed barely human. Apparently everyone else in the apartment thought so, too, including the bully, who had not said a word. Certainly, the parents hadn't objected to the punishment Bailey had handed out to their son.

When they got back in the car, the sergeant pulled out a form and wrote down something. He gave Sally an address, explaining he had to pick up a rifle from the owner because the rifle permit* had expired. The sergeant had tried to reach the man earlier in the day, but he hadn't been home. Bailey had left a message at the owner's office that he would be by that night. In fact, Bailey said, this was the third time he had tried to confiscate the rifle and he had little doubt the owner was avoiding him.

They reached the address, a renovated brownstone on one of the nicer blocks in the precinct. They walked up a short flight of steps to the front door. There was no intercom, so apparently the brownstone was a single residence and not broken up into apartments, a rare luxury in that part of Manhattan. Sergeant Bailey knocked on the door.

The man who opened the door seemed surprised to see a police officer, but greeted them politely. Bailey informed him that they had come to pick up a rifle because the permit had expired. He explained the weapon would be held at the precinct for thirty days and the owner could get it back as soon as he had another valid permit.

"You can't just come to my house like this," the man said. "I'm a lawyer and I know the law. You have to conduct this during business hours, not at night. You can't invade a private residence whenever you feel like it."

"We're not invading your home, sir," Sergeant Bailey replied. "I left a message with your secretary this afternoon. This, you will recall, is the third time I've notified you about this rifle and the expired permit."

"I don't do business at my home," the man responded, still angry. "If you want to see me, you can come to my office on Madison Avenue. I'll show you the permit and license for the rifle."

"I can't do that," Sergeant Bailey explained. "That's not my precinct and that's not the address on the permit. Our records show the rifle permit issued for this address has expired and has not yet been renewed. Until it is, your possession of that weapon is a violation of New York City's gun control laws and I am authorized to confiscate it. I don't want to make trouble for you, but I'm just doing my job.

"If you do not surrender the rifle, I will have to arrest you." Bailey looked the man in the eye. Sally stood to one side, listening to the conversation, amazed at the sergeant's ability to stay calm and unruffled while being abused by someone who should know better, if he really was a lawyer.

The rifle owner apparently knew he was not in a position to argue because he backed down, saying he would get the weapon. He closed the front door, leaving Sally and the sergeant standing on the front stoop. When the lawyer returned, he handed the rifle to Sergeant Bailey and got a receipt in return.

"Thank you for your cooperation, sir, and have a good evening." The sergeant's voice held just the slightest hint of sarcasm, but the lawyer ignored it.

"You haven't heard the last of this," the man said. "I'm going to write the police commissioner about this."

"Yes, sir, that's your privilege. My name is Sergeant Sheldon Bailey, One-Six precinct. Good night." Bailey turned and walked back to the car with Sally following him.

As they drove back to the precinct, she heard the sergeant muttering, "I'll bet that's another complaint at the CCRB." He turned to Sally with a smile. "Sometimes, I'm not sure which are worse, the mutts we arrest or the upstanding citizens we're supposed to protect."

They walked into the stationhouse, with the sergeant carrying the rifle under his arm.

"It was busier than I'd expected," he said to Sally. "You got your money's worth tonight. Do you still think you want to be on patrol?"

Sally wasn't sure what to say. She had enjoyed the night, but didn't think that was what he wanted to hear.

"Yes, sir," she said. "It was fascinating. I learned a great deal. I like the challenge of it, having to do so many different things, respond to so many different situations and people. I think I'll like patrol, too."

"You'll be okay, kid," Sergeant Bailey told her. "If you need anything when you get out there on your own, just ask. You're through for today. You working tomorrow?"

"No, sir," Sally answered. "It's my weekend."

"Well, that will change when you go on patrol." He grinned. "You can't expect Saturdays and Sundays off anymore. Have a good weekend."

"Thank you, sir," she said. "See you next week."

# CHAPTER 14

**W**hen Sophia got back to work on Saturday afternoon, she found a message from Geri. Knowing Geri had weekends off, she called her at home.

"Do you remember meeting my ex-partner, Alex Grandey, a few years ago?" Geri asked her.

"Not really."

"He sure remembers you," Geri said with a laugh. "I met him for drinks a couple of nights ago. He asked about Mary Frances and then about you. He's divorced now and was hoping you were available."

"Tell me more," Sophia said.

"Why don't we meet for a drink one night and I can go into detail?" Geri suggested.

"Sure, how about Monday? I should be off by midnight unless we get a collar," Sophia said.

"That sounds good," Geri answered. "I'm catching that day, so I'll be in the office. Give me a call and tell me where and when. I'll hang around until I hear from you."

"Fine. Have you talked to Mary Frances since we met last week?"

"No, I haven't had a chance," Geri said. "On the way home,

she was more like herself, just trying to find a way out of the round-the-clock schedules. How about you?"

"Oh, I'm back to normal, I guess," Sophia answered. "I was just pissed off that night, but it was no different than a dozen other times. Remember more than two years ago when I hurt my knee fighting with a cabbie who was on angel dust? I needed two operations to get back to normal and the DA refused to prosecute the bastard. This time wasn't as bad as that. I just needed to let off steam."

"I don't remember that. What happened?"

"It started because the cabbie tried to cut me off making a right turn across traffic," Sophia explained. "We were in an unmarked car, but I showed him my shield and ID and told him to go around the block. He continued to turn and I told him to pull over. He did and his passengers got out. My partner came up on the passenger side and I went to the driver, identifying myself again and asking for his license and registration.

"He got very belligerent, maybe because we weren't in uniform. I was willing to give him the benefit of the doubt and called for a sector car on the radio. I said it was an emergency and that turned out to be a good thing," Sophia continued.

"I wasn't going to give him a ticket, just let him sit for a few minutes to learn a lesson. He kept carrying on and refused to give up his papers. By this time a crowd had gathered and he still refused to hand over his license and registration. I said, 'That's it. You're under arrest.' I went to take him out of the car and he started jumping around.

"My partner came around to help me and we're trying to get the cuffs on him, and he's jumping and moving so we're all against the trunk of his cab. He grabbed the cuffs out of my hand and took a swing at me, so I kicked him in the balls. And nothing happened." Sophia repeated it for emphasis. "Absolutely nothing.

"My partner and I were struggling with him, just trying to cuff him without hurting him. He tried to grab my partner's gun—with all those people around. The cabbie was kicking us and I hit him with my radio, sending the battery flying across the street. He kicked me so hard I ended up on the hood of the cab.

"Finally, a couple of sector cars showed up," Sophia recalled. "It took six cops to put cuffs on this guy. Later, he said he knew we were cops, he just didn't feel like giving us his license. My partner and I both ended up in the hospital and the DA never called me about it. They just decided not to prosecute and didn't even bother to explain why to us."

"Yeah, this is the only job I know where you gain power and lose your rights," Geri remarked with a tinge of bitterness. "How was your weekend?"

"The usual," Sophia said. "Did they tell you when you called that it was my day off?"

"Yeah, why?"

"Oh, it's one of my pet peeves around here," Sophia replied. "When someone phones one of the guys, the caller is always told he's out on patrol, even if he's on vacation. When someone calls for me, they get chapter and verse on where I am: she didn't come in, she went to court, she took off early, whatever."

"I know what you mean," Geri said. "That's because they don't want to give away anything to a guy's wife if he has a girlfriend, or vice versa. You should feel complimented. They don't think you're doing anything wrong or immoral."

Sophia laughed. "Yeah, that's what I've told them. I'm the upstanding citizen and you guys are all creeps. But it's annoying. There are some people who don't need to know the details of my life."

"Hey, if that's your biggest complaint on the job, you've got it made. I'll talk to you Monday evening." Geri hung up.

Sophia pulled out a notebook to jot down the date with Geri, then looked around to see if Norm and Van had come in yet. She had been working on a team with Norm for nearly two years now and they were good friends. Van joined them about six months ago, when their old partner got his gold shield. She liked working with them and knew from talking to some of the other girls who worked Anti-Crime that her partners were better than a lot of the other choices available.

Norm was standing by the soft drink machine, talking to Sergeant Camillo. Norm had only a fringe of brown hair, but a full bushy beard. Van had one, too, but wore his in a goatee.

Most of the guys working plainclothes in the precincts seemed to have beards, probably because they were not allowed to have them in uniform. Men let their beards grow and women usually let their hair get longer once they were no longer controlled by the regulations for uniformed cops.

Van came in the door. As usual, he was wearing jeans, a sweatshirt and cowboy boots. He hated wearing suits and ties because he was a body builder and had enormous chest and arm muscles. He looked as if he was strangling, even in specially tailored clothes. He was a wrestling nut and moonlighted during the summer as a lifeguard. He claimed that's how he met all his girlfriends.

After hearing some of his stories about the girls he dated, Sophia didn't doubt it. She thought most of them sounded as if they barely had the brains to get dressed in the morning. She had said something like that once and Van replied that he liked women that way. Sophia didn't think the comment was worth arguing about, so she usually just tuned out when he and Norm talked about girls.

Norm was married and actually not too much more interested in talking about women than Sophia was. His passion was Star Trek. He went to all the conventions and got all the newsletters. He seemed to think the old TV series represented some kind of universal truth. Sophia had tried to watch it a few times so she could at least talk to him about it. But she found the show boring and realized Norm was perfectly happy just rambling on about the show without a comment from his listeners. She noticed that Van also tuned out when Norm went into a monologue on the value of Trekkie culture.

Despite their oddities, they were good guys and good cops. All three of them liked to work and their team had a good record. When one of them had a court date or was on vacation, the replacement was usually worse and had even odder quirks.

"Okay, everybody, let's settle down." It was two o'clock and Sergeant Camillo began the Anti-Crime Squad's briefing for the day. After making sure everyone in the squad was there, he made a couple of announcements. There had been a rash of purse snatchings in the Columbus Avenue restaurants, so one team each day would be assigned to a stakeout. The other announcements were just routine police business, including assignments for the upcoming Thanksgiving Day Parade. Everyone would be in uniform for parade duty.

They were dismissed and Sophia, Norm and Van gathered their things, signed out their radios and got ready to leave.

"What car do we have today?" she asked.

"The one without heat," Norm answered. "Dress warmly."

They went out to the dark sedan they were assigned. Norm flipped Van to see who would drive. Norm won, so Van got in the backseat with Sophia. Norm began the random circling, allowing Van and Sophia to do most of the surveillance. It was cold and the usual Saturday crowds on Columbus Avenue were smaller than normal. They had been patrolling for more than an hour when Central notified all police units in the area to be on the lookout for three suspected child abusers.

The descriptions were sketchy: two black men, one heavyset, the other short, and a black woman in a green coat, last seen running south on West End from Seventy-second Street. Norm called Central to ask if they had any more on the suspects. The dispatcher said that was all so far, then added that the descriptions came from the victims, two kids in the playground at Riverside Park and Seventy-fifth Street. The sector cars were still there with them.

"Maybe we can learn more if we go talk to them ourselves," Sophia suggested. As an Anti-Crime team, they had more leeway than uniformed officers, although they had to stay in their precinct. Norm agreed and headed for the playground a few blocks away. Two patrol cars were parked on the asphalt when they arrived.

Sophia and Van got out of their car and walked over to where two patrolmen were talking to two girls and a boy. There was no one else in the playground. One girl appeared to be about twelve years old and was just starting to develop a bust. The other was about a year younger and the boy was not even eight. The two girls were in tears and the two uniformed cops seemed unsure of what to do with them.

Sophia asked one patrolman what had happened. He explained that the girls said they were attacked but managed to get away. They had been smart enough to pull a fire alarm box. The fire trucks had arrived, notified Central that it was a police job and waited until the first patrol car got there. The girls had been able to tell them what happened generally, but were too upset to go into more detail or to describe their attackers.

"Let me try," Sophia offered. "They may be frightened because of the uniform. Maybe they'll feel more comfortable talking to me."

"Go ahead."

Sophia walked over to the two girls, motioning the other cop away. She took them over to a set of swings and knelt down next to them, handing each a Kleenex.

"Here, wipe your noses and try to calm down," she said. "You had a pretty scary experience, but it's over now and you're safe. We won't let anything happen to you. Your parents will be coming to get you soon and everything is all right now."

The girls nodded, used the Kleenex and managed to stop crying.

"Do you think you can tell me what happened?" Sophia asked gently.

"We were playing on the swings with my little brother," the older girl stated. "These three people came up to us and started talking dirty. We got scared and tried to run away, but the big man grabbed me from behind."

"Do you remember what he looked like?" Sophia questioned.

"He was real big and fat," the girl said. "I think he had on a tan coat. He had very dark skin."

"That's good," Sophia praised her. "Then what happened?"

"He carried me over there, inside, and closed the door." The girl pointed to the public restroom a few yards away. "I screamed and yelled, but he was holding me too tight. He tried to get his hand into my pants and under my sweater. I kept shouting and kicking and screaming. I kicked him once in the stomach and he yelled and let go of me. I ran out the door. I looked back once and I think he had a gun, but he didn't use it. He did throw a brick at me, but it missed."

The other girl nodded in agreement. "I tried to help Maria, but the other man was holding me and I couldn't get loose. He kept touching me all over. I could hear her yelling and I tried to help her, but I was so scared."

"That's all right, honey," Sophia said to soothe her. "I would have been scared, too. Do you remember anything about the man who was holding you? What he was wearing or what he looked like?"

"He wasn't as big as the one holding Maria," she said. "He was skinnier and shorter and he had on a blue jacket. I think it had a white stripe on the sleeve."

"That's very good," Sophia reassured her. "You said there was a woman, too. What did she look like?"

"She was talking to my brother." The older girl pointed to the boy, who had not said anything. "She was fat. She had dark hair but it was yellow in front, and she wore a green coat."

"You've both been a big help," Sophia praised them again. "We're going to find those people who tried to hurt you. When we do, you'll have to tell us if they're the right ones. But don't worry, they won't be able to get close to you and they won't hurt you again. You've all been very brave and you did exactly the right thing."

Sophia left the three children on the swings and beckoned to one of the uniformed officers. "I have better descriptions now. You take them back to the precinct and call their parents. We're going to find those three mutts."

She walked back to where Norm and Van were talking with the other patrolmen. "Did you learn anything?" Norm asked.

Sophia nodded and gave them the more detailed descriptions the girls had provided. Norm called Central with the new information and the three of them got in the car. They went south on West End Avenue for several blocks, then started driving back and forth along the side streets between West End and Broadway.

They were on West End when Sophia thought she spotted a man in a blue jacket with a white stripe, walking around one of the buildings at Lincoln Towers, a middle-income high-rise development just north of Lincoln Center. The complex was made up of several buildings, separated by lawns and sidewalks, taking up eight square blocks. West End divided the site, but the only other access for cars was driveways leading to underground garages or the smaller outdoor parking lots in front of each building.

Norm stopped the car and Sophia and Van got out, trailing the man in the blue jacket on foot. He noticed them and began running toward a low-income project a few blocks away. Norm followed their radioed directions in the car, turning east to get to Columbus, then south to reach the project.

By the time he arrived, Sophia and Van had found all three suspects. "Any trouble?" Norm asked.

"No, they stopped when we identified ourselves," Sophia answered.

Van was frisking the big man while Sophia held her gun on the other two. Norm got out and began searching the second man as Sophia checked the woman for weapons. The trio matched the descriptions given by the two girls exactly.

Van found the gun in the man's pants pocket. He put it in his own belt, handcuffed his prisoner, then called Central to report they had the suspects in custody. He requested a patrol car to take them to the precinct.

"Why you bothering us?" the big man asked.

"You're under arrest for attempted rape and carrying a gun without a license for starters," Sophia answered.

Two patrol cars arrived and they put the short guy and the woman in one and the heavyset man in the other for the ride back to the One-Six stationhouse. After getting their names and birth dates, Van checked the computer for outstanding warrants while Norm and Sophia took the three to a back room. They pushed them into chairs and handcuffed them to the chairs. Norm stayed with them, but Sophia left when a uniformed officer beckoned to her through a window in the door to the room.

"We've got the kids," he said. "Do you want to do a lineup?"

"I don't think that's necessary," she answered. "It would take too long to round up enough other people for the lineup. The kids can just look through the window and tell us if they're the ones. Just give me a minute to warn Norm. Don't bring the girls here until I come out again."

"Okay."

She went back into the room and walked over to Norm. She pulled him into a corner and whispered that the kids were there and would try to ID the three through the window. He agreed and went to turn their chairs so they wouldn't be directly facing the door, but could still be seen.

Sophia left the room and walked down the hall to the muster room. The three children were there with two of the patrol officers from the playground. They looked even more scared than when she had first seen them, but the older girl smiled when she saw Sophia. Sophia smiled back and called them over to her. "I want you to look at some people in an office in the back. You won't have to go into the room, just look at them through the window, so you don't have to be frightened. Do you think you can do that for me?"

All three children nodded. Sophia led them to the back room. Maria was tall enough to see through the window by herself, but Sophia had to ask one of the uniformed cops to lift the younger girl and the boy so they could see. All three children said the three people sitting inside were the ones who had attacked them in the park.

Sophia brought the children back to the front of the precinct. A very worried-looking man and woman were standing at the desk when they came down the hall and the children ran to them. The couple hugged and kissed all three, then asked if they had been hurt.

"Your children are fine," Sophia answered. "They have been very brave and very smart. They helped us find the people who tried to hurt them, but they also acted courageously on their own. You should be proud of them."

Both parents still looked concerned, and Sophia drew the father aside and explained what had happened. "None of the kids were hurt physically," she said when she finished. "But you may want to talk to a psychologist to be sure there is no emotional damage."

"Thank you, officer," he said. "Is there any more we have to do right now?"

"No, not if the desk officer has your address and home phone number," she answered. "Thanks to the descriptions the girls gave us, we were able to pick up the creeps who bothered them. The children just looked at them through a door and identified them. We'll take it from here, but we will need your permission for the children to testify against them in court."

The man looked troubled. "I'm not sure I want to put my kids through that."

"I can understand your feelings, sir," Sophia answered. "But remember, if we don't have their testimony, we'll have to let those three go. They'll be free to bother other kids."

"I'll talk it over with my wife," he replied. "We'll probably follow your suggestion about seeing a psychologist and ask about it then, too."

"Well, it's your decision," she told him. "In some cases like this, the judge is often willing to let the children testify on videotape. And please remember, without their testimony, these three creeps will be released."

"I'll remember," he said. "And thank you for everything." He went to his wife and children and shepherded them out of the precinct as Sergeant Camillo entered.

"I hear your team got a collar," he said to Sophia. "What happened?"

She told him and he praised their work. Sophia told him about the conversation with the father and the sergeant shook his head.

"Let's hope he decides for us," he stated. "Now, let's go see these mutts." He started toward the back room when Van came up and said the computer showed outstanding warrants on sex charges against the two men.

"Well, at least we can keep those two for a while," the sergeant said. "Let's get them processed and downtown."

Two hours later, Sophia, Van and Norm were guiding the prisoners to the entrance to Central Booking in the basement of police headquarters in Lower Manhattan. Sophia hated the place, which she imagined must resemble medieval dungeons.

The walls were tiled, as was the floor, so there was nothing to absorb noise. The place was filled with a constant sound of metal: cell doors clanking shut, handcuff chains rattling, coins clinking as they were dropped. If you spoke in a normal voice, you couldn't be heard, even when it was relatively empty.

On a busy night, the main room sounded like bedlam, with prisoners yelling to each other, cops shouting back and forth, telephones ringing and doors slamming. She often wondered how the cops assigned there could put up with it.

Sophia and her partners led the prisoners in through the garage under the building, stopping at a long table once they got inside the heavily guarded doors. They told the prisoners to empty their pockets. It was still early, so there was no line and the two holding cells on either side of the central aisle were empty.

One by one, each of the three was carefully searched. Everything in their pockets, including money, was taken out and placed in an envelope with their name on it. All metal jewelry was removed, and after the handcuffs were taken off, the three walked through a metal detector that was like those used at airports but much more sophisticated. These detectors could be set off by a suspect wearing denim pants with metal studs.

From there the prisoners were taken to other holding pens to await transportation to the courthouse where they would be arraigned. The two men went in a large cell in the corner of the main room, the woman to another one in the next room.

Sophia and her partners walked up to the desk sergeant. They told him about the charges against the three prisoners, and he looked over their arrest forms to be sure everything was filled out correctly. Then he sent the three officers to the computer room for a check on the rap sheets of the prisoners. After a few minutes, the computer reported all three had long records for sexual abuse, robbery and just about everything but murder. The woman had a record of prostitution and narcotics as well.

While Sophia, Van and Norm were waiting for the computer printout, a couple of Street Crimes* cops came in with a group of teenagers. Sophia spotted them first and nudged Norm.

"Look at the group that just came in," she said. "Isn't that our old friend Wishbone?"

The name caught Norm's attention and he turned to look at the prisoners being searched.

"Yeah, that's him. Hey, Van, look, it's Wishbone."

Van turned around. "That brings back an unpleasant memory, right, Soph?"

She nodded, thinking about the time she had nearly shot Wishbone and Van as well. It had been near the end of a tour on a hot weekend earlier that summer. They were just about to go back to the house when a call came over of a robbery at gunpoint on a side street just off Lincoln Center. The description of the suspects was brief, two male black teenagers, one wearing dungarees and a blue T-shirt.

They were just north of the area, so they started cruising the streets. Sophia pointed out that the pair had probably run from the scene and it was a hot night. She suggested that the kid had probably taken off the T-shirt, so they should be looking for someone who was sweaty and bare-chested. They drove down Broadway and spotted a teenager of that description walking down the sidewalk on the Columbus Avenue side of the small triangular park that separated Broadway from Columbus, in front of Lincoln Center.

Sophia and Norm got out to follow him on foot while Van drove on, turning west on Sixty-third Street to cut him off. The kid stopped as Van pulled up at the intersection with Columbus in front of a restaurant on the corner. Luckily, it was nearly midnight, so the plaza across the street was empty of the usual tourist crowd. But the sidewalk café of the restaurant was full and the diners had a front row seat for what happened next.

The teenager turned around when Sophia and Norm yelled at him to stop. They called out that they were police officers and both of them had their guns out and police shields and ID's hanging on chains around their necks. The youth reached into his pants, as Van moved to come up behind him and grab his arms. Sophia started pulling the trigger back when she saw him put his hand in his pants, sure he was going to pull out a gun. The report from Central had said a robbery at gunpoint; this kid met the description of a suspect and he stuck his hand in his pants as soon as he heard them say, "Police."

Even as she pulled the trigger back, Sophia realized that if she fired, the bullet would probably not only hit the kid, but also go through him and hit Van as well. She managed to stop herself from shooting in time. Van was able to control the struggling kid and Norm came up a second later. They pushed him against a car and tossed him, searching for the gun. Instead, they found the blue T-shirt.

Sophia shook for ten minutes afterward, especially when a patrol car showed up with the robbery complainant. He couldn't identify their prisoner positively and the uniforms in the RMP told them that Central had just reported the other suspect had also been caught and he had the gun. She could just imagine the headlines in the tabloid newspapers if she had fired: "FEMALE COP SHOOTS UNARMED TEEN."

Even now, almost six months later, she got nervous thinking about it. She still couldn't believe that she had thought that fast at the time, remembering that the rounds used by the NYPD were powerful enough to go through more than one body and that Van would be in danger if she fired. All of that had gone through her head in an instant, even as she was pulling the trigger back. Seeing Wishbone brought the whole horror of the incident back again. It was not one of her favorite memories.

Sophia shook off her unpleasant thoughts and suggested that they go over to the District Attorney's office to detail the case against today's prisoners. Norm and Van agreed and they left Central Booking. With luck, they could be through with the DA in an hour or so and could go home. They had a good case against the trio: ID's by the complainants, outstanding warrants, long rap sheets. There should be no problems and if Central Booking wasn't crowded, there shouldn't be a long wait for an ADA either.

They completed their responsibilities and went back to the precinct. Sergeant Camillo was waiting for them and congratulated them again on their good police work. He had heard from the uniforms how Sophia had been able to calm the frightened girls and get a more detailed description of the suspects. He said he was proud of them, and their quick action and teamwork.

Sophia went back to her desk, where she glanced at her calendar and saw her upcoming date with Geri. That reminded her of their conversation earlier. She tried again to remember Alex Grandey, but just couldn't place him. Still, if Geri was willing to set them up and had been his partner, he couldn't be too bad. Sophia was between men at the moment and more than willing to meet him. At least it was something to look forward to.

# CHAPTER 15

**M**ary Frances got to work on Monday wondering who would be riding with her, since Paul was taking the day off. She hoped the tour would be more interesting than the one the day before had been. Sunday had been slow, just a series of car alarms and a couple of aided cases, none of which were emergencies. Paul was lucky to have today off, she thought, if it was going to be another day like yesterday.

But that was what she liked best about the job, never knowing what she would have to confront in a day. She parked her car, waved hello to everyone in the muster room as she walked through and went upstairs to change clothes. Sally Weston was already in the locker room.

"How are things going?" Mary Frances asked.

"Great," Sally replied. "It was terrific driving Bailey last week and when I went past the desk a few minutes ago, he said I'd be on patrol today, too."

"I told you he was a nice guy," Mary Frances said. "He's one of the real old-time sergeants, but he doesn't have the usual attitude about women. Did you learn anything with him?"

"Yeah, I learned that I don't want to be a sergeant," Sally said with a laugh.

Mary Frances smiled as she buckled on her equipment belt.

"I know what you mean. Patrol sergeant is a tough job. You're responsible for everything that goes on out there. I'm not sure I'd want it either. Neal is thinking about taking the next test, but I'm not sure if I like that idea."

They walked downstairs together to find the usual crowd in the muster room waiting for roll call. Sergeant Bailey called them to attention, then read the announcements of the day. He reminded them of the rash of restaurant purse snatchings and warned everyone to be on the lookout for suspects. An Anti-Crime team would be staking out one of the Columbus Avenue places that had been hardest hit, so they should be listening for possible chases. He went through all the usual stuff, then announced the daily assignments. Sally would be riding with Mary Frances in Sector H.

After Bailey dismissed them, Mary Frances turned to Sally with a smile. "Well, I guess it's you and me, partner. You get the radios and I'll get the car keys." Sally nodded in agreement. They met outside, in front of the radio car assigned to them that day. Mary Frances made her usual check of the backseat and found it cleaner than usual. Sally refused her offer to drive first.

They checked the radios to be sure they were working, then drove to their assigned patrol area. Mary Frances complained about her boredom the day before, and insisted that Paul was probably seeing more excitement at his son's wrestling match.

"I wondered what happened to him today," Sally said.

"He had some time coming and this was the kid's first match on the varsity team, so he wanted to be there," Mary Frances informed her. "He told me you did real well last week when you rode together."

"That's nice to hear," Sally responded. "I admit I'm a lot less nervous about being on patrol than I was a week ago."

"It just takes some getting used to," Mary Frances said. "Have the boys been giving you any more trouble?"

"Not really trouble," Sally answered. "But I really don't like Frank Gordon." She told Mary Frances about his calling her an empty suit the week before.

"Too bad Bailey didn't hear," Mary Frances commented. "Once, when I was driving a sergeant, someone called me the sergeant's bimbo. I didn't say anything, but at the next precinct party I went up to the guy and his wife and asked if she was his bimbo. He got real pissed, screaming at me not to talk that way in front of his wife. I just reminded him that I was someone's wife and he had called me the same thing. He never tried that on me again.

"Gordon's the same kind of jerk. In the old days, before there were women on patrol, he argued the loudest against allowing wives at the precinct parties. He was the one who used to arrange the raffle for blow jobs and line up the strippers. Now that the commands are co-ed, he brings his wife to everything and glares at anyone who uses a four-letter word in her presence."

"I thought it was just me he didn't like," Sally said.

"I told you last week, some of those guys are real dinosaurs." Mary Frances frowned. "I don't say that about many people, but there is no other way to describe some of them."

The radio called for one-six Henry. Sally answered and they were sent to a report of a woman screaming on West End Avenue and Seventy-fifth Street. When they arrived, they saw an elderly woman with a shopping cart filled with ragged bags and boxes. She had long, stringy gray hair, wore several layers of tattered sweaters and coats, and had on boots held together with string. She was sorting through the garbage in a litter basket and screaming at the top of her lungs about Nixon and Watergate.

"It's Mabel," Mary Frances said. "She's sort of a regular EDP* in this neighborhood." She parked the car and got out, approaching the woman slowly, talking to her in a soft voice as she neared.

"What's the matter, Mabel?" Sally heard Mary Frances ask as they got near the old woman. Sally could see the woman's hands, twisted by arthritis, with long, uneven nails black with dirt. She was pawing through the newspapers and other litter and didn't look up, but she stopped screaming.

Mary Frances asked her again what was wrong and Mabel finally glanced at her. "There's no soda cans here. No one is throwing away cans anymore. How can they expect an old woman like me to live if they don't put their soda and beer cans in the garbage? So, can I get the nickel refund? It's all that Nixon's fault. He got the country in trouble." Mabel started screaming again.

"Are you hungry, Mabel?" Mary Frances asked, trying to distract her from her complaint. "I can get you some soup if you want."

"Yeah, that would be nice." Mabel grinned toothlessly at Mary Frances. "I like soup. Make sure it's real hot. I like real hot soup."

Mary Frances nodded, then turned to Sally. "There's a deli on Broadway. Here's a buck. Go get her a cup of whatever soup they've got and a buttered roll. I'll stay here and talk to her, keep her calm."

Sally left to walk the short distance to Broadway and Mary Frances turned back to Mabel. "Where are you living now, Mabel?"

"Nowhere," the woman answered. "I go to the shelter some nights when it's really cold and they make me. But I don't like it there. They want me to live in a hotel, but I don't want all those screaming kids and junkies around me. I like the streets. Nobody bothers me on the streets. They think I'm just a crazy old lady and they leave me alone."

Mary Frances was not surprised by what she said. She had caught the sour smell that signaled too few baths. Mabel was one of the thousands of mental patients released from state hospitals several years before on the grounds that she wasn't dangerous. She wasn't, but neither was she capable of taking care of herself. The state was supposed to provide community residences for the released patients, many of whom were like Mabel. Instead, they were just turned out of the hospitals and hundreds of them had ended up on the West Side, where cheap hotels offered one room with a communal kitchen and bathrooms down the hall.

A few years later, the West Side became the "in" place to live and the rooming-house hotels, known as Single Room Occupancies or SRO's, closed down; their interiors were renovated and they reopened as luxury apartments. The previous tenants were evicted and, like Mabel, could find no new place to live.

Mary Frances had seen many of the homeless people who just stayed in the area they knew best, afraid to go to the shelters or even to welfare offices.

Sally returned with the soup and roll and handed the bag to Mabel. The old woman grabbed it, taking the top off the cup of soup and gulping it down hungrily. She smiled again at Mary Frances, holding the soup and the bag with the roll in one hand and pushing her cart with the other. She shuffled off to find a place to eat in peace without a backward glance at them or even a word of thanks.

Mary Frances and Sally walked back to the patrol car. "She's a harmless old lady," Mary Frances said. "One of the eight million stories in this city. I met the social worker who tries to help her. He told me she had been a schoolteacher who suffered a nervous breakdown and never got better. She has no family that anyone has ever been able to find and she's been wandering the streets ever since she was forced out of her SRO a couple years ago.

"Everyone in the precinct knows her and we all buy her soup and a roll whenever we can. That's usually why she starts yelling on the streets," Mary Frances said with laugh. "I guess she's not as crazy as she acts. She knows if she screams, someone will call the police and whoever comes will buy her soup and something to eat."

Sally called in a 10-91* to report what had happened to Central, then entered the incident in her memo book. Mary Frances resumed their random patrol of the area, but a few minutes later they heard a call for one-six George, a 10-29, possible rape. They heard George answer and Mary Frances called Central to say Henry would go as backup.

The other patrol car was there when they arrived at the old tenement building on Amsterdam, in a block that had not yet been gentrified. Two kids were standing in the doorway and let the two women in, telling them the other cops had gone to a fifth-floor apartment. Sally and Mary Frances climbed five flights of poorly lit, twisting stairs. Mary Frances commented that as bad as the smell of urine was in the staircase, she was at least glad they weren't in an enclosed elevator, where it was worse.

At the top, they found a door open. They could see Larry Holland and Jeff McMichaels talking to a crying woman. She had bruises on her face and some chairs were overturned in the apartment.

Larry and Jeff came out as Sally and Mary Frances reached the landing. "She came home from shopping to find a burglar," Larry explained. "He attacked her, tried to rape her, but she screamed and fought him off. He went out the window with the fire escape and she thinks he went up to the roof. We're going to search up there for him."

Mary Frances nodded and beckoned Sally to follow them. They climbed another flight of stairs and pushed open the sliding bolt that locked the door to the roof. All four cops unbuckled their holsters. Larry, who was in front, was the only one who took his gun out. The others kept their hands on the butt of their guns, but didn't draw them. That was procedure. If a cop tripped while holding a gun, it could accidentally fire and hit the officer in front.

Larry cautiously pushed open the door, peering around the frame before edging out on the tarpaper. It was a cold day, and that high up, the wind was biting. Like most New York City apartment roofs, this one had a number of pipes, chimneys and other structures. The door was part of something that looked like a shed. A similar shed stood on the other side of the building, a closed padlock guarding its door. In between were the legs of the water tower.

Larry and Jeff took one half of the roof, Mary Frances and Sally the other. The building abutted another one, which was a few feet lower, its roofline edged with barbed wire. An agile person could have jumped down from one building to the other without hitting the barbed wire. Or he could be hiding in the water tower.

Mary Frances and Larry, the two senior partners from each team, looked at one another. It was just getting to dusk and someone would have to climb the water tower before it got completely dark. Sally realized it almost as soon as they did. She hated heights, but she was the lightest. She knew no one expected her to volunteer. She also knew that she was the most logical person to make the climb.

"I'll do it," she heard herself saying. She didn't want to wait to be ordered up. A good cop, they had taught her at the Academy, should see the obvious and do it without being told.

She holstered her gun and walked to the ladder that went up one of the legs and started the climb. She tried not to look down or to think about the wind. It was even colder than on the roof and the gusts of wind seemed to have increased to gale force. She climbed carefully but steadily, and with every step, heard the refrain from a favorite childhood nursery book in her head.

"I think I can, I think I can, I think I can," echoed round and round in her mind. She concentrated and changed the chant slightly: "I know I can, I know I can, I know I can." She was near the top and managed to get her gun out again, climbing with it in her hand. Larry had said the mutt might have a knife.

There was a narrow ledge circling the rim, for maintenance work on the tower. Sally climbed out on to it and edged slowly around the tank, strangely remembering the joke that rooftop water tanks were New York hot tubs. She used her flashlight to check the sloped roof of the tank for holes big enough for a man to get in, but there were none. She reached the ladder again and turned to begin her descent, calling down that she had found no sign of the suspect. Sally holstered her gun and climbed down slowly, looking up the whole time.

She got off the ladder and found she could barely stand up, her knees were shaking so badly. Mary Frances moved close to Sally, unobtrusively helping her stand. She looked around to find Sergeant Bailey and Bill standing nearby with Larry and Jeff. She told them again she had found no sign of anyone. Bailey said they had already sent a description of the attacker over the radio. He must have escaped over the next roof or down the fire escape.

The sergeant pretended not to notice how badly Sally was trembling. He praised her for seeing the need to check the water tower and taking quick action to do so. He informed them that detectives from the Sex Crimes Unit were on their way to talk to the victim and they would take up the investigation. Larry and Jeff smiled at her and they all walked back to the door and into the building again. Mary Frances went last, stopping to slide the bolt on the door to the roof closed.

Back on the street, the six police officers went off to their cars. Bailey suggested softly to Mary Frances that she and Sally take a few minutes to pick up a cup of coffee. Mary Frances nodded and called Central to report one-six Henry on a personal. She waited a few seconds for Sally to take out her memo book and when she didn't, reminded her to make a notation.

"Oh, yeah." Sally smiled weakly. "I'm still in a state of shock. Maybe I shouldn't admit it, but I've never been so scared in my whole life. I've always been afraid of heights and climbing that tank, even without thinking someone might be up there waiting for me with a knife, terrified me."

"You don't have to be ashamed of being scared," Mary Frances pointed out. "Anyone on this job who won't admit they're afraid some of the time is lying. The problem comes when you allow the fear to stop you from doing what you should be doing. Think of fear like the cold water in a swimming pool; just dive in and get it over with. That's what you just did."

"I guess so," Sally said. "But I'm still shaking."

"That's natural," Mary Frances answered. "But the next time you have to make a climb like that, I bet you find you're less afraid. That's one of the things I like about this job. It sort of throws you into life. You can't avoid it." She drove to Broadway, parked at a fire hydrant in front of a coffee shop and asked Sally what she wanted.

When Mary Frances returned with two teas and a couple of donuts, she found Sally writing up the incident in her memo book. She put Sally's tea on the dashboard until she finished and opened her own to note the break.

"I thought there was an unwritten rule among cops not to talk about fear," Sally said when she looked up.

"It's carved in granite, but invisible," Mary Frances replied. "Actually, it's not a good idea to go around telling everyone that you were scared. But you can talk to me and most of the other girls about it. Like I said, anyone who doesn't admit being afraid some of the time is a nut case.

"But if you're terrified all of the time, then you should get out. I don't see that with you. I don't think you're walking around worrying that someone is going to shoot you in the back. Something like the water tower, there's nothing wrong with being afraid of heights, as long as it doesn't stop you. I hate going into abandoned buildings. They terrify me. But that doesn't mean I refuse to search them when it's necessary," Mary Frances remarked.

They sat silently, sipping the hot tea for a few minutes.

"I've heard some of the guys in the precinct talk about a woman sergeant who locked herself in the car, responding to a 10-13,"* Sally said suddenly. "They seem to think all women will do that."

"I know that story. Everyone does." Mary Frances frowned. "It happened more than ten years ago, just after they put women on patrol. That sergeant had been on the job for several years, but she hadn't really been trained for street work. But they put her out there and when the call came about another cop needing assistance, she panicked.

"There have been plenty of men who have shown cowardice since that incident, and women, too. The trouble is, no one talks about the men, but every time a woman does something like that, all the women on the job are assumed to be cowards with some personal exceptions." Mary Frances turned to look at Sally. "Are you afraid of this job?" she asked.

"No," Sally answered. "I don't really think about being afraid. This was one of the few times I can say I was. And it wasn't because I might have found the guy up there. I knew the rest of you were there to back me up if I had. I'm just afraid of heights and it was the climb."

"Then I wouldn't worry about it." Mary Frances smiled at her. "Just remember, no one expects you to do more than you can. Even someone who isn't nervous about heights would have been uncomfortable climbing that tower. You're not supposed to be Superwoman, just a cop.

"That doesn't mean you can look the other way if a big strong guy jumps your partner. That's the one unforgivable sin on this job," she went on. "Always back up your partner. If there's a fight, call for help on the radio, then join in. You may get a few bruises and stuff, but the backup will be there in seconds. But if you don't help, if you come back neat when your partner is hurt, that will be remembered and held against you as long as you're on the job."

Sally nodded. They finished their tea and donuts just as someone tapped on the window next to Mary Frances. She turned around to see a well-dressed woman peering in with another right behind her. Mary Frances rolled down the window and heard the first woman say: "I told you. I was right. You owe me ten dollars." The second woman agreed: "You were right. You won."

"What's happening?" Mary Frances asked.

"I told her there were two women in this car and she didn't believe it," the first woman said. "She didn't think they would let two women patrol together."

"Oh, they do it all the time," Mary Frances answered. The women waved and walked away, chattering together.

While Sally put the garbage in a litter basket on the corner, Mary Frances called Central to report they were going back on patrol. A minute later, the dispatcher called to send them to a reported family dispute in an apartment house on Columbus.

Neighbors had been hearing screams and what sounded like a loud argument in a twelfth-floor apartment in one of the new buildings on the avenue. Mary Frances acknowledged the assignment, got the exact location and they drove to the address. When they got off the elevator, they could hear an argument.

Sally moved to one side of the door, Mary Frances to the other. She pounded on the door with her nightstick, calling: "Police, open up." The shouting stopped and the door opened in a few seconds. A tall blond man with the beginnings of a potbelly stood in the doorway. He was wearing sweatpants, a T-shirt and sneakers.

"May we come in?" Mary Frances asked. "We were called about a fight here." She could see the man didn't want them in the apartment. "We were told someone heard screams coming from here. We have to make sure everyone is okay," she insisted.

The man stepped back into the room reluctantly and she

followed him, with Sally behind her. A woman was sitting on the couch, tears running down her face. She looked as if she had the beginning of a black eye.

Mary Frances turned to the man, motioning to Sally to go to the woman. They maneuvered the pair to stand back-to-back so Mary Frances and Sally could see each other. That was one of the tactics taught at the Academy, separating the fighters while maintaining eye contact with your partner.

The man still looked angry and unlikely to calm down. The woman had stopped crying and was sitting quietly. Mary Frances looked around. An expensive stereo sat on a bookcase otherwise filled with books and records. A VCR was next to the TV with boxes of tapes below them. The floor was covered with a plush rug, plants hung in the windows and the sofa was new. A coffee table held expensive art books and magazines and several newspapers littered the floor, as though someone had just tossed them down as each section was read.

"What's the problem?" Mary Frances asked.

"I came home from work and she hadn't done anything all day," he said loudly. "She hadn't even started dinner. I don't get home until eight at night and I can't even get a decent meal when I get here. I slapped her to teach her a lesson."

Mary Frances was stunned. She had been to other family disputes, even abuse cases, but most of them were in low-income families. She knew that the experts said wife-beating crossed economic class lines and she had heard other cops talk about wife-beating cases involving professional people, but until now she had never really believed that well-educated, intelligent, middle-class men beat their wives. She could see that Sally was equally shocked.

"You hit your wife because she didn't have dinner ready?" Mary Frances knew she shouldn't be taking sides, but she couldn't help it. This guy weighed nearly two hundred pounds. He had big hands and even if he was starting to go to fat, she could see he still had muscles.

"I should know a woman would take her side." The man started yelling again. "If someone is going to butt into my business, I want a real cop here, not two more lousy broads. I get enough all day from this bitch, I don't need to hear more from you two."

"We are the officers sent in response to this call," Mary Frances said calmly. "We're going to stay here until this is settled. You can begin by understanding that and also by understanding that if your wife wants us to, we can arrest you for assault right now."

The woman standing next to Sally heard that and shook her head, indicating that she did not want to press charges. She hadn't said anything yet and she didn't really look as if she was afraid of him, but Mary Frances couldn't be sure.

"The hell with it," the man said. "This is disgusting. I can't expect anything from you two. I'm getting out of here. I'm going to get something to eat."

"That's a good idea," Mary Frances answered. "I think it would be better if you left until you calm down. Hitting anyone is assault. You do not have the right to cause physical injury to another person just because you're angry. It would be wise of you to remember that."

The man went to the closet near the door, pulled on a coat and stormed from the apartment without another word. Mary Frances closed the door behind him and turned to the woman. She definitely had a black eye.

"You'd better put some ice on your face," Mary Frances suggested. "We'll wait for you." The woman walked into a small kitchen just off the living room. Sally and Mary Frances just looked at each other while they waited. The woman came back within a minute, holding a thick towel to her eye. When questioned, she repeated the story the man had given them. She didn't seem surprised or even angry that he had hit her.

"Does he hit you all the time?" Mary Frances asked, astonished.

"No," she said quietly. "I guess he had a bad day at work. He hasn't hit me in a couple of months. He doesn't do it often and he doesn't mean to hurt me. When he comes back later, he'll probably have flowers and candy and be very apologetic." She apparently didn't mind the beatings.

Mary Frances informed her about the shelters available for battered women if she wanted to leave. She also explained how to get an order of protection from a judge, but the woman wasn't interested in that either. She assured them she would be all right and that her husband would not hurt her again. Sally and Mary Frances left.

"I can't believe it," Mary Frances said as they went down in the elevator. "Why would she put up with that? I've been on jobs with other women much less abused who demanded we lock the bastard up."

"I know." Sally seemed as upset as Mary Frances. "I never thought I'd see something like that. They were rich people, or at least they seemed better off than middle class. And there were some legal books on the bookshelf. He might even be a lawyer and he wasn't even ashamed to admit that he had been hitting his wife."

"I'm glad he was annoyed that we were women and taking her side," Mary Frances said. "It accomplished our purpose: to get him out of there. We offered her help and she turned it down, but at least we separated them for the time being. I would have hated to call a backup if he had decided to make trouble and refused to leave."

"I know what you mean," Sally remarked.

"When I worked in the Bronx, before I hooked up with a regular partner, I would sometimes ride with this big black guy," Mary Frances said. "He was huge—tall and nearly two hundred and twenty pounds—but all muscle, with big hands and shoulders. He had a real system on family dispute calls.

"We'd get to the apartment or the house or whatever and I'd come out of the car, screaming at the top of my lungs. He would be real quiet like Gary Cooper in *High Noon*. He'd take the guy aside and say to him, 'Listen, my partner over there, you hear her, the bitch is really crazy. I can't control her. And she really hates wife-beaters. We'd better do what she says, because I can't afford to get involved in any more shootings.' " Mary Frances giggled.

"The guy would look at this huge cop, like Rosey Grier but not as fat, and then at me, screaming and yelling and carrying on about men who beat up on women. The guys would always nod their heads and go along with anything. We ran some real numbers on people," she finished, laughing.

"Sometimes, I'd go into the routine and he would try to calm me down, knowing everyone was listening, saying, 'Now, now, Mary Frances, don't shoot this one. Don't get into trouble again.' " She laughed again. "We'd really do some scenes. It helps calm things down. The people who are fighting stop what they're doing to hear what you're doing and pretty soon, they forget they've been fighting."

Sally laughed, too. "I can't believe anyone would think of you as a crazy uncontrollable bitch," she noted.

"Don't forget, I'm Irish," Mary Frances commented. "If I get my Irish up, I can be just as irrational as the next person. And these people were strangers. They didn't know what I was really like, they just knew what they were seeing at the time. Speaking of time, it's time for our meal. Where do you want to eat?"

They decided on a nearby deli, reported to Central that they were on meal and went into the restaurant. As usual, most of the other customers stared as they found a booth to sit in and hung up their jackets and hats. Two women officers together attracted even more attention than two male cops, but Mary Frances and Sally ignored it. A waitress came and both ordered corned beef sandwiches. They also got French fries to share and tea.

"You're lucky to have Paul for a partner," Sally remarked.

"I know," Mary Frances agreed. "My other longtime partner, Doug Green, was also a great guy. I've worked with some real losers, but I just ask out fast if it's not working.

"When I first came on, I was riding with a guy one night on a midnight. He was just a couple of years older than me and we were both single. I noticed he seemed uncomfortable the whole time. I finally asked him what was wrong and he told me he felt that he was on a date, riding around with a girl late at night.

"How does your husband feel about your going on patrol with other men?" she asked Sally.

"We haven't really talked about that yet," Sally replied. "He wasn't happy when I told him I was going to ask to be put on patrol, but I explained that to him. Since he's not on the job, I guess he won't really know what having a partner is like."

"You get real close to someone you spend eight and a half hours a day with." Mary Frances nodded in agreement. "You probably spend more waking time with your partner than with anyone else in your life. Doug and I are still close friends although it's been three years since we split up when I took time off to have the baby.

"He was divorced last year," Mary Frances continued. "All that time we were riding together he would talk about his wife and the problems they were having and they finally split for good.

"I threw him a shower," she said, laughing. "I knew he didn't have any of the things you need to set up an apartment, not even basics like linens or towels or even dishes and pots. I invited all of our friends from our old precinct and had a shower for him. It was fun. He told me later his ex-wife was jealous because no one had thrown a party for her."

"Was she jealous of you when you worked with him?" Sally asked.

"At first she was," Mary Frances replied. "But after I met her, she was okay. She knew I wasn't interested in him as a boyfriend and that he was trying to fix me up with friends of his. I like her, even if he doesn't. She calls me every once in a while, just to chat and catch up. She just never adjusted to him being a cop. That's a real problem on this job."

"I know," Sally said. "It worries me sometimes. Jim has been pretty good so far, but he hates going to police parties. I've explained how important they are, how that's where you meet the people who can really help your career. But he's uncomfortable being around so many cops.

"And he gets annoyed when I can't always get time off to come to his office gatherings or the out-of-town conventions. Those are important in his work, but I can't just take a few days off to go with him." Sally frowned. "So far, he makes his own plans and if I'm off I go with him. Otherwise, he goes alone."

The waitress came with their sandwiches and they started to eat.

"It's not any easier when you're married to a cop, just a different kind of problem," Mary Frances pointed out. "For the past few months, I've barely seen Neal because we always seem to be working opposite shifts. Just this weekend we came up with a solution and we're hoping his CO goes along with it. But Neal's been talking about going back on patrol and if he does that, we'll be right back where we started."

"Would you care if he had a woman partner?" Sally wanted to know.

Mary Frances looked startled and hesitated before answering. "I hadn't thought of that. Now that you mention it, I have to admit I wouldn't like it. I don't like saying it, but I sure wouldn't be happy about that."

Sally looked surprised. "How can you say that, Mary Frances?"

"Like I said, it didn't occur to me before," she admitted sheepishly. "But I wouldn't like it. I wouldn't make a big stink and demand that he change or anything like that, like some of the civilian wives have done. But it would be hard to get used to."

"Why?"

"Because of what we were saying before," she answered. "You get very close to a partner. You spend a lot of time with them and being that close to someone else has to put a strain on the marriage. I guess if it happened I'd learn to live with it. I wouldn't want to be responsible for making another woman on this job feel unwanted, but it wouldn't be easy. And he puts up with my having partners."

"Still, I'm surprised to hear you say that," Sally said.

"I am, too," Mary Frances admitted. "And a little disappointed in myself. I thought I was stronger than that. And it's not that I don't trust Neal. But it would be hard to get used to."

"Have you had any real problems with male partners?" Sally asked.

"No, because when I see it isn't working, I request a change," Mary Frances answered. "There was one guy who always criticized my driving. If I stopped for a light, I should have gone through it. If I turned right, he wanted us to go left. If I cruised slowly, I should go faster. If I went faster, I should be driving more slowly. After a couple of months, I asked out of that car.

"And when Doug and I first started riding together, he insisted on keeping the radio turned to whatever baseball or football game was on," she said. "It drove me crazy. Finally, I told him, 'When I drive, I decide what we listen to; when you drive, you can pick the station.' He agreed and we didn't have another problem about the radio after that."

Mary Frances spread her hands out. "My partners all worry about my nails." She laughed. "I guess I do that to them, bitching whenever I break one. Now, whenever we finish a job that has been a little rough, Paul will ask me if they're okay. Doug used to ask, too. It's become almost a joke."

"I can never get my nails to grow," Sally said. "They break off all the time."

"Drink more milk and eat lots of dairy products," Mary Frances recommended. "Jell-O helps too or gelatin capsules. Come on, our hour is up. Time to go back to work."

They paid the check and got back in the car. Sally drove and Mary Frances called Central to report they were back from their meal. They cruised randomly for about an hour, finding nothing in particular. Mary Frances groaned and complained about boredom, but Sally was just glad to be out of the office.

The radio sputtered. They heard a woman's voice reporting that one-six Ida had spotted a van with three males answering the description of the suspects and vehicle wanted for a robbery in the next precinct to the north a couple of hours earlier. One-six Ida was following and requested backup for a stop. They were on West End going south toward Seventy-second Street. Mary Frances replied that one-six Henry would back up. Another voice said one-six Frank would also.

Sally turned west on Seventy-seventh Street, then south on West End. Mary Frances looked behind them and saw the other patrol car a block or two away. The radio reported that one-six Ida had pulled the van over at Seventy-second and Riverside, next to the road leading to the West Side Highway. Sally turned at Seventy-second Street and they saw the patrol car, parked at an angle in front of the van. Ellen Fletcher and Clare Roberts were already out of their patrol car, approaching the van with their guns drawn.

Sally stopped and Mary Frances jumped out, taking out her gun. The third radio car was right behind them with Karen Nathan and Suzy Chamberlayne. Sally was out of the car by now and they all had drawn their guns. Ellen and Clare had the doors of the van opened and were ordering the men out.

Three men climbed out, their hands up. Ellen, Clare and Mary Frances pushed them up against the side of the van, kicking their legs apart in the frisk position while Sally, Karen and Suzy stood to one side, keeping the trio under guard.

The three were searched. Mary Frances found a knife, and Ellen came up with a switchblade. Clare's prisoner didn't have a weapon. The prisoners were muttering to themselves as they were handcuffed. One started talking louder, saying the lousy cop bastards would never have caught him if he had had his gun with him. He would have shot first and asked questions later. He was tough and he wasn't afraid of lousy cops.

Two more radio cars had arrived by now, including Sergeant Bailey. He smiled at the sight of the three handcuffed men and the six women who were responsible. He came up to them in time to hear the one belligerent prisoner bragging.

"Yeah, you mutts are real tough guys," Bailey agreed. "That's why you let a bunch of women nab you." He laughed.

One of the handcuffed prisoners turned his head. The six women were ranged behind him, smiling to each other. The other uniformed cops were standing off to one side, trying not to laugh out loud.

"Shut up, you fucking idiot," the prisoner snarled to his loudmouthed pal. "If this gets out, we're really going to look bad." At that, all ten cops broke up.

Bailey stopped laughing first. "What have we got? These guys sure fit the description of that robbery that came over a while ago. Anything in the truck?"

"We haven't had a chance to look yet, sarge," Ellen said.

"We found two knives on these mutts." Clare went to the truck and looked in the back.

"It's full, sarge," she called. "VCR's, TV's, car radios, you name it."

"You guys planning on going into business?" Sergeant Bailey asked. He turned to the women who were keeping an eye on the prisoners. "I guess Clare and Ellen get the collar. But split them up to go back to the house. When you get them there, call the complainant in today's robbery, and see if he can come down for a lineup. And notify the Robbery Squad.

"One of you drive the van back. On second thought, you girls stay with the prisoners in your cars. One of you guys drive the van back. Let's go. I'll make the call to Central to cancel the alarm for these mutts. Nice going, girls." He grinned again.

"Come on, you creeps, get in the cars," Bailey said to the three prisoners. "I guess you guys are really ba-a-a-d to be taken by such big strong cops." He started laughing again.

Mary Frances sat in the back with one prisoner, the only one who hadn't said anything. Sally drove and on the way back to the precinct, one or the other of them would start to laugh while the prisoner sat glaring at them.

"You're doing pretty good for the new kid on the block," Mary Frances told Sally as they escorted their prisoner into the stationhouse. They pushed him in front of the desk.

Sally looked pleased. "I just wish I'd gotten a collar," she said.

"Don't worry, you will," Mary Frances reassured her. "You haven't been on the job all that long. It will happen."

# CHAPTER 16

Sophia called Geri during her meal Monday evening. It was a quiet night and they made arrangements to meet at eleven at a small bar and restaurant near the precinct that specialized in late-night desserts. The rest of the tour was as uneventful as the first half and Sophia got to the restaurant a few minutes early.

She had forgotten the purpose of the meeting, because she now wanted to talk to Geri about the collar she had made two days before. She couldn't forget how scared those kids had been and she was still upset about it. She didn't understand how Geri could deal with sex abuse cases all the time. She knew it would help to talk to the more experienced woman about it.

Sophia sat at the bar waiting for Geri. She really didn't feel like drinking and ordered a club soda. She only had time to light a cigarette and take a few sips before Geri sat down next to her.

"You want to stay here or go sit at a table?" Sophia asked after greeting Geri.

"A table, I think. I feel like eating something terribly fattening."

"Good, that's the way I feel," Sophia answered. She picked up the glass and followed Geri to a table in the back. Geri lit a cigarette and ordered espresso and marble cheesecake when the waitress came by with the menus. Sophia decided to have a cannoli and the waitress left.

"I'm glad we'd already planned to meet tonight," Sophia said. "I would have called you if we hadn't already had plans."

"Why?"

Sophia told her about the children who had been attacked in the park and the three people who had been arrested.

"I saw the case," Geri said. "I didn't realize you had been involved. Why is it bothering you?"

"I'm not sure. Maybe it's just the usual frustration of dealing with these creeps, knowing they've done it before and will probably do it again. This time, I saw the victims. I haven't been able to think about anything else since Saturday."

"You've been on the job too long to let things get to you," Geri reminded her. "Wasn't it you, less than a week ago, who told another woman not to take the job home with her, to learn to leave it in her locker with her uniform? You're not wearing a uniform anymore, but that doesn't mean you can forget rule number one."

Sophia laughed. "Yeah, I guess that was me. I don't know why this particular thing got to me. Maybe because the kids were young and those two guys who tried to rape them were so big. How do you stand it, hearing nothing but rape stories all day long?"

"If there's anything I dislike about this assignment, that's it," Geri said, frowning. "On the other hand, I feel a great deal of satisfaction when I can put one of these mutts away for a while.

"Let's change the subject. Do you remember Alex?" Geri asked.

"Nope, I can't say that I do. Are you sure I met him?"

"Yes. It was right after you and Mary Frances got out of the Academy. We were meeting for dinner and he dropped me off and came in to have a drink and meet my little cousin."

"I don't remember a thing about it. Tell me about him."

Geri blew a smoke ring as she thought about how to describe Alex Grandey to Sophia. "He was my partner in Brooklyn before the layoffs. He stayed on. Now he's a detective Second Grade with the Major Case Squad.* He's forty, thin, with a kind of craggy face."

"Doesn't ring any bells," Sophia said. "What's he like?"

"I'm not sure how to answer that," Geri answered. "I like him, I always have. When we first started riding together—and don't forget how long ago that was—he wasn't at all condescending. He was willing to let me prove myself. If I hadn't, I'm sure he would have asked for another partner immediately. But once he knew I would back him, we were really equal partners. He spoiled me. I thought all male cops would be like Alex."

"No ego?"

"Don't be silly." Geri laughed. "Of course he has an ego and a big one, but somehow it never got involved with how I did the job. He tried to come on to me, too, but I convinced him we made good partners but would be lousy lovers."

"And he accepted that?"

"Yeah, he seemed to know I didn't mean it personally or as a put-down," Geri said. "We've been real good friends ever since."

"He sounds like the perfect man," Sophia remarked. "I don't think I've ever met a good-looking cop who didn't think he was God's gift to women." The waitress put down their order and both started eating.

"I know what you mean," Geri said. "But for some reason, Alex never assumed that all women on the job were either nympho, gay or frigid. He's really a good guy. Not that he doesn't have his faults."

"Like what? I knew he was too good to be true."

"Well, I don't know all of them." Geri grinned at her. "If you decide to go out with him, you'll probably find some that I never saw. But he's a terrible tease. He's got a great sense of humor, but sometimes he just doesn't know when to stop.

"We would be riding around and he would make some kind of sexist comment about every woman we saw—look at those knockers, boy, she can really swing that ass—that kind of thing. He knew it was annoying me and the more upset I got, the more comments he made. But I learned how to deal with him."

"How?"

"Respond in kind." Geri laughed. "He'd comment about some big-chested broad and I'd spot a guy that looked like he was hung like a bull elephant and say so. Or comment on some guy having a cute little ass. Or ask him if he thought the CO wore his on the right or left."

Sophia laughed with her. "That worked?"

"For a while." Geri smiled at a thought. "The first time I commented on how some kid looked like he had huge balls, you should have seen Alex's face. I thought he would explode. He turned bright red, then purple. He couldn't believe I was talking like that. I pointed out that men have sexual attributes and women have eyes to look at them. That shut him up for almost a week."

Sophia doubled over, laughing. "I can imagine."

"The next time he started to make his comments, I started a discussion on why some men wear their cocks on the right side of their pants and some on the left, and how it didn't seem to correlate with where they wore their gun." Geri was laughing again. "I thought he'd choke that day."

Sophia was almost hysterical. "If he put up with that, he must be a good guy," she finally managed to get out.

"Well, like I said, he's not sexist at work," Geri answered, still smiling. "But I'm not so sure about his personal life. He's been divorced a few years. I liked his wife. She was one of the few civilian wives I've known who weren't jealous of a woman partner. But that might be a result of not really caring. They were having problems for a long time, I know that."

"What happened?"

"She went back to school to get a master's in fine arts," Geri explained. "Then she got a job in a SoHo gallery and decided she wanted to be on her own. Whenever we talked about it, Alex seemed more upset at the idea of not seeing his kids as often—he's got two boys, but they're both in college now—than about the marriage itself. They had both been miserable for so long, I guess they finally decided to end it."

"Is it possible he's still carrying a torch for her?" Sophia asked.

"I don't think so," Geri replied. "I never got that impression. He's very interested in you and you're the opposite physical type from her. She was tall and a bit overweight. Very motherly looking, but in a youthful way."

"How did he happen to become a cop?"

"After the Army, he didn't want to go to school, although he's since gotten a degree at John Jay," Geri said. "I think I remember him telling me he couldn't figure out what else to do at the time and afterward, couldn't think of anything that would be as challenging and as much fun."

Sophia nodded and finished her pastry. She lit another cigarette and leaned back in her chair.

"If he's willing to go out with a female cop, he can't be too much of a chauvinist, even in his personal life," she pointed out.

"I'm not sure he is," Geri replied. "But I'm not sure he isn't either. I just don't want you to go out with him and then call me the next day with stories about your miserable evening. I'll tell you what I told him: I don't want to hear from either of you about the other. I like you both and I'm not going to get caught in the middle if something doesn't work out."

"Fair enough," Sophia said. "Has he gone out with a cop before?"

"I'm not sure. I don't think so. He's never mentioned anyone to me." Geri repeated Alex's comments about women in the Army and on the job. Sophia frowned.

"He may be right, much as I hate to admit it," she said. "I can't figure out why else some of these girls have come on. But that doesn't explain the boys."

"I know what you mean," Geri agreed, relieved to have something besides Alex to talk about. "I'm glad I won't be working with some of these kids until they grow up a little. It's easy to see why they're here. They get to carry a gun and ride in cars with sirens and flashing lights. They're not only terrors behind the wheel, but, from what Mary Frances tells me, they're real bastards in the precinct."

"I've heard that, and not just from Mary Frances," Sophia said. "I don't see many of the new boys either, but I do talk to some of the girls. They bitch to me about harassment as well as complaining about hours and working conditions or the locker room. I don't know what they expected when they came on this job—nine-to-five hours with weekends off, maybe."

Geri laughed. She told Sophia that she had heard from an unimpeachable source that a sergeant was now assigned to the street in front of the Police Academy. So many of the students had fathers on the job who were coming to pick up their precious darlings after school that the street was always blocked. A rank-and-file cop wasn't heavy enough to get some of the bosses to move their cars, so a sergeant was given the post.

Sophia shook her head. "These kids are really something. I hate talking like this, because it makes me sound like I'm a hundred years old, but I really don't understand them."

"I get the same feeling," Geri said, frowning. "They look, and act, like babies."

They both smoked quietly for a few minutes, then Sophia looked at Geri. "What did you think of Sally Weston the other night?"

"Okay, I guess. I haven't really given her too much thought. Why?"

"I don't know," Sophia answered. "I had the feeling there was something she wasn't saying."

"I'm sure there was," Geri said. "I had the feeling she was uncomfortable because I was there. At a guess, I would say she was nervous about the job and whether she could do it."

"That's a pretty good guess," Sophia remarked. "The next day, she asked to be taken off clerical and put on patrol. Mary Frances told me she ended up riding with Paul Randall the next night when Mary Frances made an early collar."

"So, how did she do?"

"Okay, I gather," Sophia answered. "Paul apparently told the sergeant he would ride with her again whenever Mary Frances wasn't there."

"If she impressed Paul, she must be okay," Geri commented. "He's one of the best guys in uniform I know. I know a lot of bosses who would like him to go further, go for a gold shield or for sergeant. They think it's a waste of a good cop for him to just ride patrol."

"Yeah, too bad Paul can't train all these little brats," Sophia suggested. "They sure could learn something from him."

"Most of them will be okay," Geri said. "Give them time to outgrow the need to be macho, and to learn to laugh at themselves. Don't forget, for these guys, when they make a mistake in front of an old-timer like Paul or the others, it affects their self-image, and therefore their manhood. They're afraid and can't talk about it, which makes it worse."

"I know," Sophia agreed. "That's why I think we need more women on the job. They're willing to talk about their feelings. Their self-confidence isn't threatened every time something goes wrong."

"These kids are just learning," Geri said. "And most of them are still terrified when they go out on the streets. They can't admit it so they try to show off, at best; at worst, they try to divert attention to another minority."

"Aren't you afraid?"

"Sometimes, especially if someone is shooting at me," Geri said. "But not like when I first came on the job. And nothing like when I worked in Narcotics."

"That's where I'd like to go." Sophia's eyes lit up. "I'd really like to be picked up by Narcotics. You liked it, didn't you?"

"I loved it," Geri answered. "But I was terrified most of the time."

"More than when you first started on patrol?" Sophia asked.

Geri nodded.

"Why?"

"Every time I went out to make a buy, there was a knot in my stomach," Geri explained. "Fear on patrol was easier to handle. I knew I could call a backup and it was something you learned to live with unless it was an extraordinary situation."

"So what's so different about Narcotics?"

"You're on your own," Geri said. "The whole investigation centers on you, how you handle it. It's not just fear of your own safety, but fear of screwing up. The whole investigation could have gone down the tube if I had done something wrong or said something wrong. It's a different thing entirely.

"Especially when you're doing street buys and you've told them some story and you're meeting them again to make another deal," she went on. "Just before you go out, you review the whole thing in your head and hope you have your story straight.

"This is still a macho job, even if we're the ones doing it," she continued. "You can't admit to anyone that your knees are shaking and your stomach hurts. Sometimes I thought I was keeping the Rolaids company in business. You can't believe how much money I've saved since I got my gold shield and left Narcotics," Geri said with a self-deprecating laugh.

"But you liked it?" Sophia asked again.

"Oh, I loved it." Geri nodded. "You can be creative, use whatever will work. It's just trying to keep it all straight in your head, what you told to who. And there was a safety factor, too. If I was making a big buy, meeting some dealer in a hotel room or apartment, I didn't dare wear a gun or even a wire. If they had searched me, it would have been all over. So I went in clean and kept my fingers crossed."

"I still think that's where I want to go," Sophia said.

"You'd be good," Geri told her. "I don't know too many people in Narcotics anymore, but I'll make a call for you. How long have you been in Anti-Crime?"

"Two years," Sophia replied, her eyes glowing. "I'd really appreciate it if you can help me get there."

"Like I said, I think you'd be good there," Geri repeated. "But don't forget what I just said. I'm not doing you any favors."

"Well, I'd take it as a favor," Sophia said. "I've always wanted a woman rabbi."*

"Now, why would a nice Italian girl like you need a rabbi?" Geri grinned at her and Sophia laughed. "The more I think about it, you really would be good. No one would ever make you for a cop and you can easily pass as Hispanic. But I would think your Anti-Crime team would hate to lose you."

"Norm says I can sit in the guy's pocket and they don't make me," Sophia commented smugly. "I sit down next to mutts on a park bench and they tell me how they're going to pull a job."

"Well, I'll call over there, but I don't have a hook for making any promises," Geri said. "And I don't want to hear about it if you get there and don't like it. But I'll listen if you want to talk about being out there alone."

"It's a deal," Sophia replied.

"Now that we've settled your career, what about your personal life? Should I tell Alex to call you?"

"Sure," Sophia said. "I'll try anything once. Which reminds me, what does he like to eat?"

"I'm not sure he has any preferences," Geri replied. "I've gone to all kinds of restaurants with him. Why?"

"An old friend of mine who is now a psychologist says that's a sure way to tell how good a man is in bed," Sophia said with a grin.

"I'm not sure I understand that," Geri remarked. "But you're not leaving here until you explain."

"It's really simple," Sophia answered. "A guy who only likes the food he grew up with is equally unimaginative in the hay. If he's willing to try something new to eat, he's willing to try something new in bed as well."

Geri laughed and stood up. "I'll remember that one. Now that I think about it, you may have something there." They left money on the table for the check and walked out still laughing.

"I've got my car, I'll drop you off," Sophia offered.

"I accept," Geri said. "And I'll tell Alex to call you. At home. No sense letting the One-Six Anti-Crime Squad know who you're dating before it's necessary."

"You're a very good detective," Sophia said. "You think of everything."

# CHAPTER 17

When the four-to-midnight squad was dismissed after roll call and inspection on Tuesday afternoon, Sergeant Bailey told Mary Frances that Captain DiMilano wanted to see her. Mary Frances couldn't imagine what the CO wanted her for. She knew she hadn't done anything to get a reprimand. She had made her fair share of collars lately, two in each of the last few months; no more or less than anyone else. She checked to be sure her shoes were shined, her uniform pressed and her hair tucked up under her hat. She didn't bother to ask Sergeant Bailey what it was all about, but instead knocked on the door to the CO's office.

"Come in."

"You wanted to see me, sir?" Mary Frances saluted and stood at attention.

"Yes. At ease." Captain DiMilano looked at her carefully, and then, without preamble, said, "I'm putting you in Anti-Crime, starting in two weeks."

"Thank you, sir." Mary Frances wasn't sure if she was pleased or not. The change she had been wanting had come through before she had had time to look for it. Her first thought was that the afternoon/evening schedule would go better with Neal's. But being in Anti-Crime meant she would no longer have Paul as a partner. She wasn't happy about that at all. "I'm glad you have confidence in me."

"I always have," DiMilano said. "I've been waiting for an opening there for you, and with this rash of purse snatchings and robberies we've decided to beef up the unit. You'll start in two weeks, as I've said. Sergeant Bailey knows of the change in your assignment and so does roll call. That's all for now. Good luck."

"Thank you, sir." Mary Frances saluted again, turned and left his office.

Paul was waiting for her when she came out. He had picked up their radios and the keys for the patrol car. "Well?"

"I'm going to Anti-Crime in two weeks," she said.

"That's great. Congratulations, partner." He grinned at her. "But I'll sure hate to lose you. And I'll hate even more having to break in a new partner."

"If I know you, that's what you'll dislike the most about it," she teased him. "If it weren't for the trouble of finding someone to replace me, you wouldn't mind losing me at all."

"Mary Frances, you know that's not true." They had left the precinct and were walking toward the car. She just grinned at him as she slid into the passenger's seat.

"How do you feel about it?" he asked.

"I'm not sure," she replied. "I'll hate to lose you as a partner, but the hours are much better for me. But, boy, will I have to go shopping. I don't have the kind of civilian clothes I can wear with a gun."

"I'll bet Neal will be delighted," Paul said.

"About my new assignment and hours or about my shopping?"

"The hours, of course." He called Central for a radio check, then started the car while she checked hers. "We've had some good times. I'm really going to miss working with you."

"Thanks," she said. "I'll miss you, too, but it's not as if I'm going to another command."

"Yeah, but it won't be the same. How often do you see Sophia at work?"

"I know." Mary Frances looked unhappy. "But you've spoiled

me. None of those guys can match your standards as a partner and Sophia told me some of those Anti-Crime guys are really lousy. I just hope I get a couple of guys who want to work and will let me work with them."

"You can handle that, partner," Paul said reassuringly. "I'll put in a good word for you. I think it's a great move for you."

"Why don't you try for something else?" she asked.

"Come on, Mary Frances, we've talked about this before," he answered. "I worked Anti-Crime years ago. I asked to go back to uniform. I like it better. I'm happy riding in a car for eight hours and then going home. I like patrol work. I'm going to wait until you make deputy inspector and then call and ask for some special assignment."

"It's a deal," she said, laughing. "If I ever get important enough to be a rabbi, you know I'll help you get whatever you want."

"Still, this may be a good move for you, but it's going to be tough on me," Paul remarked.

"Come on, how many partners have you had over the years?"

"Enough to know how hard it is to break in a new one," he answered. "But I'll manage. I just can't see that any of the new kids look very promising."

"How about Sally Weston?"

"That's a thought," he replied. "I'll have to consider it. But I don't think she'll be like you and threaten some kid with an attempted murder charge because I had to chase him."

"I think you're still mad at me about that," Mary Frances said, smiling at him. "I just wanted to scare him a little bit. We had to chase him three blocks after he grabbed that purse and I didn't think it was fair of him to make an old guy like you run so hard. With your weight and all the smoking you do, you could have had a heart attack. He apologized to you, didn't he?"

"Yeah, thanks, partner," Paul said sarcastically. "I really appreciate your taking care of me."

The dispatcher reported that a suspected mugger was seen running along Central Park West in the seventies. They were heading west on Seventy-seventh Street and turned south. Paul drove slowly, looking for a man in a plaid jacket and dungarees, wearing workboots. At Sixty-ninth Street they spotted another patrol car and the two officers from it frisking someone who met the suspect's description. Paul pulled up to ask if everything was all right, got an okay and continued on.

"Remember those guys we picked up around here?" he asked.

Mary Frances nodded. His question brought back an incident she had almost forgotten. A little more than a year ago, near the end of a four-to-twelve tour, they had been driving on Central Park West when she thought she heard something. Paul stopped the car and she again heard cries for help coming from inside the park.

The sound had come from around the playground near the entrance to the restaurant. A couple of footpaths and the bridle trail crossed the area. Mary Frances got out of the car, her flashlight in one hand, her gun in the other. Paul was right behind her. The cries had stopped, but she thought she heard someone groaning and someone else panting.

She swung the flashlight toward the sounds and saw one person on the ground with someone else lying on top of him; they were both facedown. The area was near the section of the park known as the Ramble, a hangout for homosexuals. At first, Mary Frances thought she had stumbled across a case of male rape. She yelled, "Police! Don't move!"

In order to get her radio out while she still held her gun, she tucked the flashlight under her chin. Its beam pointed down, but still cast enough light so that she could see the person on top of the pile when he stood up. Paul was no longer behind her and she wasn't sure what had happened to him. The man getting up was big—very big—and she called a 10-85 forthwith* on the radio for help. Just then, Paul had reached the group, looking somewhat disheveled. He stopped near the second person on the ground, and the guy grabbed Paul around the knees to haul himself up.

Mary Frances could hear the sirens of the other units coming toward them and ordered the large man to lie down again. It was an unusual posture for searching someone, but there was nothing for him to lean against. The big man had started yelling that he had been robbed, and so did the smaller one.

Mary Frances began to frisk the bigger one, who was screaming that he was an innocent victim. She told him to be quiet and when he continued to yell, she kicked him in the groin. That produced another sharp yell, then silence. She muttered, "I guess I finally got your attention. Don't move again, or I'll kick you again."

Paul, by this time, had frisked the small man, who was claiming he had been robbed by the big man. Both men were handcuffed and taken back to the precinct. On the way, Mary Frances and Paul tried to figure out what had happened, but decided to wait until they could question the pair in comfort and with enough light to see if they were lying. They both figured it might be a drug deal gone sour.

They marched the two into the precinct and got their first good look at them. The smaller of the pair, the one who had been on the bottom, was Hispanic. When questioned, he claimed he had been walking through the park from the East Side, on his way home. He insisted the bigger man had stopped him as he reached the western edge of the park, asking for a cigarette. He had not only given him a cigarette, but stopped to light it. But when he turned away, the big man grabbed him, started hitting him and demanded his money. The attack made him drop the rest of his pack of cigarettes.

The big man had a slightly different story. He had been walking through the park, too, but from west to east. He said he had stopped at his cousin's house to pick up a pair of shoes his wife had loaned to his cousin. He claimed the smaller man had approached him and asked if he wanted to party. Afraid of getting AIDS and not attracted to homosexual sex, he had been angered by the invitation and started to beat up the Hispanic man.

While Paul and Mary Frances were listening to the two stories and trying to decide which to believe, the desk sergeant came looking for them. A third man had come into the precinct, to see if the police had picked up the big guy whom he had seen attacking a little Puerto Rican in the park. To this third man, it looked like a mugging, but that didn't confirm the little man's story.

Mary Frances asked that a sector car go back to the place in the park where the two had been fighting and look for either the pack of cigarettes the smaller guy claimed to have dropped when attacked or the shoes that had not been on the big man when he was arrested. The search unit came back empty-handed, which didn't help them decide which story was true.

An ambulance was called because both men claimed to have been hurt in the fight. The Puerto Rican announced he was sure he had bitten his attacker on the hand and the EMS technician found the bite marks. The smaller man had bruises on his face from being punched.

After conferring with the lieutenant, listening to the two stories again and watching the pair glare at each other, Paul and Mary Frances decided to believe the smaller man's story of being mugged. When she talked with the assistant district attorney on duty, who ultimately had the authority to decide what the formal charges would be, she explained the conflicting stories and the confusion. The ADA agreed with their interpretation, so the big man was charged not just with assault, but also with attempted robbery.

The whole situation had been like something out of a vaudeville routine and everyone in the precinct had laughed about it for days afterward. Paul was furious because he had gotten dirty, having tripped on his way into the park. That's why he had taken so long to catch up with Mary Frances. He had come back to the precinct looking as if he had been dragged through the mud, feet first, while Mary Frances was still neat and clean. It had been one of their funnier collars, mostly because of the confusion and the screaming and the time it had taken to sort everything out.

Mary Frances smiled again, remembering the incident, but decided not to tease Paul about tripping. They were just cruising the sector and the dispatcher sent them to a noise complaint, a car alarm sounding. When they got to the location they found a new Mercedes with the alarm screeching and the headlights flashing. Just as they pulled up, the alarm shut itself off, so they kept going.

They drove a while longer, then heard a sector car from One-Six report they were following a possible rape suspect on Broadway. The suspect was in a beat-up blue Ford missing one front headlight, heading south from Eighty-sixth Street. Paul turned at Seventy-ninth Street and waited at the intersection. When they saw the car, he turned on the lights and siren of the patrol car for a few seconds, to get the driver's attention and motion him over. The other sector car was right behind the Ford and also pulled over.

Ellen Fletcher and Clare Roberts got out and came up to the car. The driver was ordered out and told to put his hands against the car roof. Ellen explained that he might be the guy who had been beating up hookers and stealing their money. At least, that's what the girls on Broadway had told them.

"You should have seen them," she said, still laughing. "About ten of them, all wearing those white boots with spike heels, running down the street in their tight little skirts and holding their boobs to keep them from bouncing, flagging us to chase this car. They told us he was the one, so we went after him. You want the collar?"

Mary Frances looked at Paul, then shook her head. "No, he's yours. You were after him first, we just backed you up when we heard you on the radio."

"Thanks." Ellen and Clare handcuffed the driver and put him in the back of their patrol car. "Can one of you drive his car back to the house? We'll decide what to do with it later."

Mary Frances nodded and got into the Ford. She checked the glove compartment and under the seat for possible weapons, but didn't find anything. The car would be more thoroughly searched at the precinct. She parked it in the tiny lot behind the building. Paul followed her, she got back in the RMP and they resumed patrol.

"I'm sorry I missed that," Paul said. "It must have been something, to see those hookers running down the street." Mary Frances laughed.

"Yeah. I like most of the girls who work Broadway," she

remarked. "They're not vicious like some of the downtown whores. Most of them are just kids. I'd like to get them straightened out, but they won't help themselves."

"Well, if you're going into Anti-Crime, they can help you," Paul pointed out. "Keep up your contacts with them. They're the best source of information on the street. A lot of cops don't like them, but I've found if you treat them fairly, they'll be straight with you, unless they're junkies."

"I've gotten along fairly well with them so far," Mary Frances said. "I listen to their stories. One of them told me she charges ten times more for a lay than a blow job because she has to get undressed. That never occurred to me."

Paul looked embarrassed but didn't say anything, so Mary Frances decided to tease him a bit. "Another one was showing me how she keeps a rubber in her mouth for blow jobs. She said it was cleaner. She gave me one and I was trying to learn how to do it when the lieutenant walked in. I thought he would turn purple. I was pretty red myself," she finished, laughing.

"Will you stop?" Paul mumbled. "A nice Catholic girl like you shouldn't know those things."

"Come on." Mary Frances was astonished. "Paul, I'm a married woman with a kid. I'm not right out of the convent. I've been a nurse and a cop. You sound like I'm barely old enough to wear a bra."

She watched as he turned even redder. He just shook his head and changed the subject. "You won't have to do any more dishes for DOA's now that you're going to Anti-Crime. That should be easier on your nails."

Mary Frances went along with him. "You're not going to let me forget that one, are you?"

"Why should I?" he replied. "First you tell me how you make Neal do the dishes because you don't want to mess up your nails, but when we go to a DOA what do you do but wash the dishes. That's nuts."

She didn't bother answering him. Paul was referring to an aided case they had been called on, a possible heart attack. When they got to the apartment, the man had already died. His wife was hysterical. She kept crying that her husband was dead and her mother-in-law would be coming over and the house was a mess. Mary Frances could understand how she felt. The two male EMS attendants and Paul were close to laughter that the woman was so worried about her housekeeping when her husband had just dropped dead.

But Mary Frances had understood and she went into the kitchen, did the dishes and straightened up. Paul teased her for months, but Mary Frances understood what was upsetting the woman. Her husband's sudden death was enough in itself; the fact that her kitchen was dirty and her mother-in-law was coming over was just more than she could handle. It was just the kind of mundane problem people suffering from shock and grief fixate on. Men somehow couldn't understand how much something like that would bother a woman at such a time.

That got her thinking about DOA's. Probably because of her training as a nurse, she had not been as upset by them as most new cops were. She had seen bodies before she came on the job, so they weren't as gruesome to her. She remembered when their class at the Academy toured the Medical Examiner's office. Even Sophia had turned slightly green and come close to losing her breakfast, but Mary Frances hadn't been upset. She found the tour fascinating, although she didn't think she would like to work in the autopsy room.

When they first walked in, the place reminded her of an operating room with the bright lights and the bodies laid out on tables. But the pathologists didn't wear masks, and the atmosphere was devoid of the sense of urgency surrounding surgeons who were cutting live tissue. This tissue was already dead and the blood just drained to the floor. Some of the bodies were near the end of the examination procedure, so there were gaping holes in the chests with organs sitting next to them on the tables. Brains were exposed and ropes of intestines draped on the edges of gurneys. The whole scene looked like a mad scientist's lab.

But Mary Frances wasn't bothered by the blood or the sight of lungs, hearts and stomachs. She was more appalled by the casual treatment of the bodies. Old women, children, young men of all races, all lay totally naked and exposed on the metal gurneys, waiting their turn to be cut open. Tags hung from the toe of each corpse to identify someone's child, lover, parent. Now, they had no more dignity than the carcasses in a butcher shop.

The class had passed a huge cold storage locker, just down the hall from the autopsy room. The door had been open and Mary Frances had seen naked bodies stacked on the shelves that circled the room from floor to ceiling. There were no longer any separate identities for a naked, dead body stored next to a dozen others. She had been bothered by that more than the sickly sweet smell of the place or the sight of blood everywhere.

Intellectually, Mary Frances knew that in a city of eight million, a lot of people died every day. She understood that autopsies had to be performed whenever there was a question about the cause of death or evidence that a crime had been committed. The sheer number of such cases required an assembly line–like operation, but she preferred not to see it firsthand. As a nurse she had learned to respect the dignity of the dying and the dead and the scenes at the Medical Examiner's office had not been easy to forget.

The radio in the car crackled, calling for one-six Henry. Paul answered and they were sent to a car alarm again, in the same location. When they arrived, they found the same Mercedes with its alarm screeching again. This time, it did not shut itself off right away. In typical New York fashion, people were hanging out of the windows yelling, "Turn it off." Paul got out of the car and tried to get into the Mercedes to turn off the alarm. It stopped again before he could do so.

"I hate car alarm complaints," Mary Frances said when he got back in the RMP.

"I know. I do, too, but they are annoying to people in the neighborhood," Paul answered. "A lot of them go off for no reason. Too bad we can't do what the Fire Department used to do."

"What's that?"

"I guess you're too young to remember," he replied. "But years ago, if there was a fire and a car was parked at the hydrant, they would break the windows with their axes and pull their hoses through the car. They're not allowed to do that anymore."

Mary Frances laughed. "That is too bad. When I was still in the Bronx, we had a noise complaint, a car alarm. We managed to get the car's door opened, but we couldn't get the damn noise turned off. I took a knife and just cut every wire I could see under the dashboard. That did it. The neighbors had been hanging out their windows, yelling, like they were tonight. When we got out of that car after the noise had stopped, they applauded us."

"Did you get in any trouble?"

"Not really. I left a note in the car. The owner filed a complaint with the CCRB, but I had done the paperwork and I was covered. They dropped the complaint," she explained.

"Lucky," he commented. "That damned Civilian Complaint Board never seems to take our side. They'd rather believe some jerk off the street, no matter who he is, as long as he's not a cop."

"I know," Mary Frances said. "Do you remember that do-good lawyer who tried to interfere when we arrested that little punk from the subway?" Paul nodded, grimacing at the memory.

It had been one of the collars that had bothered him the most—three kids, the oldest only ten years old, had robbed a blind newsdealer and run away through the subway tunnel. They surfaced at Seventy-second Street. Paul and Mary Frances heard their description on the radio and saw them as they ran toward Central Park.

They had grabbed the three children and found a gun on the ten-year-old. Paul was handcuffing them to each other and Mary Frances was standing a few feet away, holding the gun taken from the kid, when a resident of the area came along, yelling and pulling on her gun arm.

"What are you doing with those children? I demand that you let them go."

Mary Frances had stayed calm, turned to the man and asked him to identify himself. He did, adding that he was a lawyer and repeated his earlier statement: "I demand that you let them go."

"You can demand all you want," Mary Frances answered. "I don't have to tell you anything. As a matter of fact, under the law, I'm not allowed to say anything about the charges against them because they're juveniles." She turned back to the children.

He had carried on for several more minutes while they waited for another patrol car. Mary Frances finally got tired of listening to him and turned back to face him.

"Mister, if you don't go on about your business and leave us alone to do our job, I'm going to arrest you for obstructing governmental administration."

The lawyer backed off somewhat. "You had your gun out on these children. As a citizen, I have a right to know what you're doing. I'm not going to stand by and let some cop shoot a child on the street."

That made Mary Frances angry and she informed the man that he was under arrest. She wrote the summons and told him when he was due in court to answer the charges. He walked away, still muttering about police brutality to children and the injustice of arresting Good Samaritans. Paul and Mary Frances took the three suspects to the precinct and turned them over to the Juvenile Division.

When the case came up in court, Mary Frances brought the file on the three juveniles with her. The judge listened to the lawyer's story, then asked Mary Frances why she had her gun out. She explained the situation, then added that the lawyer had pulled on her arm and interfered with the arrest process. She showed the judge the folder, explaining that the three children had been referred to Family Court and because they were juveniles, the details of their cases could not be read in open court. She had the minutes if he wanted to read them. The judge fined the lawyer five hundred dollars.

Mary Frances thought about that case occasionally. She wondered if the lawyer really believed she, or any cop, liked arresting children. Mary Frances knew that even the most hard-nosed, cynical bastard on the police force could get upset about the kids. The children, like those she arrested that day, bothered everyone. Where did a ten-year-old get a gun? And what made a six-year-old go along with an armed robbery? Being on the street, seeing children like that who had almost no chance at a life within the law, was the hardest part of the job.

"You're very quiet tonight," Paul remarked.

"Just remembering," Mary Frances said. "Isn't it time to eat?"

"Yeah, any preferences?"

"No, anything is okay," she answered. "But pizza sounds pretty good."

"Okay, there's a new place down the street." He called Central to say they were going on meal and looked for a parking space. There weren't any, so he put the car by a fire hydrant and they got out. They decided they were both hungry enough to split a small pie.

"Did I ever tell you about the guy in the One-Six, before you got there, who pulled a trick on Internal Affairs?" Paul asked Mary Frances.

She could tell he was also in a mood for reminiscing, probably because they had just been told they would soon be splitting up. "I don't remember it. What can you do to IAD that won't get you into more trouble?" she asked.

"He got pissed because someone reported his partner for taking a free cup of coffee or something," Paul started off. "The partner wasn't on the pad* or anything; it really was something like a cup of coffee, and it was admittedly a dumb thing to do after all the stories about the crackdown on corruption. But the IAD investigation really pissed this guy off. His partner was suspended for thirty days without pay and he decided to show them."

"What did he do?"

"He always ate in the same coffee shop when he was on patrol, so he made a deal with the owner," Paul explained. "Instead of paying every time he ate, he ran up a tab and paid it every two weeks, when he got his check. After a while the owner agreed to mail the bill to him at home.

"So he ate there every day and every day he walked out without paying." Paul grinned. "Sure enough, someone called IAD and they sent an investigator. The IAD guy sat in the coffee shop every day for a month or more, making notes on what this guy ate and how often he was there and when he left without paying.

"Finally, they had enough evidence and they called him down for a hearing," Paul went on. "When he got the order to go downtown, he knew what it was, of course, and he was all prepared. He had the canceled checks with him, and he even brought the owner of the coffee shop along to testify that he paid his bill in full every two weeks. He explained innocently to IAD that he didn't like to carry money with him when he was on patrol."

Mary Frances laughed. "He's lucky they didn't get really pissed and tail him for the next six months." The pizza came and while they ate, the conversation moved to their families. Paul's son had won his first varsity wrestling match and she congratulated him. He asked if Stevie had shown any interest in sports yet, and Mary Frances laughed, pointing out that at two, he was still having trouble walking and running.

They talked for a few more minutes, then went back to the car to resume patrol. Mary Frances drove around randomly, hoping something would come over the radio for them. After an hour of cruising, the dispatcher sent them to a dispute in one of the last SRO's left on the West Side. It turned out to be a loud radio annoying someone. They convinced the owner of the radio to turn it down.

On their way out, while they were waiting in the hall for the elevator, Mary Frances noticed a man standing in the stairway at the far end of the hall who seemed to get angry when he spotted the two police officers. Paul was watching the elevator floor lights and hadn't noticed him, but Mary Frances was watching the man. She heard him say: "Suck my black dick, motherfucker." She turned toward him and he took off down the stairs. She followed, calling Paul.

The man was tall and had long legs; he seemed to leap down the stairs, but she was only a flight behind him. She could hear Paul lumbering after her, calling, "What's wrong? What happened?" The chase continued out of the building and into the next one, a six-flight tenement with no lock on the front door.

The long-legged man was getting ahead of her, and as Mary Frances reached the fifth floor of the tenement she realized she had no reason to arrest him if she did catch him.

She stopped running and started back down the stairs, finding Paul on the second-floor landing, still coming up. "What the hell happened?" he said angrily. "I was standing there, waiting for the elevator, and you took off like a shot. Where did you go? And why? Were you chasing someone?"

She explained what happened and Paul started to laugh. "This is the partner that doesn't like to chase anyone? That's what it takes to make you run, huh. I'll have to warn your new partners about that. What were you going to arrest him for? Using foul language on a nice Irish girl?"

"I don't know what happened." She grinned sheepishly. "I heard him say that and I just flipped out. He ran and I took off after him. I was just mad."

They walked back to the car in time to hear the dispatcher call them with a noise complaint, another car alarm. The address was the same one they had already checked twice that night. Paul grimaced as Mary Frances answered Central. When they got to the Mercedes, its alarm was screaming again. It had apparently been going for a while. The neighbors, or someone, had tired of hearing the alarm and had taken their own revenge. The windows were broken and the door panels of the car were scratched on both sides.

Paul called Central for a check of the license plate. The answer came back in a few minutes. The owner lived a few blocks away, so they drove over to tell him his car had been vandalized. He was furious. They tried to explain that they had responded to the car alarm three different times that night and apparently someone had just gotten sick of hearing it.

Mary Frances offered to write up a report on the vandalism. The owner went back with them to where the car was parked. He was even angrier when he saw the amount of damage. Paul and Mary Frances questioned people on the street, but of course no one remembered seeing anyone near the car. They filled out the forms, recommended the man put his car in a garage after he got it fixed and drove back to the precinct.

"Anti-Crime will be more exciting," Paul pointed out. "You won't be complaining about being bored anymore. They're the ones who are expected to make the collars, so you'll have to work."

"I know," Mary Frances replied. "The only thing I regret about the whole thing is leaving you."

"It's always nice to know I'm appreciated." Paul smiled at her. "I'll miss you, too. But no one deserves this chance more. You work hard and you're a good cop, Mary Frances. This is a chance to really get somewhere on this job. I've been expecting you to get this for a while now. I knew DiMilano was watching you. This is the first step up and I'll be expecting big things of you."

She smiled. "Well, I've still got two more weeks riding with you, so we have some time to do big things together."

"Not anymore tonight," he said. "But there's always tomorrow."

# CHAPTER 18

**A**lex Grandey called Sophia before she left home on Tuesday. She agreed to meet him for a drink after work at one of the quieter places on Columbus Avenue. They made the date for 11 P.M. with the understanding that if something delayed Sophia, she would call him. She hung up and felt like a teenager. He had sounded very eager. Geri must have just called him and he hadn't waited even a day to call her for a date.

She decided to wear good slacks instead of her usual jeans in honor of the occasion. She would have liked to really get dressed up, but knew that would not only cause comments from the guys at work, but also make her job more difficult. But as a cop, Alex would know why she had to dress in slacks all of the time. If this date went well, she would have other opportunities to dress up, times when she would not be coming from or going to work.

Sophia remembered how much she hated wearing a uniform when she was still on patrol. The pants were made for men and had to be fixed by a tailor to fit. Even so, she always felt awkward and self-conscious in the uniform. She used to tell Mary Frances that the women in uniform looked as if they were wearing blue Hefty trash bags. She couldn't wait to get a plainclothes assignment, but that was almost as bad. There was the never-ending problem of finding something to wear that would hide her gun. And she hated always having to wear pants for work. Sometimes she felt like a construction worker.

One time, while she was still on patrol, she and her partner had gone out in response to a call from a woman who said she had been hit in the head by her boyfriend. After they had called the ambulance and cleaned up some of the blood, a really good-looking guy from the next apartment stuck his head in the door to see what was wrong. Since the others were taking care of the woman, who had stopped bleeding, Sophia stood in the doorway, talking to this guy. He turned out to be an actor in one of the soaps that she liked.

She remembered thinking about her lousy luck in meeting a guy like that when she looked her worst. Her hair was tucked up under her cap; she had no makeup on; she wasn't wearing any jewelry and she had fifteen pounds or more of hardware around her hips. Other women could look their best at work, but policewomen looked terrible. She liked dressing up and looking feminine, but just couldn't do so as long as she stayed on the job.

When she got to the office, she learned that Norm had called in sick. Van said he wasn't sure who would be riding with them to fill in that night. He had tried to ask Sergeant Camillo, but there had been an important conference with Captain DiMilano about the purse snatchings. They would just have to wait for roll call.

Sophia nodded and looked around the squad room. Most of the other teams were present and complete. Only Eddy Bott was standing alone, off in a corner. His partners had recently been transferred and he was still waiting to hook up with another team. Sophia had a feeling he would be riding with them tonight. Going back to when they were both still in uniform, she had never really liked him.

Eddy was the kind of guy who wouldn't take no for an answer, no matter how many times she refused his invitations. He was married and his wife was very jealous, but Sophia wouldn't have gone out with him if he had been single. Eddy couldn't understand that. He had a big mouth and made a comment about every woman in the precinct. If a girl went out with him, she was a slut, a bimbo. If she refused once, she was frigid. If she continued to refuse, as Sophia had done, then he reported that she was gay.

He wasn't much better when it came to the job. He didn't like to work with women, of course. He got out of riding with one whenever he could. Although departmental policy frowned on refusing partners because of gender, most sergeants would find a way to change the pairings. That didn't bother Sophia. Whenever she had been assigned to ride with him on patrol, she herself had asked to switch, even agreeing to take a foot post sometimes to get out of being with him.

Sophia was also offended by the way Eddy worked. He seemed to think he was the Rambo of the NYPD. He acted as if he could handle anything and Sophia thought that was dumb. There was always somebody bigger, tougher, stronger, even crazier for that matter. As a woman and a small one, she didn't go into a situation expecting to overpower it.

Eddy would walk into a dispute and talk tough. Someone would usually react and he would make a collar for resisting arrest, assaulting an officer, whatever he could add. Sophia thought that was dishonest. She preferred to go in soft, trying to settle the dispute. She figured she could always get tougher, call for more backup, invoke the authority of the uniform and the NYPD. But if she was going to make an arrest, it would be for something that had really happened, not because someone was reacting to something she had done to aggravate their behavior.

Sophia and Norm had talked about it a few times. He didn't like Eddy either. Norm agreed that cops who talked too tough got themselves into trouble, and he had not argued with Sophia when she pointed out that it was usually male cops who worked that way. Norm was a big guy, but he wasn't always trying to prove something. He often said he wanted to go home to his family every night. He insisted he wasn't on the job to make some doctor's career.

Sophia wasn't sure how Van felt about Eddy. There were times when she got the feeling that Van put up with her only because Norm did. Originally, she and Norm had been working together with another partner. When their first partner was transferred, Van joined their team. Sophia liked Van, but she wasn't sure he was all that comfortable with her. All in all, she didn't think this was shaping up as a fun evening for her.

As she expected, Eddy was riding with her and Van. The sergeant didn't have too much more in the way of announcements. He issued another warning about the purse snatcher on Columbus, explaining that the guy was getting bolder and had hit a couple of places a night. Either he or a copycat was starting to show up in some of the Broadway hangouts as well.

They got in the car and Eddy confirmed her fears about the coming tour within a minute. "Hey, it's Steel Tits. How are you doing, sweetheart?" She nodded and slid in the backseat. Eddy got in next to Van, who was driving. Sophia didn't mind the crude name. When she came to the precinct, she spent the first year refusing all invitations, even those for a drink with other cops after work. Steel Tits was only one of the names she had been called. She was also known as the Iron Maiden and the Ice Queen.

She had realized her divorce was common knowledge and she was determined no one was going to be able to say anything about her or spread any rumors. Now she would go out occasionally for a drink with her partners and one or two other guys on the squad, but she was still very careful not to give anyone reason to talk about her.

Van cruised down Columbus Avenue, talking with Eddy. They commented on the women on the sidewalk, the women in the precinct and the women they both knew. Van got cruder with Eddy's encouragement. Sophia sat quietly in the back, trying to ignore them. This was going to be even worse than she had expected.

Eddy was so busy talking, he didn't seem to be watching the street. He kept Van distracted, too. He proposed they go up Riverside Drive. Van turned at Seventy-second Street. Sophia started to ask what they were supposed to be looking for on Riverside when the people were on Broadway and Columbus, but she just kept quiet, knowing she was outnumbered. They moved up Riverside, took a service road and made a turn to make the trip south.

"Those kids coming up out of the park look dirty,"* Sophia said, pointing at a group of teenagers who were running in a pack. They crossed Riverside and disappeared down a side street. Van kept driving south. He hadn't even looked around when she pointed out the group of teenagers. Eddy also ignored her and Sophia sat back again.

Was this the way it was going to be all night? she wondered. They would treat her as if she didn't exist, just ignoring anything she said. Were they going to spend the night acting as if she didn't know anything, couldn't possibly see something they had missed? It had happened to her before in radio cars. She got out of those situations as quickly as possible. Well, this was only for one night, but it was sure to put her in a bad mood by the time she met Alex.

What was wrong with these guys? Were they really so insecure that they couldn't even admit the possibility that a woman would say something worth listening to? She couldn't think of any other reason for the way they were acting. Norm had once tried to explain it to her. He thought some men were so afraid of being found inadequate, they lived in a fantasy where they were strong, brave and smart and all women were weak, defenseless and irrational. Sophia had to laugh. She knew how illogical Van could be. He never could figure out how credit cards worked and finally got so deep in debt the year before that he had come close to going bankrupt.

This was going to be a very dull tour if they were going to continue like this for the next eight hours. Eddy was directing Van now, and he seemed to be suggesting only the spots away from traffic and crowds, places unlikely to produce anything. Sophia was surer than ever that her instincts about him were right. He was the kind of cop who did as little as he could get away with, who didn't mind being mediocre as long as he could slide by.

Sophia had run into that attitude before, and not just on this job. When she had worked in an office, there had been a few people like that, too. She couldn't understand that attitude. She always wanted to be the best at whatever she did. She liked the recognition she got and the satisfaction of knowing she had tried her best.

She wondered how Eddy had got to Anti-Crime. It wasn't exactly an elite unit, but they were expected to do most of the arrest work in a precinct. Uniforms were too obvious to bad guys, too easy to spot. Anti-Crime cops worked in plainclothes, trained to spot potential troublemakers, followed them and arrested them in the act. The Anti-Crime squads accounted for 75 percent or more of the arrests in most precincts and they were deployed whenever special situations developed, especially robberies, auto thefts, muggings and similar crimes.

Do-nothing cops rarely got assigned to Anti-Crime. If they did, they were often sent back as soon as their disinterest became obvious. A few always slipped through, of course, usually because they knew someone higher up. Sophia wasn't sure whom Eddy knew, but she had no doubt someone was protecting him. He was always commenting on how other people got special deals because of hooks. He sounded too defensive about it to Sophia.

They had left Riverside and were now driving down Central Park West. It was the middle of the afternoon and Central Park West, like Riverside Drive, was filled with mothers pushing strollers and carriages, leading children by the hand or carrying them in their arms after an outing in the park. At this time of the day, most of the action would be on Broadway, Columbus or Amsterdam, the streets with restaurants and stores. Those were the places where teenagers hung out after school, where commuters stopped to pick up dinner on the way home or waited on line at a new chic bar.

Sophia thought about suggesting a new direction for Van's aimless cruising, but didn't. They wouldn't listen to her. Van knew the pattern they usually followed at this time of day. He was driving and chose to follow Eddy's directions. Had he objected or wanted to do more, he would have said so. So she sat back and watched the streets, waiting to see what would happen.

As she expected, they drove for a couple of hours without

finding anything. Sophia spent most of the time wondering about her date. She still couldn't place Alex Grandey, but going on Geri's recommendation, she was looking forward to meeting him. She hadn't gone out on a date for a couple of months. Her work didn't lend itself to meeting many new men, except other cops, of course. There were very few of them she found interesting enough to see on her own time.

She had been dating a civilian for a few weeks, but that hadn't worked out. Sophia had the impression he looked on her as a sociological exhibit; he was always questioning her about the job, but didn't seem really interested in her as a person. He had also been uptight about the gun, always asking if she had it with her. On their last date, he had suggested it might be safer if he carried it. *That* comment had convinced her not to see him again.

A voice on the radio reported a foot chase after a purse-snatching suspect. The suspect was running toward Central Park West on Eighty-fifth Street. Van had stopped for a red light at Eighty-sixth and Central Park West. Sophia jumped out of the car and ran the block south, not even bothering to see if Van and Eddy were following. Whoever had called on the radio would be coming from the other direction. Looking down the block, she could see a man coming toward her, walking fast, wearing a dark gray jacket and wool hat. He matched the radioed description.

She spotted the Anti-Crime team that had called in the chase way down at the Columbus Avenue end of the block, dodging pedestrians as they tried to catch up with the suspect. He was apparently hoping to lose himself in the park before they caught up with him. He started moving even faster, twisting to look behind him to see how close the chase was getting. He wasn't paying any attention to Sophia, who was standing next to the cars parked on the curb directly in his path.

The suspect ran past her and she swung out between the cars, grabbing his arm and throwing him off balance. At the same time, she kicked him in the shins. He fell and rolled over a couple of times on the sidewalk, but Sophia followed him, kicking him again when he tried to jump up and run off. At first, he clearly thought she was just a passerby who had collided with him accidentally. As she approached him, he started to apologize for knocking into her. He just kept saying, "I'm sorry, lady, I didn't mean to run into you."

He was still apologizing when Sophia got out her handcuffs and pulled his hands behind his back. As the metal rings snapped on his wrists, he stopped in the middle of his apology and started cursing: "Jesus Christ, you're a goddamned cop. Just my fucking luck to run into a goddamned woman cop!"

The three cops who had started the chase had reached them by this time. So had Van and Eddy, who had apparently decided to follow her. The three other cops were swearing, too. They thought Sophia was going to claim the collar, but she surprised them by handing the suspect over to them, saying, "I guess this one's yours." They were pleased and grateful.

Van and Eddy looked annoyed, but she ignored them. She exchanged handcuffs with one of the guys who took the suspect, and walked back to the car. The collar really wasn't hers. She had just been there as backup. The other team had started the chase. They had seen whatever precipitated it and gone after the suspect. She had just helped out.

Van started the car again, but before he moved into the traffic, he turned to look at Sophia. "Why did you give that collar to those guys? That was your collar. You shouldn't have given him up. That was really a dumb thing to do."

"He wasn't mine in the first place," Sophia replied as calmly as she could. She was furious at Van for even suggesting it. She knew the subject wouldn't have come up if Norm had been with them. "The other guys started the chase, and I came in as backup. We work as a team in this job."

Eddy didn't say anything, not that she had expected him to. Still, after all his put-downs of women cops, he could at least have acknowledged that she had taken action, subdued a suspect much taller and stronger than herself, and had not needed the help of another officer. Then she laughed at herself. If he was as insecure as she suspected, the last thing he would do was publicly acknowledge that someone smaller and lighter than he had been able to act effectively. She sat back and waited for the tour to end.

Sophia realized suddenly that she was lucky that Van and Eddy were acting the way they were. If Norm had been there, they would have been really working the streets, looking for troublemakers. She could have easily gotten involved in a long drawn-out arrest that would have meant breaking her date. This way, the odds were good that she would not be stuck working overtime and could meet Alex as planned. She figured she could at least be grateful to Eddy for that.

When she had accepted the date, what had been in the back of her mind, Sophia realized, was to give any collars to Norm and Van and go on her way after the tour. She would probably still do that if something happened, but she really disliked the thought of giving Eddy a free ride.

When their meal hour came up, Sophia listened as the two men debated Italian versus Chinese. Neither bothered to ask her what she wanted, and she didn't say anything. They finally decided on pizza and she went along without an objection. She didn't mind pizza, even though she resented not being asked. But then, she resented the whole day. The part that really upset her was the whole new side of Van she was seeing. Sophia thought about talking to him about it once Norm was back, but realized that wouldn't do any good. What did she expect, an apology? For what? She decided just to forget the whole day, but made a promise to herself never to work with Eddy Bott again.

After dinner the night continued as the afternoon had gone. Eddy was driving, and he aimlessly cruised the streets least likely to have any action. They had never even asked her if she wanted to drive. Sophia spent the rest of the shift trying to tamp down her building resentment and anger. She hadn't been faced with the kind of chauvinistic, arrogant attitude she had been hearing all day for a long time. She really hoped she didn't take it out on Alex.

Eddy drove back to the precinct, commenting gleefully on how little work they had done. She caught the first flash of annoyance on Van's face. However he felt about women, Sophia knew that Van liked being a cop, liked the work and usually complained the loudest on slow days. Apparently, he really hadn't realized that Eddy had been trying to get out of doing anything. Now, she got the impression Van was feeling he had been used. And he had been. Van had been having a good time laughing and joking and making dumb comments, and hadn't really paid attention to the pointlessness of their cruising. Maybe he had learned something.

"It's been a charming evening, gentlemen. Let's do it again sometime," Sophia said sarcastically as she got out of the car. Eddy didn't react, but Van knew her well enough by now to give her a strange look. She didn't really care if he knew she was angry or not. She was and it was largely his fault. It would be interesting to see what he said about it, if anything. But they had the next day off and when they came back to work on Friday, it would be forgotten. She hoped Norm would be back by then.

Sophia went up to the women's locker room. She wasn't going to change clothes, but she had to take off the bulletproof vest she was wearing. The damn thing was like a corset. She washed her face and put on some mascara. She had stopped wearing mascara at work years before, after getting sprayed with Mace. Her eyes had teared for ten minutes and the mascara had run down her face, so that she looked as if she had painted lines on her cheeks.

She was meeting Alex in the same place she had seen Geri the night before. Sophia liked the restaurant. It was convenient to the precinct, had a bar but no jukebox and offered something besides hamburgers to eat. Her car was parked near the stationhouse, but it wasn't worth trying to find another parking spot. The restaurant was only a few blocks away. Sophia walked quickly. She was early, but it was cold out and she preferred to wait for him inside.

She saw no slender men with graying hair at the bar and none sitting alone at any of the tables. She sat down at the bar and after a moment's thought decided on a hot apple cider with rum. It came in a glass mug with a stick of cinnamon and reminded her of Halloween parties she had been to as a kid. She sat sipping the warm, sweet drink. Someone sat down next to her and she glanced up to see a vaguely familiar, smiling face.

"Geri said you might not recognize me, but I assured her I would know you," he said. "I'm Alex Grandey." He put his hand out and she shook it, returning his smile.

He sat down and ordered a drink for himself. They chatted for a few minutes, making small talk and discovering some mutual acquaintances on the job. After about thirty minutes, Alex asked about her tour that day.

"It was pretty awful and I've been sitting here trying to forget it so I wouldn't take it out on you," she replied honestly.

"Well, I know it's kind of soon, but Geri always says I'm a pretty good listener," he offered. "I promise not to take it personally, and maybe it would make you feel better to talk about it. Since you weren't late and didn't call, it couldn't have been a collar that upset you, so it must have been one of our colleagues."

"Now I know why you made detective," she said with a smile. "You're right and it's all really dumb and not worth talking about, except that I've spent the last eight hours biting my tongue and I'm not sure I can swallow any more blood."

"That bad? Then I insist you talk about it. Otherwise, I'll leave you and take a raincheck until you're in a better mood."

"Okay," she agreed, smiling. "But remember, this wasn't my idea. Or maybe it was and I apologize in advance. I'm grateful for the offer to listen." She told him about Eddy Bott and how they had wasted the tour riding on streets that were empty of potential problems. She didn't mention Eddy's attitude toward her or his constant comments about other women, but Alex apparently guessed that part of it.

He was sympathetic and understanding. He suggested that Eddy probably felt insecure and unsure of himself around her and had to act tough so no one would guess how uptight he was. Sophia agreed, but said that didn't make it any easier to accept when she had to listen to Eddy Bott for eight hours.

Alex smiled. "Let's find a table, unless you want to sit here?" She nodded, and they found a table. After glancing at the menu, Alex announced that he intended to eat and Sophia realized she, too, was hungry. She lit a cigarette after they ordered and he frowned.

"I've been nagging Geri about smoking," he commented. "It looks like I'm going to have someone else to nag."

"You don't smoke?" Sophia ignored the hint that they would be seeing more of each other, although she realized she was pleased to hear it.

"No, I stopped two years ago," he answered, then returned to the original subject. "I've had several women partners since Geri. I'm always amazed at the male cops who refuse to work with women. I wouldn't work with just any woman, or just any guy for that matter, but I've found all of my women partners have had an unusual perspective."

"What do you mean?" Sophia was intrigued by his offhand observation.

"I was working with one woman and we had a job, a shot fired that turned out to be a murder. At first, it looked like random violence. It was about twelve years ago in Brooklyn, the Prospect Park section. The area wasn't fashionable yet, but some brownstones had been renovated. A banker and his wife had been visiting friends in one of them. They came out to find their car with a flat tire. While he was fixing it, someone walked up to him, fired at him several times and ran into the park.

"We were the first car on the scene and the guy was lying there, still bleeding. His wife was standing next to him, sobbing into a handkerchief. She told us what happened and we roped off the scene and put in a call to homicide. Another radio car came by and they searched the park. They didn't find the killer, but they did find the gun." Alex liked telling stories and talking about work, Sophia could tell.

"The detectives arrived and they discovered that the air had been let out of the flat tire. They began to suspect this wasn't just a random shooting. Anyway, our job was done there and we left to go back on patrol. As we got into the car, my partner kept saying the wife knew about the murder."

Alex seemed to be waiting for a reaction, so Sophia asked, "What made her say that?"

"That's what I said." He grinned. "She said the wife wasn't

really crying, just pretending. A few days later, the story made the papers. The gun had clear prints and the detectives picked up the killer. He admitted he'd been paid to kill the banker." He leaned back and waited.

"Who?"

"The wife's relatives," he said triumphantly. "The husband had been running around and was talking about getting a divorce. She was angry and told her family. They decided to bump him off. She knew it was planned, but didn't know when and how it would happen. And it was my partner who noticed that she wasn't really upset even while he was bleeding at her feet."

"Nice story," Sophia said. "Too bad we can't tell it to every cop, not that it would make a difference."

"I know," Alex remarked sympathetically. "I've been listening to Geri and other women friends on the job for years. Like I said, I don't understand the cops who aren't willing to give you girls a chance.

"Maybe things were different in the old days, before radios and when people knew they would get a knock on the head if they didn't listen to The Man,"* he continued. "But those days are long gone and with walkie-talkies, backup can be there instantly. And I know, as do most other cops who are really honest with themselves, that it's not very often that you need brute strength."

"I've found I need common sense a lot more frequently than strength," Sophia offered. "Not that there haven't been a few times when I would have liked to be bigger or stronger. But, as you said, I can always use the radio and more cops will be there in seconds."

"I think you're just the right size, if that helps," he said, grinning at her. "But it must be hard for you girls. Especially knowing there are so many things on the job that you do as well as, if not better than, most men. And to see so many men who aren't doing the job right but get away with it, while the women who are lousy are always the center of attention, must be frustrating as hell. Especially when all women are lumped together under the least common denominator."

"I guess that's what makes me maddest," Sophia agreed.

"My partners like me and like working with me, although after tonight, I'm not so sure about one of them. Norm, at least, doesn't paint all women with the same brush, but I'm sure Van wouldn't hesitate. And if he thought of me at all, it would be as the exception who proves the rule."

"Funny how many exceptions I know," Alex said. "I had three women partners before I made detective and they were all good cops. And I've been working with women in the Detective Bureau and they're all good, too. Of course, a lot of the men I know think all women get their gold shields by sleeping with a chief.* But some men will admit women can do the job."

"That's nice of them," Sophia muttered sarcastically.

"Come on. I don't feel that way," Alex said. "The women I've worked with provided a different perspective—they saw things differently. I would see a billboard and she would see what was written on it. Women see more detail, they pick up on things that men don't see and hear things that men ignore. I like working with women."

"I know all the men on this job aren't hairbags, but the ones who are just add to the other crap you have to deal with," Sophia said. "I am so tired of it all, the red tape and the petty bureaucracy, the bosses who don't back you up and the nit-picking rules and all the other stuff. And then to have to deal with stupid partners as well. I've been wondering lately if it's worth it."

"Let's talk about something else," she suggested. "I've had enough of the Police Department for one day."

"I agree," Alex said. "What do you want to talk about?"

They started with films, went on to favorite books and then to places they liked in New York and things they liked to do. Both loved the city and the diversions it offered. They sat talking until the restaurant closed.

Alex drove her back to her car and they made another date for Friday night. Sophia went home feeling better than she had thought possible a few hours earlier. Alex Grandey was a definite improvement over sitting at home alone.

# CHAPTER 19

After her tour on patrol with Mary Frances, Sally spent the next three days back at her desk. She found being back inside after the excitement of being on patrol especially hard, but comforted herself by remembering that it was only for a few more days. On Friday, Sergeant Bailey told her she would be needed on patrol again. At roll call, she learned she was assigned to ride with Frank Gordon, whose regular partner was at the police firing range for the day, taking the semiannual firearms qualifying course.

After inspection, Sally stood to one side, wondering how she could ask Sergeant Bailey for another assignment. She really hated the thought of riding with Frank. Maybe she could volunteer for a foot post? While she was still trying to make up her mind, she saw Frank go up to the sergeant. She heard him say something about his wife and suspected they were talking about her because Bailey was glancing her way.

Sally walked up to them and said that she preferred to walk a foot post, if there was a problem. Bailey sighed with relief, nodded and looked around. He motioned to Ellen Fletcher, who had also been assigned a foot post. Her partner had a court date and extra foot posts had been ordered because of the purse snatchings. Bailey told her about the change of assignment, but

Ellen apparently knew Frank, too, and said she also preferred the foot post.

One of the men was finally given the seat with Frank, and Sally was assigned to Seventy-ninth Street, from Broadway to Columbus. Ellen had an adjoining post, Central Park West to Amsterdam, Seventy-seventh to Seventy-ninth, so they walked from the precinct together. They had the same meal hour, and made plans to meet at a small coffee shop on Broadway and Seventy-ninth. Sally was a little nervous, but Ellen reassured her that the foot post would be no different than a radio car.

"Talk to the store owners," she suggested. "They'll be glad to see you. Walk very slowly; you see more that way and it makes it harder for someone to follow you. Spend most of your time at the Broadway and Columbus Avenue ends. There's a subway stop on Broadway that's a potential problem and on Columbus there will be tourists coming from the museum and walking along the street. And if you get bored, you can always chase the street vendors who don't have licenses." Sally nodded.

Ellen walked along Seventy-ninth Street with her to Columbus, pointing out corners that might conceal muggers or drunks once it got dark. They both checked their radios and parted at Columbus Avenue, Sally to make the return trip to Broadway, Ellen to walk south to Seventy-seventh Street before starting her rounds.

Sally liked Ellen, but she didn't know her very well. From listening to her in the locker room, Sally knew she was smart and funny. Ellen was a tall, thin woman with long dark hair. Her lanky body looked good in the uniform. She was one of the few women Sally knew who looked attractive in the outfit. When she was on duty, she wore her hair in two long braids pinned to the top of her head. Ellen always seemed to know what to say, too. Sally knew that none of the men made sexist remarks to her anymore, because her replies were always such good put-downs.

It was a cold afternoon, but crisp, without a hint of rain. Sally waved to a couple of merchants, who smiled and waved back as she walked. A man was selling flowers in front of the subway station and she looked for his vendor's license. When he couldn't show her one, she told him he would have to move. He argued that he was there every evening.

She sympathized, but explained it wasn't legal for him to be selling without a license. As long as no one said anything, he had been okay. But she was on this post tonight and if the sergeant came by and he was still there, she would be in trouble. He understood and packed up his flowers without a further argument.

A crowd came out of the subway exits and she stood on the corner, watching as people walked passed her. There hadn't been anyone hanging around the stairs to the train platform, so she didn't expect trouble. The streetwise thieves usually waited at the street-level exits, grabbed a purse or briefcase and ran off before the victim realized what had happened. So far, this subway crowd was just an ordinary group of people returning home from work.

When they reached the top of the stairs at the subway exit, they spread in all directions, heading for their individual destinations. After a few minutes, the crowd diminished, then disappeared, and the subway stairs were empty again. Sally started to walk east, toward Columbus, this time on the north side of the street. She passed some kids playing hopscotch who tagged after the "lady cop" until she reached the corner. They went back to their game and she crossed Amsterdam, continuing toward Columbus.

The two blocks of her foot post were among Sally's favorites in the precinct: a typical West Side mixture of big old apartment houses, restaurants and stores. Seventy-ninth Street was a major crosstown street, with an exit from the West Side Highway at one end and the American Museum of Natural History at the other. Traffic was two-way to Columbus, where the museum grounds interrupted the street. There were some brownstones on the Broadway to Amsterdam block, old-style narrow houses with apartments on the upper floors and everything from a Chinese-Thai restaurant to a veterinarian on the street level.

A big apartment building on Amsterdam and Seventy-ninth that had been an SRO hotel had recently been renovated to a luxury condominium. A fancy restaurant had replaced the lumber store that used to occupy half the ground floor and a trendy boutique now had the space that once belonged to a hardware store. Across the street stood the Gloucester, one of the first of the new apartment buildings on the West Side. A twenty-story brick structure that had seemed out of place when it was constructed, the building now was typical of the area.

The next block, from Amsterdam to Columbus, was made up of mostly older buildings that had more ornate exteriors than the new ones. Sally liked to look at the gargoyles and carvings that decorated them. Many of the upper floors had tiny stone balconies and most of the people who lived there put out flowering planters in the warm months. They added some color and charm to the neighborhood.

Sally reached Columbus, looked up and down the street, and was about to turn and walk back to Broadway when she heard someone calling to her: "Officer, officer." She turned and saw a couple with two children, waving from across the street. She crossed Columbus when the light turned red and neared the four, who were standing just inside the fence that enclosed the grounds of the museum.

The man came up to her. He spoke with a thick Southern accent and asked if it would be okay if they took her picture. She agreed and offered to pose with the children. They were delighted, especially when she gave her uniform hat to the little girl to wear for the picture.

The children's father backed up, looked through the camera, then suggested they stand with the museum in the background. They repositioned themselves and he took the picture. His wife, in the meantime, told Sally that they came from a small town in Georgia and had never seen a woman police officer before. They had heard there were some in New York, but couldn't really believe it. Wasn't she afraid?

Sally talked to them for a few minutes, showing them her radio and explaining that police cars were constantly cruising the area so she could get help almost immediately. That surprised them, but she assured them she felt perfectly safe and didn't worry about being shot or attacked.

The man was surprised to see she had only a .38-calibre

revolver, but she explained that was the only gun allowed by the department. He seemed to know a great deal about guns and said he expected the New York Police to carry heavier automatic weapons for safety. Sally explained that big guns were too dangerous to use in the city because they could too easily endanger bystanders. He said he hadn't thought about that, thanked her for allowing them to take her picture and left.

Sally walked back toward Broadway, thinking about what he had said. It was true that the .38 was an old-fashioned gun. Criminals often carried much more powerful weapons, .357's or even submachine guns, but then, they didn't worry about hurting bystanders.

The .38 was bad enough as far as Sally was concerned. She had been carrying it for more than six months now and she was used to the ten pounds it weighed, but the idea of having a gun with live ammunition still made her nervous. She knew it was a necessary tool on this job, but she had never even held a gun before she came on the Police Department. Sally remembered the day they had received their guns at the Academy, how most of the men in the class had seemed to sit up straighter, strut when they put a gun on, even fondle it.

Most of the women had had very different reactions, she thought. Some of them were familiar with guns and just took it as another part of the job, another piece of equipment. The others were like her, unused to having a gun and a little afraid of it. She had felt some awe as well, knowing she now had the means in her hand to end a human life. She just hoped she never had occasion to use it.

Sally could still remember how she felt the first time she had fired her gun. She had been with her company at the Police Academy and they had gone up to Rodman's Neck, the police firing range in the Bronx. The instructors had carefully taught them how to take the gun apart, clean it and load it. They had explained its potential and repeatedly warned the new recruits about safety precautions. The best position for firing the gun was described: knees bent, feet apart, both hands holding the grip.

When they had finally begun firing, Sally had been surprised at the recoil even after all the warnings. She had squeezed, not pulled, the trigger, surprised at the strength needed to move it. When the gun had fired, her hands jerked back, though she had been expecting a recoil. She fired again, determined this time to keep her hands steady, but she couldn't. It took practice and experience before she was able to control the reaction.

She found the target practice fascinating. She seemed to have a good eye, because she had no trouble hitting the target and from the beginning had scored well. The department used a target that outlined a snarling man in a crouch, with a gun in one hand and the other hand in a fist covering his chest. Sally hit the fist more often than not. Her problem came in shooting within set time limits.

The NYPD expected not just accuracy but speed from its officers. Once the new recruits were used to the feel of the gun and firing it, they began the real training: standing on the firing line, firing six shots, reloading and firing again. The best marksmen could do the whole sequence in fifteen seconds with 95 to 98 percent accuracy from seven yards away. But that took practice.

The department also required everyone to qualify with the off-duty revolver the Patrol Guide specified they carry. Also a .38 but with a shorter barrel, it was a much lighter gun, but had an even stronger recoil. Sally found the firearms training harder than she had expected and she wondered if the twice-a-year repetition was enough to keep her familiar with her guns. She knew that most police officers never fired their guns in the line of duty.

She walked back and forth on her post several more times, finding no problems. She waved at the kids playing hopscotch when she was on the other side of the street, and walked with them when she was on their block. The storekeepers all waved every time she passed by and occasionally a car horn tooted at her, but it was mostly quiet. The time passed quickly and Sally was surprised when the sergeant came by to sign her memo book and mentioned she had only a few minutes until her meal.

Walking to the coffee shop where she was meeting Ellen, Sally realized she was hungry. She found Ellen waiting and they ordered without delay. Ellen's tour had also been quiet so far. She asked Sally if switching from clerical to patrol had been her choice and Sally explained that it was. She knew Ellen usually worked with another woman and wanted to know if they had any problems.

"No," Ellen said. "We work well together. I've been with some men who were okay, but I find they expect to do everything and want you to stay back and let them take charge. Then they complain to the rest of the guys that you won't do anything. Personally, I'd rather work with a woman. Neither Clare nor I have an ego problem; we're not worried about being macho.

"I know some of the guys in the command don't like me. But I have news for them, I don't like them either," Ellen said with a smile. "I listen to them say they'd never work with a woman because they were worried she wouldn't or couldn't back them up," Ellen went on. "I've got news for them: men can be cowards, too. I prefer to work with someone who's not out to prove how tough they are all the time, who's not looking for an excuse to start a fight and break someone's head open."

Sally nodded in agreement. Ellen told her about a male partner she had had in another precinct, a real gung-ho type who waved his nightstick around and was always trying to make street people back off in confrontations. He received a lot of civilian complaints about brutality and intimidation. He also got in trouble with bosses and once, she got a Command Discipline* because she was his partner and should have stopped him. She had only lost a couple days of vacation, but she had been furious because she had tried to calm him down and he had just ignored her. After that, she changed partners.

Her next partner was an older man and they worked well together, but his wife objected to his having a female partner. Finally, she made such a big deal about it that he requested a change.

"She was really something," Ellen said. "I met her at the first precinct party after we became partners and she wouldn't even talk to me. I couldn't believe it. I was in my early twenties and her husband was in his mid-forties. And she thought I found this 225-pound overweight mass of blubber attractive!

"I spent eight hours a day riding in a car with this guy who hadn't brought his uniform home to be cleaned in so long his shirts stood by themselves. He spent the night belching from the stuffed cabbage she fed him and smoking a smelly cigar." Ellen shook her head. "He may have been the man of her dreams twenty years before, but he was the man in my nightmares."

Sally laughed at her vehemence. "Well, I don't think I'll have that problem because I'm already married."

"Is he on the job?" Ellen asked.

"No, he's a civilian."

"Well, I don't want to sound negative, but that can be a problem, too."

"I know," Sally answered. "He isn't happy about the crazy hours or the overtime and working holidays and weekends, but he thinks the job has been good for me. He's a pretty understanding guy, so I think we can work things out."

"I wish you the best," Ellen said, but Sally noticed there was some doubt in her voice. She decided not to pursue the subject and was glad when their hamburgers arrived.

They made small talk as they ate, but just as they finished Sally asked, "What do you do about comments from the street?"

"Well, if they're from civilians, you can just ignore them," Ellen said. "If they're from your fellow cops, you just have to have an appropriate response. One cop started a conversation with me by saying he couldn't understand why they allowed women on the street. Then he asked what I would do if he came after me, and I told him I'd shoot his balls off. That shut him up."

"I don't think I could say something like that," Sally remarked.

"You don't have to say that," Ellen answered. "Just say you're big enough to pack a .38."

"Now *that* I could say," Sally agreed.

"I've gone on jobs and someone will look at me and say, 'I want a real cop.'" Ellen grimaced. "I just look at them and tell them I'm the officer assigned to the job. I tell them if they don't want to deal with me, I'll leave. But I also tell them I'm trained to handle their problem and I'm not going to waste another officer's time by calling for them. Usually, they'll stop arguing and start talking about the problem."

Sally nodded. "Yeah, I ran into that occasionally when I was in NSU. Once they saw we could open a car and turn the alarm off, they stopped complaining."

"You meet all kinds of people on this job," Ellen said. "And some of the guys think they know it all, and you find out they don't know from beans."

She told Sally about riding with a more experienced male cop once when they were called to help a woman giving birth. The woman had called a gypsy cab when she went into labor, but it wasn't her first child and the baby started coming before the driver could get to the hospital. They made it to the emergency room entrance, but it was too late to move the woman and she was still in the backseat of the cab. Hospital regulations prohibited the doctors from helping and the gypsy cab driver was petrified.

Ellen's partner assured her he had attended other births and knew what to do. He got out of the patrol car and into the backseat of the cab, where he cradled the woman's head in his lap. Ellen pushed the woman's skirt up and could see the baby's head. She turned to her partner, but he was still holding the woman's head. She realized she would have to deliver the baby herself. The woman had another contraction, pushed and the baby slid into Ellen's hands.

"That's what this guy knew to do," she said now, laughing at the memory. "His idea of helping with a birth was holding the woman's head. When we got back to the car, I pointed out that the action was at the other end. He just looked at me as if I couldn't expect him to get involved with that." Sally giggled.

They checked their watches and still had fifteen minutes to their meal, so they each ordered another soda and continued talking. "Have you done many frisks?" Ellen asked.

"No," Sally answered. "I haven't been out of the office much."

"Well, that's another whole thing," Ellen said with a laugh. "When I worked with a male partner and we arrested a guy, the skell would often say he wanted me to search him. Half the men I toss* have hard-ons. You get used to it after a while."

"I'm not sure about that," Sally said, looking embarrassed.

"Oh, you will," Ellen assured her. "Once I arrested this guy for stealing a woman's wallet, one of those long kind, you know, the French purses?" Sally nodded.

"He had taken it from her handbag at a dance studio, stashed it and come back," Ellen went on. "We arrested him at the scene and searched him quickly there. He was big, about six feet two, and skinny, only a hundred and fifty or so. At the desk in the stationhouse, I was going through his pockets more carefully to see what kind of money he had.

"I went into his rear pockets, his jacket pockets, nothing. Then I felt into his right front pants pocket and I felt this thing, like a rock, long and hard. I thought, holy shit, he stashed the wallet in his pants and they missed it when they tossed him." She had a grin and Sally could see what was coming.

"I mean this was hard, like the table here." Ellen's grin got bigger. "I said to the other guys, 'Look at this son of a bitch.' He wasn't wearing a belt so I pulled his pants away from his body, expecting to see the wallet, and it was his cock, a big long one that reached up to his beltline.

"He was laughing hysterically by that time," Ellen said, grinning at the memory. "He got hard while I was searching him and by the time I got to that part, it was like a rock. You should have heard everyone in the stationhouse roaring." Sally laughed at the story, but it made her a little uncomfortable. She wasn't sure how she would handle a similar situation.

Ellen realized her embarrassment and reassured her again. "You'll get used to it once you're out here regularly. Some of these mopes, I think that's the only excitement they get. These jerks are always playing with themselves. Think of it as their problem, not yours."

"I guess so," Sally said. "I just never thought about that part of it."

"Like I said, you'll get used to it," Ellen answered. "Has anyone told you about the little things you need to know when you're on patrol?"

"I'm not sure. What do you mean?"

"Well, first of all, going to the bathroom," Ellen said. "In case you haven't discovered it yet, that can be a problem when you're on a foot post that's some distance from the house. That's why I told you to make friends with the merchants. They'll often let you use theirs. Or try a bar or restaurant on your beat. But be careful. I went into a bar once and got caught with my pants down when the toilet overflowed."

Sally laughed and agreed that might be a problem.

"Then there are other special problems for women," Ellen continued. "If you use tampons, you'll be all right. You can carry them in a pocket when you need them. But I used pads and could never figure out a way to carry them with me. Once, I thought I had a brilliant solution stuffing them into my socks."

"What a good idea!"

"I thought it was at first," Ellen responded. "But then I found out it only works if it's not raining. With enough rain they get wet and you're back where you started.

"And don't forget to buy some long underwear," she suggested. "If you're going to be on patrol in the next few months, you'll need it. It really does help keep you warm. Get the thermal kind, it's worth the extra cost." Sally nodded. She would not have thought about that either.

"You wear your hair short," Ellen commented. "That's fine, but if you decide to let it grow, you'll probably have to get a new hat. I have half a dozen, in different sizes, so that one will fit no matter how I decide to wear my hair.

"And it's not a good idea to wear too much makeup on the job when you're on patrol," she said. "First of all, you can't keep putting on lipstick or whatever. And it can cause you problems, especially if you're wearing mascara and someone uses Mace around you."

Sally's eyes widened. That was something else she hadn't given much thought to. Everything Ellen was telling her was important, she realized, and she was lucky not to have to find it out for herself. "Anything else?"

"Oh, there are some general cop tricks," Ellen said. "If you're on a foot post in the winter and it's cold out, try to find a place to stay warm, but where you can see the sergeant coming. Or listen to your radio so you know when he's near and can come out before he gets there. And leave your jacket outside. Some of the old-timers will touch your shield to see if it's cold to make sure you've been on your beat."

Sally grinned. "That sounds like a good idea, but I'm not sure I'd have the nerve not to stay where I'm assigned."

"Oh, I don't mean the whole tour," Ellen explained. "You have to walk around some. But if it's quiet and there are no problems, and you can find somewhere to keep warm, it's kind of silly to suffer." Sally nodded again.

"You're lucky you're in this precinct," Ellen said. "If you had an East Side house, you'd probably get stuck guarding one of the UN consulates. Then you'd have no choice but to spend eight hours in a tiny wooden shack without heat and nothing to do. And those you can't leave." With that, Ellen checked her watch. "Come on, time to get back to work."

They left the restaurant and crossed Broadway. "I'll leave Seventy-ninth Street to you," Ellen said. "I'm going down to Seventy-seventh."

Sally nodded and started east toward Columbus. Broadway was fairly quiet and there would probably be more people at the other end of the post, where the new restaurants were. She had just started to walk when an elderly man came up to her.

"Excuse me, miss policeman," he said with a heavy Slavic accent. "I can't make my key work in my door. I can't get home. I went out to buy dinner and now I can't get in again."

"Where do you live?" Sally asked. He pointed to one of the houses along Seventy-ninth Street. "There, on the top floor."

"Well, let's go try it again," Sally offered. "If that doesn't work, I'll call for help." She notified Central that she was going off post to help a civilian and motioned to the man to lead the way. He took out a heavy key ring to open the door into the building. They climbed four flights of rickety stairs covered with a threadbare carpeting. At the top landing, the man led her to one of the two doors on the floor.

Another key on his ring opened one lock, the kind with a steel bar behind the door. Sally could hear the bar sliding as

the key turned. He found the second key on the ring and put
it to the keyhole under the doorknob. The key fit, but wouldn't
turn. Sally tried it, but didn't have any more luck than the old
man had. She jiggled it a few times and tried again. It still didn't
turn.

She took out her wallet and removed a plastic credit card.
She slid it into the space in the door frame, wiggled it a few
times, felt it hit the lock, then slide past it. Sally pushed and
the door opened.

The elderly man was near tears, he was so grateful. Sally
reassured him that it was just part of her job and she was glad
she could help him. She noted the incident in her memo book,
called Central to say she was back on post, then left the building
and continued to walk her assigned position. She made another
circuit of the blocks.

The calls on the radio were busier than they had been
earlier, although there was what sounded like a lot of joking as
well. Suddenly, an authoritative voice came on, ordering everyone to stop the chatter and reminding all officers that the radio
was not to be used for casual conversations. That ended the
hilarity and the dispatcher sounded relieved.

Sally was beginning to get tired. She had been walking for
five of the last six hours, just back and forth on the same two
blocks. Most of the stores were closed now, so there was no one
even to wave to her. The kids had long ago gone inside to have
dinner and do homework.

Being on Broadway or Columbus wasn't too bad, because
there were people on the streets. Even if nothing was happening,
there was at least something to look at. But in between, she had
the long blocks to walk and she couldn't stay at just one end of
the post all the time.

At the Broadway end, she stopped by the subway entrance
for a while to watch the crowd drift up from the platform. She
could feel the pavement shake as the train they had been on left
the station. Suddenly, she heard the call on the radio—a 10-13
in the One-Six, at Eighty-second and Broadway.

Sally felt her stomach tighten, even as calls came to the
dispatcher from sector cars on their way to the scene as backup.

She could hear the sirens screaming in the distance. A 10-13 was the code for "assist police officer." That meant a fellow cop was in trouble. Sally was only three blocks away and she began to run.

# CHAPTER 20

**E**arlier that day, Sophia had been in a good mood when she reported to work. She had spent her days off doing chores and resting, reading and catching up on a couple of movies. She was looking forward to seeing Alex again that night and had dressed with some care, again resenting the need to wear pants to work. But if she had to chase a suspect, a skirt and high heels would place her at too much of a disadvantage. So slacks and a sweater it would be. She added a wool jacket and wore a shoulder holster instead of the usual bellyband.

When she got to the precinct, she heard about Mary Frances coming to the Anti-Crime Squad and left a note in her locker welcoming her. It would be fun to work with Mary Frances, even if they weren't partners.

At roll call, Sergeant Camillo announced they would all be working until midnight, two hours of automatic overtime, as part of the ongoing effort to catch the purse snatcher. Sophia's team would patrol as usual for five hours, but after their meal, they would stake out a restaurant at Eighty-second and Broadway in hopes of catching the creep. Another team would be in a Columbus Avenue restaurant that he favored.

Sophia groaned. Norm was back, she was glad to see, and she asked him to wait a few minutes while she made a call. She phoned Alex to explain the situation. He understood, and said he would catch up on his work and pick her up when she got off. She was glad he didn't want to postpone their date.

As she expected, Van didn't say anything about the day they had worked with Eddy. She decided not to say anything either. Norm, of course, didn't know what had happened. They cruised as usual, on Broadway, Amsterdam and Columbus, but there was little action that day. Even the teenagers seemed quieter than usual when school let out.

If she was lucky, it would be another quiet day and she would meet Alex as planned at midnight. The crowds leaving the subways were heavier as the homeward rush hour started. Norm noticed some kids hanging around the subway exit at Eighty-sixth and Central Park West, but they must have realized they were being watched because they broke up and moved away.

Van and Norm started arguing about where they would eat dinner. They asked Sophia what she wanted, but she said she didn't care. She had already decided she would eat lightly and wait until she went out with Alex to have a real meal. As usual, the argument was between Chinese and Italian. They compromised on Cuban-Chinese, a combination seen frequently in New York but unusual elsewhere. The food was usually good and always cheap, so Sophia was pleased with their decision. She could have soup and an egg roll, which would keep her going but still let her eat later.

After they ate, they drove to the restaurant/bar they were staking out. It was Marvin Gardens, a popular West Side hangout. Sophia had not been there before, but knew it always had a crowd on a Friday night. It was still fairly early, so they were able to get seats at the bar, the most likely place for a theft to occur.

Sergeant Camillo had explained that the owner, whose name really was Marvin, had agreed to cooperate with them. The bartender had been told not to hassle them for nursing soft drinks all night. Sophia chose a seat at the corner of the L-shaped bar, near the front door. Norm sat at the opposite end. Van was standing behind Norm, but when the crowd got denser he would move farther back.

Sophia ordered a Coke and looked around. The place felt friendly and warm. The wall behind the bar was brick and decorated with a huge macramé hanging that looked vaguely familiar, but somewhat abstract. There were ten tall director's chairs with green seats and backs at the bar. Another half dozen or so were pulled up to a shelf that stretched across the floor-to-ceiling windows that looked out on to the street.

A few more of the chairs sat under the bar-high shelf of a divider that kept bar patrons separate from people waiting for seats in the restaurant in the back. The restaurant chairs were Windsor-style and offered no place to hang a handbag, so if the purse snatcher was going to get anything in here, it would be at the bar.

There was a big television screen above the end of the bar closest to the restaurant. Sophia was glad to see it had not been turned on. There was no jukebox, but a radio station playing soft music was piped over a speaker system. She was grateful for the choice of stations. If they kept the TV off, it wouldn't be too bad. The bar was starting to get crowded and the noise level increased. All of the chairs were filled and people were standing behind them.

Sophia looked around at the customers. The crowd seemed to be the usual mix of Upper West Side young professionals. There were almost as many women as men, and most of the women were wearing suits. There were about as many blacks as whites. Everyone seemed to be in their mid to late twenties or early thirties. A few had gray hair, but even they looked young.

Nearly an hour had passed since they came in. Sophia ordered another Coke and continued to watch the crowd. She spotted a man edging near a couple sitting at the window shelf. The woman's bag was hanging over the side of her chair. Her date noticed the man moving closer and pulled the purse into her lap. The man moved away.

Sophia watched him closely. He was wearing a sport jacket

and slacks, no tie. He had been drinking a beer earlier, but he wasn't holding it any longer. As she watched, he moved near another woman who was talking animatedly to her companion. Her purse hung over the back of the chair and it was open. Someone moved between Sophia and the man she was watching as the crowd milled to take in a few more people.

The man in the sport jacket was going out the door and Sophia knew he had grabbed a wallet from the talkative woman's purse. Sophia looked for Norm and Van, but they were facing in another direction. She jumped down and elbowed her way through the crowd, knowing that her partners would be behind her as soon as they realized she was no longer sitting at the bar.

She crossed her fingers as she squeezed through the crowd. People moved aside to let her pass, apparently glad to see someone leave. Her luck was good; her suspect had been held up by people coming into the restaurant. He was waiting between the double doors for a group of six to enter before he could get free. She caught up with him and touched him on the back as he walked out on to the street.

He couldn't have known who she was; she hadn't identified herself and didn't have her police shield out. When she touched him, though, he turned around and said immediately, "Oh, I just found this purse. Someone must have lost it."

"You're under arrest. Police, don't move," Sophia said. She hadn't had time to get her gun out and the man tried to knock her down. He threw a punch, but she ducked and he kicked at her. He grabbed her hair and punched her in the face. Sophia kept moving, trying to break his hold on her hair and get free.

She managed to punch him a couple of times in the stomach, but he didn't seem to feel it. He was hitting her in the face, arms and chest. People were passing on the street and walking around them. Sophia wondered where Norm and Van were. She tried to get to the radio in her jacket pocket, but she was too busy using her hands to deflect the blows to her face to reach it.

She went down on one knee, still trying to get her radio with one hand and punch the guy with the other. Suddenly, she fell to the sidewalk and realized the man had let go of her hair. She looked up and saw Van hit the man once in the face. She heard the crack of bones, but Van just switched hands and kept on hitting him.

A crowd had gathered, but still no one tried to help. She heard one woman yelling, "What are you doing to that poor man?" Sophia didn't think the woman was worried about Van. Where was Norm?

Sophia was finally able to get her radio out. She called a 10-13 to Central and gave them the location—Eighty-second and Broadway, east side of the street. She was still kneeling on the ground trying to get her breath, but it hurt to breathe. She glanced up in time to see Norm jump on the man's back. He was punching him in the kidneys. That ended the fight. The man went down just as three sector cars screeched to a halt, sirens screaming and lights flashing. All six uniformed cops jumped out and grabbed the man, who was still struggling with Norm and Van.

Lying on the ground right next to Sophia was the wallet taken from the woman's purse inside. Sophia picked it up, then struggled to her feet with the help of one of the uniformed cops. As she stood, she heard a familiar voice calling to her, "Sophia, are you all right?"

It was Sally Weston, panting from running the three blocks from her foot post. She looked horrified as she saw Sophia. Another sector car pulled up and someone canceled the 10-13. Sophia heard the request for an ambulance for injured police officers as Mary Frances scrambled out and came running up to her.

"You've got a black eye and a cut lip," Mary Frances said as she put her arm around Sophia's shoulders.

"That's not all," Sophia said. It still hurt to breathe and she held one hand to her side. She was still holding the stolen wallet. "Give this to a blonde woman in a red sweater, sitting at the bar in there." Sophia pointed toward the restaurant. "Tell her what happened and ask her if she'll come to the precinct and fill out a 61." Mary Frances nodded and took the wallet.

Norm and Van came up to her. Van's right hand was swollen and three fingers dangled loosely. He had probably broken them when he hit the suspect that first time.

"Where were you guys?" she asked.

"I was watching someone else," Norm said. "I didn't notice you were gone until Van yelled and he was gone so fast I didn't hear what he yelled. Then I couldn't get through the crowd. What made you go after that mutt by yourself?"

"I didn't expect to be by myself." Sophia tried to smile at him. She explained what had happened, how she had caught up to the man so quickly and how he had started punching her without warning. She looked around with disgust at the crowd of spectators who still stood in a circle, although the uniformed cops were trying to move them along.

"How are you?" Norm asked.

"Okay, I guess," she answered. "I may have hurt some ribs and my left side is killing me." Just then, Mary Frances came out of the door and came up to her.

"She didn't even know it was missing," Mary Frances said. "When I handed it to her, she said, 'That's my wallet. Where did you get my wallet?' I can't believe anyone can be that numb to the world around them. She didn't even notice the fight outside." She shook her head. "You don't look too good, Soph."

"I don't feel too good either," Sophia answered as the ambulance showed up. She still wasn't in any real pain, but realized that was probably the effects of the adrenaline from the fight. That had happened to her before.

"Oh, God, Mary Frances, I just remembered something," Sophia said. "Come over here." She pulled Mary Frances to one side, so that Norm and Van couldn't hear them. They looked at her worriedly and Norm called, "Sophia, you have to go to the hospital."

"I know," she answered. "Let them look at Van's hand first. I'll be there in a second." She turned to Mary Frances. "I've got a date tonight, with Alex Grandey, Geri's old partner."

Mary Frances raised an eyebrow. "When did that start?"

"It's still starting," Sophia said, trying to smile. "We went out a couple of nights ago for the first time. He's meeting me in front of the precinct at midnight. Will you tell him what happened?"

"I'll bring him to the hospital," she said. "You didn't think I was going to kiss you good-bye here and leave you alone, did you?"

"That's my pal." Sophia grimaced, then groaned. "Is my lip still bleeding?"

"Just a little, but you really messed up your sweater."

"Oh, Christ, it's one of my favorites."

Sally Weston walked up in time to hear that. "Sophia, you can't stand here talking. Let the EMS people look at you, then go on to the hospital." Mary Frances nodded in agreement and stepped aside for the EMS attendants who had followed Sally.

"Mary Frances, you won't forget?"

"Don't worry, I won't forget. Go get yourself taken care of," she assured her. Mary Frances took Sally's arm. "How did you get here so fast?" she asked.

"I was on my foot post. I was right on the corner of Broadway and Seventy-ninth when the first 10-13 came over and I just started running," Sally answered. "I didn't know who it was, but I knew I was only a couple of blocks away and figured I should try to get there."

Paul Randall, who had let Mary Frances and Sophia talk, heard her. "I think you'll do okay, Sally," he said. "Do you want to try riding with me when Mary Frances goes to Anti-Crime next week?"

Sally smiled. "Sure."

Sergeant Bailey came up to them. He asked Mary Frances and Paul to take the prisoner back to the stationhouse to wait for Norm, who was going to the hospital with his partners. He relieved Sally of her foot post, saying she could ride back with them in the sector car.

"This may not be exactly appropriate right now, but can I talk to you, sarge?" Paul pulled him aside a few feet. "I lose my partner when Mary Frances goes to Anti-Crime in a week. I wouldn't mind working with Sally."

Bailey nodded. "Yeah, that would be okay," he said with a smile. "I don't blame you. I think she'll turn out fine, especially with you to help her."

Paul went over to the prisoner, now handcuffed, and grabbed him above an elbow to shove him toward the patrol car. Two other cars had already left. He pushed the man into the backseat, then turned to watch as the ambulance attendants lifted the stretcher carrying Sophia into the back of the ambulance. Van and Norm were already inside, Van holding his injured hand in his good one.

Mary Frances walked to the back of the ambulance. "I'll be by shortly after midnight," she said to Sophia. "Probably not alone. Don't let them give you anything to put you to sleep." She gave her a thumbs-up signal, then walked to the patrol car. Giving the prisoner a dirty look, Sally got in the backseat, as Mary Frances and Paul got in front.

Paul was driving and Mary Frances turned to look at the man, who had not said anything since he was handcuffed. "That was my best friend you were beating up," she said. "You must be a real tough guy to hit a woman half your size. You ought to feel real proud of yourself, you creep. Too bad we don't use rubber hoses anymore. I've never done it before, but I wouldn't mind watching you worked over with one."

Paul glanced at her. He could tell she was really mad. He looked at Sally in the rearview mirror and she didn't seem surprised at what Mary Frances had said. They reached the precinct and Sally jumped out of the car, grabbing the handcuffed man and pulling at him. He winced as she jerked his arm.

"Gee, did that hurt you?" she said in a hard tone. "I'm really sorry." She jerked the arm again, pulling him out of the car so fast he stumbled and fell. Sally pulled him up and shoved him in front of her, ignoring his grimace of pain. She was even angrier than she had been the night the punk had spit at her. This jerk had been beating Sophia because she had been trying to do her job. He was a thief, a criminal, a coward and deserved no consideration as far as she was concerned.

The desk officer was waiting for them. "This the creep that hurt Sophia and Van?"

"Yeah," Mary Frances answered. "Just throw him in the cell in back. Norm will be by later to book him. He went to the hospital with them to make sure they're okay. A woman in a red sweater will be in to make a complaint against him for stealing her wallet."

"We'll just add that to the charges of assaulting an officer and resisting arrest," the sergeant said with a small smile. He gave the man a strong push toward the cell, almost knocking him off balance. Mary Frances, Sally and Paul watched without reacting, feeling as furious and frustrated as the sergeant. The man had attacked a police officer and would probably get off with a plea bargain, or less if he had a good lawyer. And he would probably go right back to snatching pocketbooks and attacking the next cop who tried to arrest him.

Sergeant Bailey walked in. "It's after eleven. You guys are through for the night. Go on home or wherever," he said. "If you're interested, they're at Roosevelt Hospital."

Mary Frances thanked him and she and Sally walked upstairs.

"Can I go to the hospital with you?" Sally asked.

"Sure."

"Will they let us in at this hour?"

"That's one of the few advantages of being a cop," Mary Frances said grimly. "You get to visit your friends at all hours when they end up in the hospital. Let me call Neal and explain why I'll be late."

They changed clothes and she made her call, then decided to call Geri as well. She told her what had happened to Sophia, promised to call her again in the morning with the news from the hospital, then asked for a description of Alex Grandey.

"I vaguely remember him," Mary Frances explained. "But he was meeting Sophia in front of the precinct after work and she asked me to tell him what happened."

Geri described her former partner, sent her love to Sophia and told Mary Frances to say she would be by tomorrow to visit. They hung up and Mary Frances explained to Sally that she might have to wait a few minutes to find Sophia's date and she should go ahead if she wanted.

"If you don't mind, I'd rather wait for you."

They walked downstairs and watched the roll call for the midnight tour. The sergeant told those just coming on duty about Sophia and Van being injured and hospitalized at Roosevelt. The officers standing at attention began muttering to themselves about the details of the attack on Sophia, Norm and Van.

Police officers feel a particular animosity toward anyone who injures a fellow cop, but someone who beat up a woman was on an especially low end of the scale. They all knew that there was some degree of danger with the job, but most cops felt it was just that—a job. They were being paid to keep the streets safe, and the people who wanted to hurt them for doing that job seemed barely human.

Sally had already begun to feel close to the people she worked with in the precinct, but that night she began to understand the special bond among police officers. The training, the experiences on patrol, the reaction of the public to the uniform, the constant contact with fellow officers while dealing with the most lawless elements of society, all made for a sense of brotherhood, a togetherness, even a feeling of family. She had started to run automatically when she heard the 10-13 call, not knowing who was in trouble, just understanding that it was a fellow cop. While she waited with Mary Frances, she wondered if she would have reacted as quickly if she had known it was one of the men who had been annoying her, like Frank Gordon. She didn't think it would have mattered.

Mary Frances walked outside, glancing into the cars parked nearby. She saw a man sitting in one, walked nearer and recognized Alex Grandey.

"You waiting for someone, mister?" she said as she walked up to the window on the driver's side.

He looked up. "Mary Frances, how are you?" He smiled at her. "I haven't seen you in a couple of years, but I don't think you've changed a bit."

"Thanks, neither have you," she answered. "I've been waiting for you."

"What happened?"

"Sophia got hurt, not badly," she reassured him quickly.

She told him about the fight and that Sophia was in the hospital and that she was on her way there.

"I'll come with you," he said.

She smiled. "I figured you would. There's someone else going over with us, one of the other women. Let me go get her." She walked back to the precinct and called Sally. "Come on, we've got a ride over and he'll bring us back later."

Mary Frances got in the front seat next to Alex and introduced Sally as she climbed in the back. "We won't be able to stay too long. You won't mind bringing us back to get our cars, will you?"

"Of course not," he answered. He still looked worried. "You're sure she's not too badly hurt?"

"I don't think so," Mary Frances answered. "She has a black eye and a split lip and said she may have cracked a couple of ribs, but nothing more than that."

Alex seemed relieved and drove without saying anything more. He parked in front of a fire hydrant, put a police parking pass in the front window and they got out. They walked into the emergency room and saw Norm still sitting in the waiting area. Mary Frances introduced him to Alex and asked how Sophia and Van were.

"He's okay, a couple of broken fingers is all," Norm answered. "Soph's in X-ray now, to see if the ribs are broken or just bruised, but that's the worst of it. Of course, she doesn't look too good."

"How come she ended up fighting with the mope by herself? Where was her backup?" Alex's voice sounded hard.

Norm looked at him again. Mary Frances had just given his name, not identified him in any way. From his question, Norm assumed he was a cop, but he still wasn't sure of what he was doing there. He usually heard about Sophia's boyfriends and she hadn't mentioned anyone recently.

Mary Frances stepped in quickly. "Detective Grandey is a friend of Sophia's. He's my cousin Geri's former partner," she added.

Norm nodded in acknowledgment of the introduction, and explained how Sophia had run out after the suspect without waiting to see if he and Van were following. "She does that sometimes," he said with a small smile. "She's a great partner, but she sometimes forgets about us."

Alex smiled back. "I used to have the same problem with Geri, although I don't think she ever tried to tackle someone alone."

A doctor came up to them and said Sophia was now in a room and they could visit her for a few minutes, but she really needed to go to sleep. He explained that she had severely bruised ribs, but nothing worse. They were keeping her overnight, just for observation, and she would probably be able to go home the next day. The cops all breathed a sigh of relief, got the room number and went toward the elevator. Norm remembered Van and went to pick him up from one of the emergency rooms. His hand was bandaged, but he was okay otherwise. He would probably be out on medical leave longer than Sophia.

All five of them crowded into the small private room. Sophia looked up, one eye almost swollen shut and her lip twice its normal size. She sat up stiffly and they could see the bandage around her ribs through the hospital gown. She tried to smile, but with the swollen lip, it came out as more of a sneer.

"How do you feel?" Mary Frances asked.

"Great," she answered. "I don't even hurt that much."

"Wait until tomorrow," Norm said.

"Thanks for being there, Van. How's your hand?" Sophia asked. He nodded an okay and held up his bandaged hand. The tips of three fingers stuck out from the splints.

Sally just smiled at her. Alex hadn't said anything yet.

"Now that I know you're okay, partner, I've got to go back to the precinct and book that creep," Norm said. He took Van and they left, promising to call her at home the following evening.

Mary Frances and Sally smiled at her again. "I'll call you tomorrow, Soph," Mary Frances said. "If you're still not working on my next day off, I'll bring Stevie to visit. He'll get you out of the house."

"It's a deal," Sophia said. She waved as Mary Frances and Sally left, leaving Alex alone with her.

"I didn't think you were that anxious to break our date," he said with a smile. "You could have just called and said you were busy."

She tried again to smile. "Don't make me laugh. It hurts too much."

"Sorry," he said. "I should know better. I've had a few split lips myself. I'll come by tomorrow and take you home, okay?"

She nodded. He turned to leave, then turned back again. "Still feeling sick and tired of the job?"

She shook her head. "Not tonight. I wouldn't quit for the world after this. I'm still high from the excitement. If it were like this all the time, I could put up with the rest of it."

He moved closer to the bed and looked down at her. "You're one hell of a cop, Sophia. I suspect you're one hell of a woman, too. I think I'm going to enjoy finding out." He walked out of the room and in a few minutes, she was asleep.

# AFTERWORD

**M**ary Frances, Sophia, Geri and Sally are composite characters, not actual individuals in the New York Police Department. They are closely based on the personality traits and personal characteristics of the women I have interviewed. As I stated before, everything that happens to them and the feelings and attitudes they express are those of real policewomen.

In order to give the women I interviewed a real chance to discuss the true nature of their controversial jobs, I guaranteed them anonymity. While there may be women in the NYPD who look like the characters in this book or whose careers follow exactly the paths described, they are not the women I have interviewed. No one woman I interviewed had all the experiences assigned to Mary Frances, Sally, Sophia or Geri; rather, I assigned each of these characters a selection of the true incidents told to me by the wide range of women with whom I talked.

As I explained in the foreword, I interviewed dozens of women. They ranged from longtime veterans to women just out of the Academy. After a while I began noticing some definite personality types and patterns emerging. The four main characters in the book are based on those patterns and types. The experiences they have also follow those patterns. As an example, the things that Sally experiences in her first year are like those related to me by younger women who had serious doubts in the beginning about their abilities to handle policing as a career.

The conversations between partners in a patrol car were either reported to me by a police officer or ones I heard while I was on patrol with them. The same is true of conversations between police officers and civilians. In all matters of substance, I have kept as closely as possible to the transcript of an interview or an actual conversation. I am a journalist, not a novelist.

There is no One-Six precinct anymore in New York City. I chose the Upper West Side of Manhattan as the location for the book as a matter of convenience. While I have moved incidents from their original location, they are in the same type of place. As an example, there was a stakeout in a popular restaurant for a purse snatcher involving a plainclothes team. The suspect did attack the woman cop who first approached him and the passing civilians ignored the fight. Her partners did come to her rescue along with several squad cars, once a call for help was heard. It did not happen at Marvin Gardens, which is a real West Side restaurant.

All of the incidents described in the book happened to women in the NYPD, although I have changed the locations to put them all in my fictional precinct. In doing so, I have used actual buildings, parks and streets on the Upper West Side.

The area attributed to the One-Six is made up of the existing 20th precinct and 24th precinct. With the exception of some of the more innocuous jobs given to sector cars (which are usually incidents that I observed), none of the situations described happened in those precincts.

Finally, I would like again to thank the women of the NYPD for their help, encouragement and continuing interest in this book and for the confidence they showed in me to present their story accurately.

# GLOSSARY

**10-13:** Radio code to assist police officer. It means a police officer is in trouble and needs immediate backup.

**10-20:** Radio code for a robbery that has already been committed.

**10-29:** Radio code for a possible rape attempt.

**10-53:** Radio code for a vehicle accident.

**10-85 FORTHWITH:** Radio code for need of additional unit immediately. This is almost as serious as a 10-13.

**10-91:** Radio code for non-crime situation corrected. Used when police are called for a situation that proves not to involve a crime.

**28:** New York Police Department form to request days off.

**61:** Form filed by victim at the time of a crime with the first police officers on the scene. This form is passed on to investigators and used to compile statistics.

**ACADEMY:** New York Police Department training school for police recruits.

**AIDED CARD:** A case usually involving a sick or injured person. Police officers fill out a form with the details of the incident for departmental records.

**AROUND-THE-CLOCK:** Working a different eight-hour shift every two weeks. The normal shifts for police officers who work in uniform on patrol are 12 midnight to 8 A.M., 8 A.M. to

4 P.M. and 4 P.M. to 12 midnight. Those who work in plain-clothes may have different hours.

BOROUGH COMMAND: New York City's dozens of police precincts are combined into seven commands and are overseen by an officer, usually an inspector.

BUS: Ambulance.

CATCHING: Reviewing crime complaints from victims that are made out by the first police officers on the scene. An officer is assigned for the day to do this as the first step in the investigating process.

CENTRAL: The 911 dispatcher for police, fire and ambulances.

CENTRAL BOOKING: Collection point for prisoners between arrest and court arraignment. It is at Central Booking that past records are checked.

CHIEF: Highest ranking for police officers. Just below the commissioner.

CIVILIAN COMPLAINT REVIEW BOARD (CCRB): Panel of civilians and police appointed to look into charges of police brutality brought by civilians against individual officers.

CO: Commanding officer.

COLLAR: Arrest; a good collar is for a serious crime.

COMMAND DISCIPLINE: A punishment, usually a fine or loss of vacation days, imposed by a commanding officer on a police officer for relatively minor violations of police procedure.

COMMUNITY PATROL OFFICER PROGRAM (CPOP): Experimental program to bring back the officer on foot patrol assigned to a specific section.

COMPANY: Group of forty or so at the Police Academy, considered a manageable class size.

DAY SHIFT: Working during daytime, usually used by cops who would normally be on nights, but have had their hours temporarily changed for some reason.

DESK APPEARANCE TICKET (DAT): More than a traffic ticket, this requires a court appearance at a later date. DAT's are usually used for serious violations or minor misdemeanors.

DETAIL: Assignment; used for any police job that is not routine patrol or office work.

DINOSAUR: Derogatory term used to describe an old-fashioned cop.

DIRTY: Suspicious; usually used by cops to describe potential suspects.

DOA (Dead on Arrival): Term used by police whenever they come across a death for whatever reason.

DWI (Driving While Intoxicated): Drunk driving.

EDP (Emotionally Disturbed Person): Police shorthand for someone who is acting crazily, often a released mental patient.

EMPTY SUIT: Derogatory term for a cop who doesn't work, often used by men who dislike the idea of women on patrol to describe any woman officer.

EMS TECHNICIANS (Attendants): Paramedics who drive the ambulances for the Emergency Medical Service and are dispatched by the same 911 operator as police.

GOLD SHIELD: Badge worn by detectives as supervisors—such as sergeants and captains. The term is usually used to describe the merit promotion to detective. Rank-and-file police officers wear a silver-plated shield.

HAIRBAG: Derogatory term for an old-fashioned cop.

HOOK: Someone of higher rank who can bring someone up, provide references for better assignments or even order transfers on their own authority.

HOUSE: Stationhouse, precinct.

INTERNAL AFFAIRS DIVISION (IAD): Branch of the Police Department whose officers and detectives investigate charges of corruption against other members of the department.

KNAPP COMMISSION: Panel chaired by Whitman Knapp appointed to look into the charges of widespread police corruption brought by Frank Serpico and others in the early 1970's.

LARCENY: Unlawful taking of property.

MAJOR CASE SQUAD: Division within the Detective Bureau that investigates the most important, serious and/or publicized crimes.

MAKE: To recognize or identify, especially an undercover police officer by criminals.

MEAL: The hour during a tour guaranteed by contract for police officers to leave their post to get something to eat. If they do not get a meal because of an emergency, they get overtime pay.

MEAT WAGON: Vehicle used to take bodies to the morgue.

MIRANDA WARNING: Informing prisoners of their constitutional rights to a lawyer and their right not to incriminate themselves, based on a Supreme Court ruling.

MOPE: Derogatory term used by police to describe people with long records of petty crimes, such as shoplifting.

MUSTER ROOM: Large room on the ground floor of a precinct, used to gather officers for inspections, roll call and instructions at the beginning of each tour.

MUTT: Derogatory term used by police to describe people with records, usually for violent crimes.

NARCOTICS: Special unit within the OCCB to deal with narcotics sales on the streets. The officers assigned here work in plainclothes, and arrests are carefully planned and supervised to avoid accusations that the arresting officers steal narcotics while making arrests.

NRA (National Rifle Association): Organization of gun enthusiasts, whose members include a large number of police officers.

NSU (Neighborhood Stabilization Units): Units where new cops are sent after the Academy, to train with veteran officers, to learn about patrol. NSU assignments include patrolling in cars or on foot. They concentrate not on felonies but on low-priority problems, such as noise complaints, littering and prostitution.

OCCB (Organized Crime Control Bureau): A special division within the Police Department, this group of undercover officers and detectives concentrates on the crimes of the mob, such as narcotics, loan sharking and extortion.

PAD: Taking bribes or extorting money from people.

PATROL GUIDE: The Bible of the New York Police Department, it details the rules and regulations and the duties and forms required of all ranks in all conceivable arrest circumstances.

PBA (Patrolman's Benevolent Association): The police union.

PEA (Policewoman's Endowment Association): A social and professional organization for females in the New York Police Department.

POLICE COMMISSIONER (PC): Highest-ranking person in the New York Police Department. Appointed by the Mayor, the PC is a civilian. Most PC's have had police experience, but at least one was a lawyer whose father was a cop.

RABBI: Police term for mentor, frequently someone of higher rank or longer service who advises a junior officer or helps the younger person to get a choice assignment.

RADIO CODES: The numerical system used by police officers during two-way radio transmissions to give and get information.

RAP SHEET: Also known as a yellow sheet, this is a record of arrests and crimes charged against an individual.

RIFLE PERMIT: Special license to the owner of firearms, depending on whether the weapon is to be used for target practice, protection or hunting. New York requires the registration of all firearms within city limits.

RMP (Radio Motor Patrol): A marked police car.

ROBBERY: Forcible stealing of property from another person. A special unit within the NYPD Detective Bureau deals only with robberies, and within that there is an even more specialized group, the Senior Citizens Robbery Unit, which concentrates on crimes against the elderly.

SCRATCH: A supervisor's, usually a sergeant's, signature in a memo book. A sergeant is assigned to patrol a precinct with each tour. Besides responding to jobs that require a supervisor's presence, the sergeant also checks the memo books of patrol officers as he or she runs into them. It is a police procedure to ensure that those on patrol are doing their job.

SECTOR CAR: Marked police car assigned to patrol a specific area or sector of a precinct.

SENIOR CITIZENS ROBBERY UNIT (SCRU): Group of detectives who concentrate on crimes against the elderly.

SHORT TURNAROUND: Fewer than twelve hours between the end

of one tour and the beginning of the next. It occurs sometimes because of scheduling or overtime.

SKELL: Derogatory term used by police to describe a street person, usually an alcoholic and frequently homeless.

STEADY MIDNIGHTS: The 12 midnight to 8 A.M. shift all the time.

STREET CRIMES: Specialized detail of officers who work in plainclothes and ride in unmarked cars. They are like Anti-Crime, but can be deployed anywhere in the city and are not confined to patrolling in one precinct.

THE MAN: Old term for a police officer, used in ghettos.

TOSS: To search or frisk.

TOUR: Working hours.

TS: Telephone switchboard.

UNIFORMS: Police officers who wear the regulation uniform and are assigned to patrol functions.

UNIVERSAL SUMMONS: Multi-carbon forms kept in memo books used for misdemeanors, traffic and parking violations and offenses against the Environmental Protection regulations.